WHEN THE MOVIES MATTERED

WHEN THE MOVIES MATTERED

THE NEW HOLLYWOOD REVISITED

EDITED BY JONATHAN KIRSHNER AND JON LEWIS

Cornell University Press
Ithaca and London

Copyright © 2019 by Cornell University

Chapter 1 copyright © Molly Haskell

All rights reserved. Except for brief quotations in a review, this book, or parts thereof, must not be reproduced in any form without permission in writing from the publisher. For information, address Cornell University Press, Sage House, 512 East State Street, Ithaca, New York 14850. Visit our website at cornellpress.cornell.edu.

First published 2019 by Cornell University Press

Printed in the United States of America

Library of Congress Cataloging-in-Publication Data

Names: Kirshner, Jonathan, editor. | Lewis, Jon, 1955– editor.
Title: When the movies mattered : the New Hollywood revisited / edited by Jonathan Kirshner and Jon Lewis.
Description: Ithaca [New York] : Cornell University Press, 2019. | Includes bibliographical references and index.
Identifiers: LCCN 2018052014 (print) | LCCN 2018054550 (ebook) | ISBN 9781501736117 (pdf) | ISBN 9781501736124 (ret) | ISBN 9781501736094 | ISBN 9781501736094 (cloth : alk. paper) | ISBN 9781501736100 (pbk. : alk. paper)
Subjects: LCSH: Motion pictures—United States—History—20th century. | Motion pictures—Social aspects—United States—History—20th century.
Classification: LCC PN1993.5.U65 (ebook) | LCC PN1993.5.U65 W47 2019 (print) | DDC 791.430973—dc23
LC record available at https://lccn.loc.gov/2018052014

CONTENTS

Introduction: The New Hollywood Revisited   1
  Jonathan Kirshner and Jon Lewis

1. The Mad Housewives of the Neo-Woman's Film:
   The Age of Ambivalence Revisited   18
   Molly Haskell

2. Antonioni's America: *Blow-Up, Zabriskie Point*,
   and the Making of a New Hollywood   36
   Jon Lewis

3. "Jason's No Businessman . . . I Think He's an Artist":
   BBS and the New Hollywood Dream   51
   Jonathan Kirshner

4. Robert Altman: Documentaries, Dreamscapes,
   and Dialogic Cinema   69
   David Sterritt

5. City of Losers, Losing City: Pacino, New York, and
   the New Hollywood Cinema   86
   Heather Hendershot

6. The Parallax View: Why Trust Anyone?   101
   David Thomson

7. Cinematic Tone in Polanski's *Chinatown*: Can "Life"
    Itself Be "False"? 115
    Robert Pippin

8. "I Don't Know What to Do with My Hands":
    John Cassavetes's *The Killing of a Chinese Bookie* 130
    George Kouvaros

9. The Spirit of '76: Travis, Rocky, and Jimmy Carter 149
    J. Hoberman

Coda: What "Golden Age"? A Dissenting Opinion 164
    Phillip Lopate

Appendix: Time Line—the New Hollywood Years 177

Notes on Contributors 189

Notes 191

Index 205

WHEN THE MOVIES MATTERED

INTRODUCTION

THE NEW HOLLYWOOD REVISITED

Jonathan Kirshner and Jon Lewis

A formal announcement of a "New Hollywood" hit newsstands on December 8, 1967, as *Time* magazine, featuring a compelling Robert Rauschenberg *Bonnie and Clyde* collage on the cover, celebrated the astonishing success of Arthur Penn's film released in August of that year and predicted a turnaround in the collective fortunes of the American movie studios. The facts of filmmaking life in the years leading up to the release of *Bonnie and Clyde* were stark indeed: a 43 percent drop in box office revenues, from $1.7 billion in 1946 to $955 million a decade and a half later, with the average weekly movie attendance over the same time falling from ninety million to a low of forty million.

Complicating the box office slump were a host of problems: a 1948 Supreme Court decision (in the so-called *Paramount* case) that broke up the studios' monopoly over film development, production, postproduction, distribution, and exhibition; an industry-wide anticommunist blacklist that disrupted the industry workforce; the astonishing popularity of television that in the first decades after the war grew from a *Popular Electronics* curio to a household necessity; urban flight as the white middle class moved out of the cities and into suburbs miles away from the showcase theaters where the studios made most of their money; the emergence of a rock-and-roll music industry that attracted (and competed with the movie industry for the disposable dollars of) young consumers; an entrenched regime of censorship with strict guidelines penned by a Jesuit priest in 1930 that hamstrung American moviemakers, who faced competition from foreign cineastes working under laxer production codes; and a new and more diverse leisure culture built upon President Eisenhower's entreaty to "be happy every day . . . [to] play hard, have fun doing it, and despise wickedness." It seemed entirely possible as the sixties dragged on that the film industry, which had survived a devastating economic depression and a world war, might not survive peacetime and prosperity.

Penn's film offered an answer to the looming question shared among Hollywood's management: What do we have to do to get people back into the habit of going to the movies? *Bonnie and Clyde* enjoyed three runs at the theatrical box office: a limited first run, and then, after the Oscars—that is, after ten nominations and two wins—a second, wider, national release; and then the inevitable "sub-run" at budget-priced theaters nationwide.[1] By the end of 1967, theatrical grosses for the film topped $50 million off a production budget of just $2.5 million—enviable data for any era.

The development of *Bonnie and Clyde* can be traced back to the early 1960s in France as a New Wave emerged out of the Cinémathèque Française, with forerunners as varied as the film librarian and programmer Henri Langlois, the film theorist and *Cahiers du cinéma* editor André Bazin, and the handful of former film critics and reviewers-turned-filmmakers, including, most relevantly here, François Truffaut and Jean-Luc Godard. The screenings at the Cinémathèque were disproportionately and provocatively American, and lurking behind the style and form of the nascent French New Wave a deep affection for American genre films is plainly evident.

In 1964, when the screenwriters Robert Benton and David Newman, themselves devotees of the New Wave, began shopping around a new script for a 1930s crime film pastiche about the famous Depression-era bank robbers Bonnie Parker and Clyde Barrow, the first director they approached was Truffaut.[2] He was interested, and legend has it he sketched out the entire film for the writers before all three retired to a screening of the B-noir classic *Gun Crazy* (Joseph H. Lewis, 1950). But despite a stated interest in the project, and such a perfect New Wave backstory to the framing of a production deal, Truffaut eventually declined, deciding instead to make the adaptation of the Ray Bradbury sci-fi classic *Fahrenheit 451* (released in 1966). He suggested Godard, who had read the screenplay and responded with an enthusiastic cable to his friend, "Am in love with *Bonnie and Clyde*."[3]

It was not long, however, before the mercurial Godard left the project, which then languished until producer-actor Warren Beatty stepped in. Beatty eventually interested Jack Warner in the film, with himself as producer and star. On behalf of his studio, Warner offered $1.7 million in production financing, and Beatty ponied up the rest. The production team decamped to West Texas, where the film was shot far from the prying eyes of the studio—a wise move, because when Warner and his fellow executives had their first look at a rough cut, they hated it. Looking to limit their losses, the studio released the film "small," figuring there was no point in throwing good (marketing) money after bad (production financing). And *Bonnie and Clyde* was indeed met initially by poor notices, as Warner guessed it would, from the old guard critics at the *New York Times*, *Life*, *Newsweek*, and *Time*, where, just a couple of months before the Rauschenberg cover and the popular magazine's declaration of a new cinema, the film was panned as "aimless and tasteless."[4]

Bosley Crowther, the guardian of good taste at the *New York Times*, devoted three separate columns to Penn and Beatty's "callous and callow" film, which he excoriated as "an embarrassing addition to an excess of violence on the screen." At *Newsweek*, Joseph Morgenstern savaged the film as "a squalid shoot-em-up for the moron trade."[5] Then, at his wife (the actress) Piper Laurie's behest, the critic gave the film a second chance, this time in a crowded theater, where he watched *Bonnie and Clyde* with a young audience. After this second look, Morgenstern changed his mind and penned a retraction.[6]

The twenty-five-year-old Roger Ebert, in 1967 just getting his feet wet at the *Chicago Sun-Times*, considered *Bonnie and Clyde* "a milestone in the history of American movies, a work of truth and brilliance." The violence may indeed be shocking, Ebert noted, but "perhaps at this time, it is useful to be reminded that bullets really do tear skin and bone." Then, in a long-form review of *Bonnie and Clyde* written while she was still, sort of, writing for the *New Republic*, Pauline Kael weighed in, astutely affirming the film's Cinémathèque roots: "The French directors discovered the poetry of crime and showed [Penn] how to put it on screen in a new existential way."[7] The *New Republic* refused to publish the piece, but the review (and the reviewer) would, like the film in question, find a significant second life. Wallace Shawn, the editor the *New Yorker*, obtained and published the essay. And then Kael left the *New Republic* for the *New Yorker*, where she became an important arbiter of cinematic taste from 1967 to 1991.

By Oscar night, April 8, 1968, the importance and influence of *Bonnie and Clyde* had already become clear, even if the aging Hollywood moguls, like Jack Warner, who turned seventy-three in 1967, had no idea how or why. An uneasy truce emerged afterward in which Warner and his fellow moguls stepped back and allowed a new wave of cine-auteurs to make a New Hollywood happen.

As we look back at such an exciting decade of moviemaking, it is important to understand how clearly those involved appreciated the stakes of filmmaking circa 1967–1976; Hollywood was quite clearly at a crossroads moment, and the desperation was palpable. The desperation was alleviated somewhat by Penn's film, but it did not subside overnight; in fact, as late as 1971, Charles Bluhdorn, the CEO of Gulf and Western, which owned Paramount, negotiated the sale of the studio lot to real estate developers, a sale that, had it been executed, would have scuttled the venerable film studio once and for all. The deal didn't go through—a zoning board opposed disturbing an adjacent cemetery—so Bluhdorn hired Robert Evans to head production at the studio, a move that led first to the production of *The Godfather* (Francis Ford Coppola, 1972) and then to *Chinatown* (Roman Polanski, 1974), two consensus classics of the era, two blockbuster auteur films that saved Bluhdorn's studio and, with it, Hollywood.[8]

Movie executives are by necessity fiscally conservative. And in the late 1960s they were understandably leery about any "new Hollywood." But they made it happen anyway, because it offered a way out of a failed system—a way out of a system undermined by divestiture, by workforce uncertainty and betrayal, by a raft of awful, old-fashioned films that ignored the sensibilities of a youth culture that was seizing the day. The venture into something of a more international style, films made for (and often made by) the very youth generation that had previously abandoned American movies, was for many of these moneymen a bitter pill to swallow. But the alternative—that is, throwing more money at a failed business plan, at more bad movies no one under fifty wanted to see—wasn't in the end much of an alternative at all.

The New Hollywood

Historians of American cinema have used the phrase "New Hollywood" expansively over the years, and even in its narrowest and most traditional articulation—referring to a decade or so of European-influenced, character-driven auteur American films—its specific origins and endpoints are naturally contested. We can fairly mark the formal start of the New Hollywood with the advent of the Voluntary Movie Rating System in the fall of 1968. Or with Robert Altman's win at Cannes for *MASH* in 1970, or with the film school grad Coppola's triumph *The Godfather* in the spring of 1972. For the purpose of this volume, we begin with the December 8, 1967, *Time* cover story—a starting point additionally clarified if we consider the above- and below-the-line talent assembled for *Bonnie and Clyde*, a veritable who's who of the near-future New Hollywood: Penn (*Alice's Restaurant*, 1969; *Little Big Man*, 1970; *Night Moves*, 1975; *The Missouri Breaks*, 1976); Beatty (*McCabe & Mrs. Miller*, Robert Altman, 1971; *The Parallax View*, Alan Pakula, 1974; *Shampoo*, Hal Ashby, 1975); Dunaway (*Chinatown*, Roman Polanski, 1974; *Network*, Sidney Lumet, 1976); Hackman (*The French Connection*, William Friedkin, 1971; *Scarecrow*, Jerry Schatzberg, 1973; *The Conversation*, Coppola, 1974; *Night Moves*); the film editor Dede Allen (*Alice's Restaurant*; *Little Big Man*; *Serpico*, Sidney Lumet, 1973; *Night Moves*; *Dog Day Afternoon*, Lumet, 1975; *The Missouri Breaks*); the art director Dean Tavoularis (*Zabriskie Point*, Michelangelo Antonioni, 1970; *Little Big Man*; *The Godfather*; *The Conversation*; *The*

Godfather, Part II, Coppola, 1974; *Apocalypse Now*, Coppola, 1979); and, as a "special consultant," the scriptwriter (and in this case, most likely script doctor) Robert Towne (*The Parallax View*; *Chinatown*; *Shampoo*; *The Missouri Breaks*).

A wave of films released in the months before and after *Bonnie and Clyde* in 1967 suggested as well that there was something very new to be seen on American movie screens.[9] Robert Aldrich's war picture *The Dirty Dozen* set a new standard for pre-ratings-system screen violence. And like *Bonnie and Clyde*, *The Dirty Dozen* would establish a taking-off point for a New Hollywood; it anticipated changes in the industry's regime of censorship (forthcoming in the fall of 1968) and boasted an impressive cast bridging old Hollywood and new, bringing together the studio-era character actor Lee Marvin, the influential independent filmmaker John Cassavetes (in a head-turning performance that garnered an Academy Award nomination), and the retired football legend Jim Brown, who would become a movie star, appearing in seventeen films in the decade that followed.

Significant as well were two 1967 films steeped in the influence of the French New Wave: John Boorman's *Point Blank* and Mike Nichols's *The Graduate*. In *Point Blank*, nominally a revenge thriller featuring Marvin and Angie Dickinson, Boorman (who in 1972 would direct *Deliverance*) produced, to his studio's dismay, an enigmatic, dreamlike thriller that experimented with the fracturing of cinematic time, something, the director observed, "we associate . . . with [New Wave auteur Alain] Resnais."[10] As for *The Graduate*, it seemed to fulfill the promise of a youth-oriented new American cinema, a nod again to a more international American film style implied three months earlier by *Bonnie and Clyde*.

The Graduate, a family melodrama chronicling the existential crisis of a recent college graduate, proved to be an unlikely blockbuster, the number one box office movie of 1967. The film—and the sensation attending its release—evinced an increasingly salient generational divide, with young people lining up around the block for repeated screenings of a film that seemed to speak directly to and evocatively for them, just as some older folks left the theater feeling like they'd been insulted.[11] *The Graduate* also introduced a new type of movie star: the short, not leading-man-handsome, "ethnic" Dustin Hoffman. It showcased the talent of the hip, irreverent screenwriter Buck Henry (whose subsequent credits included script work on the adaptation of Terry Southern's ultra-hip satire *Candy*, directed by Christian Marquand in 1968; *Catch-22*; and the popular TV show *Get Smart*) and cemented the director's reputation—he had been best known as half of the groundbreaking comedy-improv act Nichols and (Elaine) May—as a New Hollywood auteur. Nichols would go on to direct *Catch-22* in 1970 and *Carnal Knowledge* in 1971.

As to a possible endpoint, we confidently offer the view that after 1976, the tide in Hollywood and in the nation in general began to turn in favor of a different cinematic and political culture. The inauguration of Jimmy Carter in 1977 would take us, in reaction, from Vietnam and Watergate to disco and the "me generation," and almost immediately from there to the early rumblings of the conservative resurgence that culminated in the Reagan revolution. The year 1977 seems in retrospect a moment of truth in Hollywood history exemplified by the sensation surrounding the release of George Lucas's *Star Wars*. At the Academy Awards in 1977, the feel-good *Rocky* (John Avildsen, 1976) won for Best Picture, capturing a shifting national mood not reflected by the tenor of its fellow nominees, which included the New Hollywood landmarks *Taxi Driver* (Martin Scorsese, 1976), *Network* (Lumet, 1976), and *All the President's Men* (Pakula, 1976)—a melancholy milestone indeed.

Endpoints can be found further in the distance, of course. The year 1980 can also mark the eclipse of the New Hollywood, coming on the heels of the auteur risk taken on by Coppola when the production of his 1979 Vietnam film for United Artists, *Apocalypse Now*, spun out of control. The shoot, which began in 1976, encompassed over two hundred days of on-location filming and over $10 million in budget overruns. The film was, when it was finally released in 1979, successful; it earned over $100 million at a time when very few films attained that mark, and its producer/director ably exploited foreign and ancillary revenues after UA executives foolishly disinvested in the film.[12] The auteur disaster presaged by *Apocalypse Now* was in fact realized a year later by *Heaven's Gate*, Michael Cimino's bloated but gorgeous western, also made on UA's dime. That film lost about $40 million and realized the looming risk of auteur projects in general. Calls for austerity followed, accompanied, not incidentally, by the rise of Reaganomics, and with it a deregulation of Hollywood that fueled the industry-wide embrace of the market- and marketing-driven blockbuster that has dominated American screens since 1980.

But this later endpoint was, we argue, anticipated in 1977. And *Star Wars*, a film itself anticipated by Steven Spielberg's *Jaws* (1975), the auteur film that invented the summer blockbuster season, seems in retrospect a turn away from the New Hollywood we examine in this book—a departure at once clear and intentional. Lucas's film certainly gave studio executives the opportunity to view movies differently, as merchandisable and franchisable, as old-fashioned divertissements shrugging off the strained seriousness of the 1970s and films that had, to a large extent, been imprinted with the turbulent social and political context of their time. The civil rights movement, the Vietnam War, the sexual revolution, women's liberation, economic distress, urban decay, and, always looming, the Shakespearean saga of the Nixon presidency seemed very much in a galaxy far, far away from *Star Wars*.

As with any effort at periodization, there are slippages at both ends. There are films that anticipate the era, such as *Mickey One* (1965), Penn's ahead-of-its-time effort to make a full-blown, enigmatic, French New Wave film in America; *Who's Afraid of Virginia Woolf* (1966), Nichols's debut feature that was initially deemed unacceptable by the censors before the newly appointed MPAA head Jack Valenti negotiated a "For Mature Audiences" disclaimer; John Frankenheimer's existentialist, envelope-pushing American-nightmare thriller *Seconds* (1966); and imports like Ingmar Bergman's influential psychological melodrama *Persona* (1966) and Michelangelo Antonioni's swinging London-set thriller *Blow-Up* (1966). Similarly, there are those later films, released in the first few years of the blockbuster era, that hark back to the New Hollywood, including Woody Allen's personal, ambitious, widely celebrated *Annie Hall* (1977); Paul Mazursky's proto-feminist *An Unmarried Woman* (1978); Scorsese's trenchant character study *Raging Bull* (1980); and Lumet's searing, morally ambiguous cop film, *Prince of the City* (1981). The contributors to this volume focus primarily, but not altogether exclusively, on the decade we've marked out for them, from 1967 to 1976; history, after all, is fluid and contextual. And practically speaking, the road from development to exhibition is long, and films are often seen a year or more after they are conceived and shot.

We are aware as well that there have been subsequent new Hollywoods: blockbuster Hollywood (1980–2000) and synergy Hollywood (2000–present), to posit just two of the many possibilities. Indeed, more nuanced and additional subcategories are available, accommodating the increasing influence and control by a handful of diversified corporations, the global financing and marketing of what are today only nominally "American" movies, the many new ways of delivering, exhibiting, posting, and viewing filmed entertainment these days, and the shift from celluloid to digital that renders the terms "movie," "film," and "cinema" at once anachronistic and obsolete. When, in 1963, Godard joked about awaiting the end of cinema with optimism, he could not have imagined how his prognostication would come true . . . but it nonetheless has.

Marginal and Marginalized Voices

The New Hollywood we discuss in this volume was in its day embraced with an intellectual energy unthinkable with regard to these newer new Hollywoods. Thus, our reexamination here is not without a degree of nostalgia for a better, smarter film culture. We are nonetheless keenly aware of the New Hollywood's imperfections. Its daring was not without limits and limitations, many of which regard the cultural constraints of the time.

In Benton and Newman's original screenplay for *Bonnie and Clyde*, for example—the version that was pitched to Truffaut and Godard—Clyde was bisexual, and the Barrow gang had a ménage à trois at its center—vestiges of which are more than hinted at in some scenes that were shot but left out of the final cut. Beatty and Penn cut this plot element, and shifted the treatment of Clyde's complex sexuality (which they were eager to explore with candor as the censorship regime crumbled) from bisexuality to impotence.

Homosexuality remained a very sensitive, difficult topic to explore in the sixties and seventies, even as the Production Code–era prohibitions against depictions of "sexual deviance" no longer prevented filmmakers from engaging the theme. (An exception here, though given some protective cover by its pedigree as an Obie Award–winning off-Broadway production—the play may have shocked audiences, but it ran for one thousand performances—was William Friedkin's 1970 gay-ensemble feature *The Boys in the Band*.)[13] Even *Midnight Cowboy* (John Schlesinger, 1969), with its then taboo-busting portrayal of gay hustlers in Times Square, never examines whether or not Joe Buck and Ratso Rizzo are lovers, despite the centrality of their relationship to that film. In counterpoint to this demure (and to some eyes, dishonest) characterization of the two male leads of *Midnight Cowboy*, Schlesinger would next work with a British production company on *Sunday Bloody Sunday* (written by the *New Yorker* critic Penelope Gilliat), which had a gay character in the lead. In contrast, the foreign-made *Sunday Bloody Sunday* treated its characters' sexuality with a confident matter-of-factness.

Other aspects of the New Hollywood were also not progressive by contemporary standards. A study published in 1980 reported that, out of over seven thousand feature films released by major distributors between 1950 and 1979, only fourteen were directed by women—a figure made even more astonishing considering that two directors, Ida Lupino and Elaine May, accounted for more than half of them. Lupino directed five films between 1950 and 1980 (*Outrage*, 1950; *Hard, Fast and Beautiful*, 1951; *The Hitch-Hiker*, 1953; *The Bigamist*, 1953; and *The Trouble with Angels*, 1966), and May directed three, all in the 1970s (*A New Leaf*, 1971; *The Heartbreak Kid*, 1972; and *Mikey and Nicky*, 1976).[14]

Thus, although the auteur renaissance introduced a new American cinema, this new generation of movie directors was still by a vast majority male. The few women directors working at the time did not benefit from the commercial Hollywood financing that their male counterparts accessed and instead were relegated to indie micro-financing and playoffs at the art house, university film series, and museum showcases. Even the best of the films made by women in the 1970s remain difficult to find and screen today. For example, in 1970, the accomplished stage actress Barbara Loden produced, wrote, directed, and starred in a terrific no-budget film, *Wanda*. The film tracks its title character as she stumbles upon a petty criminal with whom she goes on the lam. He treats her with a casual cruelty, but she stays with him anyway, because her life before she met him (drinking, sleeping around, sponging off her sister) wasn't any better. Creatively financed, shot on a shoestring, and distributed by a company otherwise specializing in martial arts imports, *Wanda* grossed on its first run, such as it was, just over $100,000.

Wanda has since acquired cult status, at least among the cognoscenti in film studies.[15] But it came and went hardly noticed as the auteur seventies got under way. Slightly closer to the commercial mainstream were two other indie features directed by women: Joan Micklin Silver's romantic melodrama *Hester Street* (1975), set on New York's Lower East Side at the turn of the twentieth century; and, released just after the decade studied here, Claudia Weill's *Girlfriends* (1978), a sentimental study of two single women navigating the sexual wilderness. *Hester Street* had a very limited theatrical run executed by Midwest Films, and it was only after its later playoff on TV (on PBS) that the film became a noteworthy title in the history of women making movies. Also on the margins of Hollywood we find the documentary filmmaker Barbara Kopple, who won her first of two Best Documentary Feature Oscars for her 1976 film about a miners' strike, *Harlan County U.S.A.*

Hollywood remained a boys' club in the New Hollywood era, but the influence of a number of female writers, producers, and actors should not be underrated. These include screenplays by Elaine May (for her own films); Carol Eastman (*Five Easy Pieces*, Bob Rafelson, 1970; *Puzzle of a Downfall Child*, Jerry Schatzberg, 1970; *The Fortune*, Nichols, 1975); Joan Didion (*The Panic in Needle Park*, Schatzberg, 1971; *Play It as It Lays*, Frank Perry, 1972); and Joan Tewkesbury (*Thieves Like Us*, 1974, and *Nashville*, 1975, both for director Robert Altman). Polly Platt (*The Last Picture Show*, 1971; *What's Up, Doc?*, 1972; and *Paper Moon*, 1973; all for Peter Bogdanovich) and Toby Carr Rafelson (Scorsese's *Alice Doesn't Live Here Anymore*, 1974) made essential contributions to production design in the era. Julia Phillips coproduced the Oscar-winning *The Sting* (George Roy Hill, 1973), *Taxi Driver*, and *Close Encounters of the Third Kind* (Steven Spielberg, 1977). And finally, a handful of celebrity actresses, such as Ellen Burstyn and Jane Fonda, enjoyed a degree of creative control over their films. It was Burstyn, for example, who insisted upon the hiring of Scorsese to direct *Alice Doesn't Live Here Anymore*; Fonda exercised enormous influence over the production of *Klute* (Alan Pakula, 1971), for which she won the Academy Award for Best Actress.

In the New Hollywood era, African Americans accounted for about 15 percent of the US population. But as market research revealed, African Americans accounted for more than 30 percent of the national first-run film audience. Since African Americans patronized what was essentially white American cinema, it seemed to many in the business that producing movies that catered specifically to the African American audience was unnecessary. For others in the business, black America offered a largely untapped resource of reliable filmgoers, a target audience starved for films about people whose lives resembled theirs.

The studios initially broached the controversial subject of race relations with *Guess Who's Coming to Dinner* (Stanley Kramer, 1967), a film produced by an all-white creative team, starring the very popular black movie star Sidney Poitier and the old Hollywood stalwarts Katharine Hepburn and Spencer Tracy. The title gave away the plot, but did so by design. Audiences flocked to the film (which ranked second in the annual box office race) already knowing the basic question the film raised: what would a white liberal couple say if their daughter brought home her fiancé for dinner . . . and he's African American? And what if he looked like (what if he was) Sidney Poitier—handsome, deeply intelligent, full of integrity? And what if, as the film further poses, he is an MD with a practice in Switzerland? Didn't every white couple of that generation dream of their daughters marrying doctors?

Also released in 1967, and also starring Poitier, was *In the Heat of the Night* (Norman Jewison), which won the Best Picture Oscar in 1968. The film tells the story of an African American policeman (Poitier) who ventures into the racially segregated South to solve a murder. His task is at first complicated by a bigoted southern lawman (played by Rod Steiger), but in the end the two men solve the crime and part company with something approximating respect, mollifying the white-liberal guilt that lay at the heart of the film's story.

The roles Poitier got to play highlighted his "blackness" and revealed how *a black person like him* might "fit in." But a rising tide of African American radicalism in the late 1960s paved the way for an alternative black celebrity and an alternative set of black narratives, dubbed blaxploitation: a compound term combining an affirmation of the anticipated audience (black America) and a celebration of a certain production style and financing and marketing scheme (exploitation). While several blaxploitation titles made money and more so seemed to forge a space in this new film culture for filmmakers and filmgoers of color, the genre was underfunded, marginalized, and ultimately short-lived.[16]

Several of the early blaxploitation stars were celebrities before they made movies, like the former professional football players Jim Brown and Fred Williamson. Brown played a series of uncompromisingly proud black men in mainstream Hollywood films like *The Dirty Dozen* and *Ice Station Zebra* (John Sturges, 1968) and then in blaxploitation films like the crime picture *Slaughter* (Jack Starrett, 1972) and the revenge fantasy *Black Gunn* (Robert Hartford-Davis, 1972). Williamson followed in Brown's footsteps, his big break coming in Altman's *MASH* as the "ringer" Spearchucker Jones. Williamson patterned his on-screen persona after Brown's: he was a no-nonsense black man with a sense of personal justice that transcended traditional white society's rules in the western revenge-fantasy *The Legend of Nigger Charlie* (Martin Goldman, 1972) and the urban crime film *Hammer* (Bruce D. Clark, 1972).

Shaft (Gordon Parks, 1971) and *Super Fly* (Gordon Parks Jr., 1972) are today the genre's most enduring titles. With an emphasis on action and clever tie-ins to the popular African American music scene (*Shaft* featured music by Isaac Hayes; *Super Fly*, music from Curtis Mayfield), the films chronicle the heroic exploits of handsome and capable black men who establish law and order despite a criminality inherent to the black urban scene. Cashing in on the success of these two "black actioners" were *Cleopatra Jones* (Jack Starrett, 1973, with Tamara Dobson playing a black female secret agent); *The Mack* (Michael Campus, 1973, with Max Julien as a pimp with ambition and Richard Pryor as his loony sidekick); the Fred Williamson gangster picture *Black Caesar* (Larry Cohen, 1973); *Coffy* (Jack Hill, 1973, introducing Pam Grier as a vigilante nurse at war with local drug lords); *Three the Hard Way* (teaming Brown and Williamson, directed by Gordon Parks Jr., 1974); and *Foxy Brown* (Jack Hill, 1974, with Grier as a "badass" sworn to vengeance after the death of her government-agent boyfriend).

Blaxploitation put African Americans behind the camera as well as on-screen, albeit armed with exploitation-level budgets. In addition to Parks (Sr. and Jr.), the genre showcased the skills of the actor turned director Ossie Davis and the writer-director-actor-composer Melvin van Peebles. Davis, a successful movie and TV character actor in the 1950s and 1960s, debuted with the action-comedy hit *Cotton Goes to Harlem* (1970), which grossed nearly seven times its production budget in its first run. Van Peebles had a hit the same year with the socially conscious comedy *The Watermelon Man* (1970), about a bigoted white insurance agent who wakes up one morning to discover that he has been transformed into a black man. But just as a move into the commercial mainstream was on offer, van Peebles turned his back on a proposed deal with Columbia and spent some of his own money and that of his friend the comedian Bill Cosby to make the alliteratively titled *Sweet Sweetback's Baadasssss Song* (1971). Van Peebles produced, directed, scripted, scored, and starred in the picture, which told the story of a black stud named Sweetback (played by van Peebles himself) who earns a living performing in live sex shows in the South-Central LA ghetto. *Sweet Sweetback's Baadasssss Song* embodies and exaggerates racial stereotypes of supersexed studs, feckless drunks, and colorful pimps but does so from a subject position and with an identity politics that put its audience in on the joke, exploiting stereotypes to critique the way such black characters had historically been used in films made by white directors and to offer commentary on the way such stereotypes reflect commonly felt fears in the white community about African American men. It was, to say the least, not the follow-up to *The Watermelon Man* mainstream Hollywood was looking for. If van Peebles was the era's most influential black auteur, as many contend he was, his brief career, which went decidedly south after *Sweet Sweetback's Baadasssss Song*, speaks volumes on Hollywood's continued reluctance, even in this golden age, to employ artists of color. All to say, the production culture in Hollywood did not much change in this era. But the productions themselves certainly did—and a new film culture emerged that proved at once exceptional and extraordinary.

The Chapters

In 1966, the film critic Stanley Kaufmann coined the term "film generation" to characterize a new American filmgoer with a "hunger for film . . . [with] the enthusiasm, the appetite, the avidity for film."[17] As Kaufmann noted, the New Hollywood was in a variety of ways ground zero for a generation of film scholars and filmgoers.

Three of the contributors to this collection (Molly Haskell, David Thomson, and Phillip Lopate) wrote compellingly about this New Hollywood at the very moment it took shape. For them, this book offers an opportunity to look back and ponder: do they still believe what they believed (about American movies) in the 1970s? Most of the rest of the contributors to this book came of age (as filmgoers and then as film historians, critics, and theorists) going to the movies during this era. And for the one or two writers contributing here who were not yet old enough to be thinking much about movies between 1967 and 1976, their formal film education was delivered by professors, historians, and film critics who would happily affirm membership in Kaufmann's "film generation," because they fell in love with the movies of the New Hollywood studied here. This collection offers, by design, an opportunity for reexamination, reflection, reconsideration, and remembrance.

Our book begins with Molly Haskell's look back at her groundbreaking American movie history *From Reverence to Rape*, which (among other concerns) argued that the star system of the classical studio period offered leading actresses power, autonomy, and a subversive feminism that was, ironically, undermined by the freedoms offered by the New Hollywood. In "The Mad Housewives of the Neo-Woman's Film: The Age of Ambivalence Revisited," Haskell reconsiders whether in fact the wayward and searching women depicted in the New Hollywood era and the actresses who played them—characters unglued and actresses without conventional star personae—can be seen as part of the general sense of rebellion against old norms and social strictures. As such, upon this second look, Haskell contends, these women (on-screen and on the set) exhibit a unique heroism.

In "Antonioni's America: *Blow-Up*, *Zabriskie Point*, and the Making of a New Hollywood," Jon Lewis examines two films by Michelangelo Antonioni: *Blow-Up*, a British import and American box office sensation, and *Zabriskie Point*, an American studio production justifiably written off as an auteur nightmare. He examines as well two simultaneous movie industry adjustments: the first, to the studios' long-running regime of censorship, and the second, to the (for the studios at least) perplexing popularity of European art films. For Lewis, these two Antonioni films evince Hollywood's reluctant and largely improvised entrée into the New Hollywood and its stumbling and mostly incompetent embrace of the very counterculture it endeavored to exploit.

Jonathan Kirshner's "BBS and the New Hollywood Dream" begins as well with industry intrigue and the studio's attraction to, but cluelessness about, the emerging counterculture. He tracks the evolution of the BBS production outfit founded by Bob Rafelson, Bert Schneider, and Steve Blauner that produced a number of New Hollywood classics, including *Five Easy Pieces* (Rafelson, 1970), *The Last Picture Show* (Peter Bogdanovich, 1971), and *The King of Marvin Gardens* (Rafelson, 1972). The B-story in Kirshner's essay attends to the underappreciated creative importance and influence at BBS of then triple-threat (writer, actor, director) Jack Nicholson, whose insouciant celebrity persona obscures this history. In addition to his status as an informal fourth partner at BBS, Nicholson had been intimately associated with Roger Corman at American International Pictures (AIP), where countless New Hollywood figures first learned their craft. Many AIP stalwarts, including the writer Carole Eastman, the cinematographer László Kovács, and the actor Bruce Dern, came to BBS via their connection to Nicholson.

In an industry given over to the so-called movie brats—university film school–educated auteurs like Coppola, Scorsese, and Lucas—Robert Altman, who cut his teeth as a director making industrials, documentaries, and episodic TV, became one of the unlikely founding fathers of the New Hollywood. In his essay, "Robert Altman: Documentaries, Dreamscapes, and Dialogic Cinema," David Sterritt focuses on "the unpredictability, the spontaneity, and elusiveness" of this unique auteur, bringing to such a study of Altman's oeuvre a range of different and complementary theoretical approaches: dialogic theory, carnival theory, and schizoanalytic theory, arguing finally that Altman's characteristically chaotic work—in particular *McCabe & Mrs. Miller* (1971), *Nashville* (1975), and *3 Women* (1977)—is usefully unpacked by such high theory.

Beginning with a practical discussion of location and logistic film work in New York City in the 1970s, Heather Hendershot examines the Big Apple as a "city of losers," a lost or "losing city." For Hendershot, films like *The Panic in Needle Park*, *Dog Day Afternoon*, and *Serpico* exploited growing national concerns about inner-city violence and law and order in general. The New York City we see in these films benefited significantly from the New Hollywood's characteristic cine-realism, a resistance to the sentimental emboldened in the post–Production Code Administration era. Key here for Hendershot is an observable distance between intention and outcome; Mayor John Lindsay wanted to use the city's film office to create a PR version of his city as "fun." What he got instead were realistic and unsentimental films about drug addicts (*The Panic in Needle Park*), hapless, sexually fluid bank robbers taking hostages and leading chants among onlookers in support of rioting prisoners (*Dog Day Afternoon*), and corrupt city cops running protection and extortion rackets (*Serpico*).

The advent and diverse output of "neo-noir" in the New Hollywood offer the context for David Thomson's and Robert Pippin's essays in this collection: close readings of Alan Pakula's *The Parallax View* (1974) and Roman Polanski's *Chinatown* (1974), respectively. For Thomson, the fundamental cynicism characteristic of neo-noir suitably frames the conspiratorial consciousness of American political culture after the JFK assassination. Filmgoers were apt in 1974 to buy into the story of conspiracy told in *The Parallax View* because they had learned a thing or two from the narrative assembled by the Warren Commission, and as well, Thomson asserts, because noir had in its first iteration in the forties and fifties prepared filmgoers for such complex and ultimately hopeless story lines. "The hero discovers the truth, but it does him little good" summarizes the plot of Pakula's film and, of course, a host of nihilistic seventies films as well. Among other notable entries in the trust-no-one thriller genre are Pakula's *Klute* (1971), *The Conversation* (Coppola, 1974), and *Three Days of the Condor* (Pollack, 1975); and with *Chinatown*, standout revisionist private eye films include *Hickey & Boggs* (Robert Culp, 1972), *The Long Goodbye* (Altman 1973), and *Night Moves*.

In *Chinatown*, Pippin posits, "what appears to be the ordinary world of rational expectations, planning, moral courage, and attempts at mutual understanding is in reality, we learn, a world where none of this really matters or is even possible," a noir scenario at once suited to 1930s Los Angeles, where the film is set; the narrative world of the 1940s and 1950s noir thriller (a genre into which the film neatly fits); and contemporary—that is, the Nixon seventies—America, in which truth is a relative concept. The exit line everyone remembers—"Forget it Jake; it's Chinatown"—refers to a world in which unintelligibility is the norm, where an "undercurrent of futility, confusion, and paranoia" prevails.

Independent filmmaking has meant different things in different eras, and the embrace of character-driven, more personal auteur work by the studios in the 1970s significantly closed the distance between what filmgoers had long defined as mainstream and independent. Thus it is on the near margins of the 1970s mainstream that we find the New Hollywood independent John Cassavetes, whose "discordant" experiments in improvisation, in genre deconstruction, in taking the personal film to extremes of self-examination and revelation occupied a unique place just outside the inclusive world of mainstream Hollywood entertainment. As George Kouvaros explores in his analysis of the 1976 film *The Killing of a Chinese Bookie*, Cassavetes successfully portrayed real people in real settings by focusing on the relationship between character and performance, by creating a small and self-contained world into which his characters *and* actors enter and interact. Kouvaros looks closely as well at *Mikey and Nicky* (1976), written and directed by Elaine May, a film that features Cassavetes (the actor) and Cassavetes's ensemble player Peter Falk cast in a complementary aesthetic.

J. Hoberman's juxtaposition of Jimmy Carter's successful presidential campaign and *Rocky*'s equally surprising and successful run for the Best Picture Oscar speaks to the zeitgeist of America's bicentennial year and offers one certain endpoint to the New Hollywood discussed in this collection. *Rocky* proved to be the start of something new but not necessarily better in American cinema, anticipating the conservative retrenchment of Reagan, as well as, in Hollywood, setting the stage for what Hoberman, a longtime reviewer for the *Village Voice*, describes as the "host of remakes, redneck and slapstick comedies, working-class inspirationals, space operas, and slasher flicks" that would arrive on American screens in the aftershock of its success. The year 1976 may well have brought "the New Hollywood epitome and cosmic bummer that was *Taxi Driver*," as Hoberman writes, but the next new Hollywood, with its franchises and tent poles, certainly had more in common with Avildsen and Stallone's and *Rocky*'s Hollywood—Avildsen and Stallone's and Rocky's America—than Scorsese's and (*Taxi Driver* scenarist) Paul Schrader's.

Our book ends with a final reconsideration of the New Hollywood as Phillip Lopate revisits his previous and decidedly underwhelmed response to the movement. He acknowledges that "in the seventies [the New Hollywood filmmakers] were the best game in town," but ultimately he doubles down on his minority dissent. Having cut his teeth as a cinephile on the greatest achievements of 1950s Hollywood and the stunning triumphs of the international fare that filled art houses in the early 1960s, Lopate can acknowledge the "vitality" of the best of the seventies, but is less impressed overall. For him, the golden era had already passed, and the ragged show-offs of the New Hollywood did not match the standards set by Hollywood masters such as Alfred Hitchcock, Otto Preminger, Nicholas Ray, Anthony Mann, and Douglas Sirk, and art house legends Antonioni, Robert Bresson, Luis Buñuel, Godard, Kenji Mizoguchi, and Satyajit Ray. For a decade of filmmaking characterized by films that purposefully broke the Hollywood mold, it seems fitting to us that we end our study of the New Hollywood with an essay expressing dissent and dispute.

Parting Glances

This book is by design selective.[18] It is not our intention to offer a definitive or comprehensive cataloging of the period. Rather, *When the Movies Mattered* is fundamentally reflective, an opportunity for a reconsideration of a decade of American filmmaking. There has been plenty written on the New Hollywood, and we—that is, the editors and contributors to this volume—are writing with that wealth of material very much in mind.[19] The project for us is fundamentally retrospective—a reconsideration of a decade of American filmmaking that proved formative for a generation of film scholars and filmgoers.

Much of what's good about modern American cinema, we contend, is rooted in the era discussed in this book. As illustrated by the chapters in this volume, New Hollywood films ranged freely over a diverse set of themes, dramatic concerns, and aesthetic criteria. Consistent with the more modern European imports from the French, British, and Eastern European New Waves in release in the United States in the early 1960s, these new American films evinced a cinematic world of hard choices, complex interpersonal relationships, compromised heroes, and uncertain outcomes—movies, as Pauline Kael described them at the time, that "don't supply reassuring smiles or self-righteous messages," but share "a new openminded interest in examining American experience."[20]

The fundamental axiom of the New Hollywood is that films were better between 1967 and 1976 because filmmakers enjoyed at the time a unique autonomy, a freedom to make the sorts of movies they wanted to make. But the looming bottom line even for such a golden age was that such an autonomy and freedom were predicated upon a fundamental capital risk; that one day the studio establishment would lock onto a safer system, one free from the risk of the inevitable auteur box office bomb. Just as, in 1972, *The Godfather* broke box office records set by *Gone with the Wind* (Victor Fleming, 1939), studio executives were already dreaming of some future *Heaven's Gate* (Michael Cimino), which realized the anticipated auteur nightmare in 1980.

Such generalizations about relative quality have come to characterize discussions of post-1967 American cinema, especially for those who came of age watching the movies of this era. Nostalgia, after all, is about loss. And we have, for sure, lost the vitality, the originality, the film culture of this golden age. With the end of this New Hollywood—that is, the American cinema of 1967 through 1976—came the beginning of another new Hollywood, one in which huge corporations merging and entering into synergistic relationships that made them bigger than ever held sway, and formulaic blockbuster films cross-marketed across the many formats and venues of the new entertainment marketplace became the industry's dominant mode. The decade of terrific filmmaking attended to here was, alas, too good to last.

In the introduction to *Reeling*, her 1976 collection of essays and reviews, Kael wrote with optimism: "A few decades hence, these years may be the closest our movies have come to the tangled, bitter flowering of American letters in the 1850s." That flowering, of course, is now of the past—the New Hollywood has reached middle age, hitting fifty in 2017. And this book looks back, for the most part in appreciation, recovering for the moment at least, to paraphrase Kael one last time, what we have lost at the movies.[21]

CHAPTER 1

THE MAD HOUSEWIVES OF THE NEO-WOMAN'S FILM
The Age of Ambivalence Revisited

Molly Haskell

In an interview on the DVD edition of *Alice Doesn't Live Here Anymore*, Ellen Burstyn describes the original script as a Doris Day–Rock Hudson movie that needed "roughing up." Roughing up the Hollywood model was what the late sixties and early seventies were all about. You might even say the New Hollywood was engaged in a collective Doris Day aversion syndrome. Not the woman herself, though her superwoman efficiency was wearing thin, as were the wink-wink plots dedicated to preserving her chastity—the last wheezing gasp of the Production Code. It was a more general rejection of studio gloss and perfectionism, the snappy dialogue, the neat resolutions, the wholesome family fare, even narrative itself. All genres were up for reinventing, crossbreeding, and besmirching in various ways: westerns as road movies, noir inflected with political paranoia, genre-bending personal films, woman's film as thriller. There was no clear division between good guys and bad guys, and boy-girl stories were out.

For one brief moment, it was the best of all worlds: American directors got to make European films with Hollywood money but without studio restraints. And it is to take nothing from their achievement to remark that it was mostly a guy thing. The venerated movies of the so-called golden age were the work of young, or youngish, *male* auteurs feeling their oats, spreading their wings, drunk on influences from Orson Welles to the New Wave. Their films were steeped in the politics of the time: the draft and the Vietnam War, the assassinations, civil unrest, Nixonian malfeasance, liberations, sexual and otherwise. The violence in Asia unleashed on television every night was met with greater violence on the big screen. Of all the anxieties at play, the renegotiation of gender was the most profound and far-reaching, yet—perhaps not surprisingly—least in evidence in the new cinema. The demand for equality from the emerging women's movement was simply too threatening; and how did one begin to deal with a phenomenon as yet so elusive and with no clear coordinates, as blurry as an ultrasound, as ungraspable as a dream, a discontent that had no name, and shape it into stories about men and women? Easiest to avoid the subject altogether, a solution facilitated by the newfound freedom from traditional marketing and storytelling demands. Now the Young Turks were under no obligation to use women at all, or make movies for that once-crucial female audience. They were free to go the limit with language and nudity, a privilege geared to the delectation of the male viewer. In other words, the sexual revolution turned out to be more about fucking than feminism.

Women were in the position of Carrie Snodgress's genteel adulteress in *Diary of a Mad Housewife*, exposing her shy lovely self to a lecherous Don Juan (an electrically sultry Frank Langella). In the rewriting of the rules of the game (as in *Les liaisons dangereuses*), women were supposed to renounce passivity and enjoy equal pleasure. They had the pill, they had the newly accredited vaginal orgasm. Husbands and wives (see *Bob & Carol & Ted & Alice*) even contemplated spouse swapping with relative aplomb. But when Snodgress embarks on the affair, she is all naïve vulnerability, he cool male defensiveness. When women went halfway in the sexual game, if they couldn't adopt the same zipless-fuck cool of their partners, they risked humiliation. They couldn't abide by the rules of disengagement. "Will you still love me tomorrow?" they inevitably asked.

There were directors (slightly older than the "movie brats") who still featured women in dynamic roles—Altman, Mazursky, Bogdanovich, Allen, Penn, Jerry Schatzberg, Robert Benton, Irvin Kershner—but the Young Turks were in flight from women in movies that took place in testosterone-fueled worlds of mean streets and open roads or crime fiefdoms and mob hangouts. And women were in flight, too, from domesticity, from husbands, from themselves—or at least from their traditional subservient selves. Both sexes were having an identity crisis, but for women the personal was, as the saying goes, political. One might say more "narrowly" personal, except that the very word implies a trivializing perspective that was coming to be seen as part of the problem. We were reexamining canons and hierarchies that consigned women's lives—and stories about them—to a lesser level of cultural significance. The reorientation was radical, not to say terrifying. A woman was allowed, expected, encouraged, to be "her own person." But what did this mean?

The Mad Housewife became its own genre—call it the neo-woman's film—with an implied *cri de coeur*: I'm not going to take it anymore. Were these domestic refuseniks mad as in angry, or mad as in insane? Sometimes one, sometimes the other, sometimes both. They were asking the question, Who am I if not a woman who lives through and for husband and children? At the end of *Diary of a Mad Housewife*, Carrie Snodgress looks into the camera as if into a mirror, asking, if not that, what?

This is the question mark hanging over emblematic movies like *The Rain People* (1969), *Wanda* (1970), *Puzzle of a Downfall Child* (1970), *Klute* (1971), *Diary of a Mad Housewife* (1971), *Up the Sandbox* (1972), *Play It as It Lays* (1973), and, in 1974, *Alice Doesn't Live Here Anymore* and *A Woman under the Influence*, movies that pivoted on women dropping out, exiting their dollhouses, or resisting male-defined roles of handmaiden or sex object. These were roughed-up versions of the old women's films: a little nudity, a lot of profanity, a bit of sleeping around, and above all, no lighting cameramen focusing on the best angles, the hollows and planes of a particular star's face. The whole flattering star-sustaining apparatus that didn't just make women look good, or glamorous, but brought them into vital connection with their audience. The persona was an intimately "known" thing, a vehicle for continuity. A Bette Davis film, a Margaret Sullavan film. A Barbara Stanwyck film. They knew who they were, so we did, too.

In 1973, I was finishing *From Reverence to Rape*, trying to assess movie roles in a period of turbulence, both on and off the screen. A decade later, in a second edition of the book, I offered an update in a chapter called "The Age of Ambivalence." Looking back now, I have to wonder: whose ambivalence? At the time I of course meant the mixed feelings of the heroines—skeptical of marriage and of happy endings, yet still wanting to believe.[1]

But yes, on my part as well. As a passionate admirer of the female stars of the thirties and forties, I'd made the point, which seemed counterintuitive at the time, that women were actually better off under the old studio system. My examples were heroines who seemed to possess power in reserve, who exuded confidence, who sounded its many subtle chords in screwball comedy, the woman's film, film noir. These stars' positions, both as professional women paid salaries equal to men, and in the male-female dynamics of movies, were hardly representative of the status or opportunities of women in general, but their very aura was a challenge and a rebuke to notions of feminine submission, indecisiveness, malleability. We can now see those screwball comedies as the upper-class fantasies they are, adventures in escapism when the country was in the midst of the Depression, or later, at war. But the feelings they tapped, the aspirations, were real. They stood for something new (women's liberation), exciting (a marriage of equals), and revolutionary (the power of speech: smart women "talking back").

The romances that contained them were what we would now consider elitist, fantasies made sustainable by two unspoken factors: the presence of money and the absence of children. The couples whose "remarriage" was the source of erotic tension and excitement were implicitly going to remain equal because they were going to stay above the muck of domesticity. They would survive as a "fun" couple because they wouldn't have to deal with a sudden divergence of roles and the recalibration of the marital contract that would come with the arrival of children.

Of course the repressed is always returning, and did with a vengeance in the traditional woman's film of the thirties and forties. Compensating for those devil-may-care butterflies and free spirits were movies about the suffering and bottomless guilt of besotted and bedeviled mothers like Mildred Pierce and Stella Dallas. Or Claudette Colbert films where suddenly maturing daughters compete for mom's boyfriend. But the neo-woman's film doesn't look back to the bitter lessons of these predecessors; it takes as its reference point, and source of disenchantment, the fables of romance and stardom central to its protagonists' own fantasy lives. *Alice* opens with a lurid reenvisioning of *The Wizard of Oz*, and a neon-lit child star (Alice) planting the seed of future ambitions as a child star in Monterey, California. On the soundtrack Betty Grable sings "You'll Never Know How Much I Miss You." (Grable will turn up later in one of her musicals with Cesar Romero on the motel television babysitting Alice's bored son.) This could be the ulterior theme song of the neo-woman's film, the old yearning side by side with the urge to move on and beyond. Hollywood romances were the handbook wherein women had learned the lexicon of courtship and marriage—lessons that were now proving about as useful as a typewriter manual in an age of computers. Two runaway couples signaled a challenge, if not a death knell, to the happy-ever-after love template: Bonnie and Clyde and Benjamin and Elaine in *The Graduate*. More shocking even than the celebratory outlaw violence of that Depression couple on the lam was the moment in *The Graduate* when The Bride runs away from The Groom, not before the exchange of vows but *after*! The sanctity of marriage, inviolable in Hollywood films from time immemorial, was being trampled underfoot, or scuttled under the bus.

Just as identity itself, so often secured by coupledom, was up for grabs, the new realism (its definition changes with the zeitgeist) now meant location shooting, improvisational performances, verismo cinematography with handheld camera, and blurry narratives, question marks rather than consummations, voyages without arrivals. Instead of heroines who knew their own minds, women were patients laid out on a therapy couch. And in a sense, how could it have been otherwise? As movies themselves observed (especially in the hip but melancholy satires of Paul Mazursky), it was as if the rules had changed overnight and we'd gone to bed believing in the foreverness of love, the sanctity of marriage, and the taboo of infidelity and awakened to a world spun on its head, swarming with nudies, hippies, cokeheads, new-age free spirits spouting self-help jargon.

Romantic love had never seemed so uncertain, and women writers and directors were emerging, tackling the confusion around roles. A lot of the juice and insight and sexual tension of two great seventies films, *Five Easy Pieces* (1970) and *Nashville* (1975), came from screenwriters Carole Eastman and Joan Tewkesbury respectively. As a performer of her own material, Elaine May had widened the spectrum of female types, and as a filmmaker, she cast a gimlet eye on masculine entitlement and bravado in wonderfully idiosyncratic comedies like *A New Leaf* (1971) and *The Heartbreak Kid* (1972). With *Hester Street* (1975), her remarkable debut film, Joan Micklin Silver added another layer to the question of identity. With a brilliant performance by Carol Kane in the lead, this Yiddish-speaking story of a Jewish immigrant couple on the Lower East Side revolves around a power struggle within a marriage, he the eager assimilationist, while the wife, the latecomer, struggles to find her place between two cultures. Through the lens of a double challenge—marriage and a new country—Silver's is a deftly observed portrait of a woman's quandary over the issue of looks and dress, how a woman can both protect and express herself, appeal to the Other while retaining some hard-won sense of self.

Actresses and models, professional beauties—Faye Dunaway as a model in *Puzzle of a Downfall Child*, Tuesday Weld as an actress in *Play It as It Lays*—awakened to their roles as objects, wrecked by a sense of futility, of fatuity, a sense of looming obsolescence in a profession based on looks and desirability. Tuesday Weld was another kind of child-woman in Henry Jaglom's *A Safe Place* (1971), lost and looking, in vain, for rescue by a man. Youth, beauty, and glamour, once unqualified assets, were now seen more ambiguously—as false friends, as ephemeral, and above all as tools of male appraisal, and part of the trap by which women were complicit in their own objectification.

Men can be more rather than less attractive as they age; men can be unglamorous and gorgeous at the same time, women rarely. This cruel double standard, this deep knowledge that looks are so much more narrowly defined and crucial for a woman, lies at the heart of ambivalence about appearance and is everywhere in evidence. Even in the most "roughed up" stories it's almost impossible for women *not* to think about how they look. It's reflexive, subliminal. Note that Shirley Knight as the runaway wife in *The Rain People* stays fairly grubby in her dress, drifting through America without a change of clothes, but her perfectly blown blond hair shines throughout. Ellen Burstyn's middle-American housewife in *Alice*, though living in isolation with a hick husband, is essentially a sophisticated performer, ready to go before the footlights on a moment's notice. And if you observe closely, the mad Gena Rowlands, home from the bin in *A Woman under the Influence*, has a perfect manicure. Only

Wanda remains utterly true to the grubby world in which she flounders. In this film, which cuts so disturbingly close to the bone, she inhabits a psychological wasteland, a world without luxuries or consumer goods that might at least temporarily appease a woman's yearnings. She remains a woman unglamorized and unredeemed by even the possibility of change, of a bad thing ending.

In the revisionist ethics of anti-romance if not anti-glamour, the ultimate challenge to female passivity and compliance was prostitution, which came to stand for freedom and autonomy: If love only and always meant surrender, then at least get paid for what most women give away for free. The business model of love pretty much sums up the philosophy of Jane Fonda, as Bree, the actress turned prostitute in *Klute*. Control the transaction rather than place yourself at the fickle whim of male desire or the degrading marketplace. The cattle call, the interview for an audition, are more dehumanizing than being a hooker, and Bree found potency in a profession where she could write her own script, choose her audience, and burnish her acting credentials in the bargain. She delights in her expertise in her new métier, how intuitively she picks her johns, anticipates their needs, fulfills the requirements of both parties at so little cost to her ego. And yet, and yet. There is a cost. She's a smart girl, a girl with character, and she's also appalled at what she's doing. She wants to quit, she tells her therapist in one of the mesmerizing, jaggedly improvisational sessions that thread through the film. She wants to but can't. Asked why by the therapist, she replies, "Because it's an act. That's what's nice about it. You don't have to feel anything, you don't have to care about anything, you don't have to like anybody. You just lead them by the ring in their nose in the direction that they think they want to go in . . . you get a lot of money out of them in as short a period of time as possible . . . and you control it and you call the shots."

Fig. 1. Jane Fonda in *Klute* (Alan Pakula, 1971, Warner Bros.)

In her Oscar-winning role, Fonda, slim and sexy in her funky-chic shag haircut and turtlenecks, gives a memorable performance as she tries on different personae. One minute she's the soft-voiced courtesan who soothes and excites her lovers; then the baffled therapy-patient, agonizing over the right words for the struggle to own her soul; and finally she's the enraged and vulnerable woman, object of a new kind of voyeurism she can't direct—the prying and probing authority of the detective played by Donald Sutherland. In her stubbornness, her wavering, she brings appealingly to the surface the agonizing dilemma that has suddenly taken on great, even unbearable relevance. Marriage, once the be-all and end-all, has come to seem a potential prison. The notion of individual freedom has taken hold; you could say it's the reigning ideology of the era, and its clarion call will only increase in volume and urgency in the years to come, expanding to include proliferating minorities and sexual diversities and antiauthoritarianism in all its guises.

The lockstep past suddenly seemed slightly alien, its beliefs and precedents increasingly useless. Now we look back in amazement: How was it that, once upon a time, women not only didn't blink twice at the implications of love and marriage, but eagerly accepted the terms of conquest, looked into the eyes of their conquerors with joyful surrender? Falling in love was the consummation devoutly to be wished, yet the very word—falling—speaks of loss. Of a kind of brainwashed state in which one's earlier hopes and dreams simply and conveniently vanish. Love defined a woman, completed her identity.

Oh, yes, men are occasionally possessed by the madness of love, *amour fou*, and the midlife crisis as depicted by social satirists of the period like Mazursky, Allen, and Irvin Kershner (see his 1970 *Loving*) often involved a messy affair. But for most, Byron's embossed epigram of emotional priorities still held true: "Love is of man's life a thing apart, 'tis woman's whole existence." Moreover it is generally the women who take on the domestic burden of marriage, who wind up in bondage to children, whose safety and security preempt all other considerations. It may be a loving bondage, even intermittently happy, but bondage all the same.

And the institution itself was changing; no longer governed by religion and community ties, it was every man/woman for himself, and the expectations were enormous, absurdly so. The pressure was twofold. Because of the credo of individual fulfillment, marriage had to be a pairing of equals, while at the same time children were coming to represent a far greater emotional and financial investment than what they had been in the relatively casual prewar years.

These hovering responsibilities, still only vaguely surmised, surely affected the attitudes and anxieties of these movies and their out-of-sorts heroines. The nullity of the marriage in *Wanda*, the cartoonish abusive marriage in *Alice Doesn't Live Here Anymore*, and Richard Benjamin's gratingly supercilious social climber in *Diary of a Mad Housewife* are obvious exaggerations, but they're the fun-house mirror distortions of feminist rage. As are the wild imaginings of the frustrated Upper West Side housewife played by Barbra Streisand in *Up the Sandbox* (1972), directed by Kershner from a novel by Anne Roiphe. A once-promising grad student, she now has fantasy affairs with the likes of Fidel Castro, while resisting her mother's attempts to turn her into a Stepford wife in the suburbs. But what is the rage about, and, to borrow from Freud, what do these women want?

I was curious to see my reactions now to films I hadn't been wildly enthusiastic about at the time, and question my own unresponsiveness. It wasn't that I wanted anything as crude as "positive images" . . . I argued against such oversimplification of roles. A bad girl, a villain, or even a well-conceived (as opposed to "mere") victim can possess interest and complexity. I think it was the passivity, the helplessness, the cloudiness of will that bothered me. It's hard to separate the symptoms—lack of self, lack of solidity—from the style of the films, the shaggy-dog quality. Joan Didion, who wrote the novel *Play It as It Lays*, can get away with affectlessness and anomie if the prose is striking enough, but a movie has to find a stylistic equivalent of that prose, a paradoxical energy in futility, resisting the sense of disposability at its core. Interestingly the least "shaggy" and most plot driven are the studio star pictures: *Klute* and *Alice*. And it's no coincidence that these two both have more or less conventional happy endings: the girl gets the guy, but on her own terms.

In the DVD interview mentioned previously, Burstyn relates how she argued with the studio executive John Calley, who wanted a happy ending with her marrying Kris Kristofferson. "You mean if she goes to Monterey by herself it's unhappy?" Calley said yes, so she and Scorsese figured out how to allow her to keep her independence and still have a man, the earthy rancher played by Kristofferson. The actor improvised the last scene, "Pack your fucking bags and I'll go with you. I don't care about the ranch."

The dream dies hard, which in a way is what all these films acknowledge. And I think Calley may have been right, at least for then. A few years later, *My Brilliant Career* and *An Unmarried Woman* featured independent-minded heroines (Judy Davis and Jill Clayburgh respectively) who rejected eminently desirable men who love them. And having seen and talked about these films with feminist audiences, I can testify that supposedly enlightened viewers were not happy. Why couldn't Judy Davis write her novel and marry rich rancher Sam Neill, too? Why couldn't Clayburgh go off to Vermont with sexy, successful artist Alan Bates? And these were the very women who'd been protesting the obligatory happy ending; now for them the flame of reason and realism sputtered and dimmed when challenged by the irrational fire of romantic fantasy. Moreover, it was precisely at this moment—a time when marriage and child rearing were staking the most exorbitant and impossible demands—that the no-less-fantasy-based phrase "having it all" came into vogue, becoming the mantra of cheerleading feminists.

The shaggiest, boldest, and the most extreme in its portrayal of a kind of despair that owes nothing to Byronic romanticism and everything to firsthand knowledge of marginalized, working-class women was Barbara Loden's *Wanda*. The actress-turned-director played the title role in a bleakly original cinematic ballad rooted in the poor West Virginia milieu of her upbringing. As a Bartleby-like waif of a wife, Wanda, with hardly a backward glance and with no discernible strong feeling, simply walks out on her husband and child. (Later, she passively hands over custody, acknowledging the husband would make a better parent.)

As she embarks on an aimless pilgrimage through a blue-collar world of bars and sex, the camera captures her on the margins of life, a lone figure crashing in someone's house, picking up a guy, traversing a vast industrial landscape. There hasn't been a film before or since that so pitilessly describes, while at the same time extending sympathy to, a character so beyond the pale of liberal thinking and conceptualizing. There is no overlay of insight, not a whiff of victim ideology, nor is there any genre framework within which Wanda would be "relatable." Yet it has that precise quality that *Play It as It Lays* lacked, what I referred to as a paradoxical energy in futility.

Fig. 2. Writer, director, and film star Barbara Loden in *Wanda* (1970, Bardene International)

Some have compared Loden to Cassavetes, but there is none of that director's histrionics—the Actors Studio improv exercises—nor the hortatory, adversarial (anti-bourgeois) political thrust. In terms of the neo-woman's film, Wanda is neither role model nor easily classifiable victim, but rather something far less sentimental—a nonentity, a woman who can't be said even to rebel, so innocent is she of causes and revolutionary conceptions, of ideology, whether Marxist or feminist. With her hair in rollers, or flowing waywardly like some untrammeled river, with her shy, child's voice, it's as if she's always waiting to be told what to do, and will try her best to do it, but that best won't be very good. So concentrated and intuitive is Loden's performance—she once said she'd learned from psychotherapy that she played the role of victim and orphan throughout her life—that there's only a sliver of light between actor and role. I was reminded of her when I saw Joel Edgerton's lovely but equally impenetrable performance as the inarticulate, redneck husband in *Loving*, Jeff Nichols's film about the marriage that led to the Supreme Court's lifting of miscegenation laws in Virginia. Like Wanda, Edgerton's husband is uneducated and barely socialized; muteness renders both these characters mysterious and unknowable, and reminds us afresh of the inadequacy of the categories by which we find meaning in experience, and thus an illusion of control through understanding.

At the end, as irresolute as ever, Wanda and the film simply stop, an enigma. It was a gutsy and shattering first film by a woman who died too soon. And it was a film that should be more widely shown and remembered, and cherished for challenging truisms that needed, and still need, to be challenged—the feminist preconception that "we"/women all have a feminist spark, that women are made what they are by an unequal society and can be remade with encouragement and legislation.

How much more genuinely working class Wanda seems, when compared to the protagonists of *Alice* and *A Woman under the Influence*, even *Klute*, who are served up by accessible actresses as fashionable victims whose plight falls within the framework of cultural thinking of the moment. Partly because Burstyn, Rowlands, and Fonda don't know such "roughed up" experience firsthand, their rebellions take on the flavor of actors' exercises. I realize that quite often cosseted, glamorous actors play lowlifes and other creatures considerably lower on the economic scale. It's called acting, and it goes with the territory, but in the realistic medium of cinema, it can make for jarring effects, and can still be tricky. We have to smile watching Jane Fonda being rejected for modeling and acting parts, like any other nonentity. Alice and Bree and Mabel stand for "authenticity" yet lack it. Still, they capture the crucial dilemma: numbness and detachment on one hand, performance on the other, or, failing that, political revolution—these were the only conceivable postures in an inauthentic world.

Running through many of these films, and practically the anthem of John Cassavetes's *A Woman under the Influence*, is the British psychoanalyst R. D. Laing's notion of madness as an appropriate response to a hypocritical world, most particularly as embodied by one's family. The toxic cluster of relatives and in-laws that surround Gena Rowlands, and bear in on her with their expectations, are like prison wardens, enforcers of conformity. They're mystified why, with all she has going for her (loving husband, good job, etc.), she can't behave like a normal wife and mother. Like the group therapy gang that attacks Carrie Snodgress at the end of *Diary of a Mad Housewife*, they haven't a clue what's bothering her, and their incomprehension drives her further into isolation. Cassavetes's cinema of embarrassment revels in breach of decorum—*Faces* was both gripping and cringe inducing, one long slog through an O'Neill wasteland of human wretchedness, but his films became more and more self-indulgent in their bullying. I'm all for films that challenge audiences, even give them a certain level of discomfort, but Cassavetes takes this impulse to sadistic extremes, and *Woman* carries a kind of threat: if we resist his browbeating tactics, we implicitly ally ourselves with the disapprovers, the prim, conventional relatives who are his version of the hated bourgeoisie. There's no denying that Gena Rowlands gives a bravura performance, and typically the most successful scenes are the most theatrical, scenes of war, screaming or smoldering.

If the left-wing philosopher Herbert Marcuse and R. D. Laing were the intellectual touchstones of authenticity, Betty Friedan's *The Feminine Mystique* was the founding text of resurgent feminism. Part of my own tepid response came from a determination, even as a teenager in the fifties, not to join the army of suburban housewives. I found my model not in Donna Reed, TV housewife, but in Doris Day tomboy movies and later in screwball comedy. As a consequence, I never read *The Feminine Mystique*; my own feminist epiphany had come earlier from Simone de Beauvoir's *The Second Sex*, which analyzed the inferior status of women from all aspects: historical, philosophical, cultural-social, and as represented in art.[2]

A Franco-Europhile from early on, I was drawn as a critic to the formal control and psychological ambiguities of European cinema, which made its own stunning contributions to the Mad Housewife genre (subspecies: prostitute). In Chantal Akerman's influential *Jeanne Dielman, 23, quai de Commerce, 1080 Bruxelles* (1975), Delphine Seyrig plays a single mother who spends the whole day meticulously performing chores, leaving time for the tricks she turns to support herself and her son. By amplifying the housewife's day under a microscope, the 201-minute movie, with its ironic, epic-minded title, gives lie to the notion of triviality of a woman's life. We are forced to bear witness to something that is grandly futile, register every repetitive domestic detail in a heroic if Sisyphean struggle that eventually, through the tiniest infraction, begins to unravel. There's a tonal consistency and dry humor in the way the movie elides domesticity and sex, until the life explodes into a murder that is treated with the same deadpan irony.

Then there are the two remarkable women's films Rainer Werner Fassbinder made for television: *Martha* (1974) and *Fear of Fear* (1975), both with Margit Carstensen as a progressively deranged housewife. *Fear of Fear* contains elements of several of the American films: Carstensen is married to a distracted husband, is pregnant with her second child, is spied on by poisonous in-laws, and can no longer recognize herself. As she takes to pills, alcohol, sex, her fear of madness becomes itself a form of madness. She goes for psychotherapy, and on the doctor's wall is a portrait of Freud. No one was a greater dramatizer and anatomist of the uses and abuses of power in sexual relationships than Fassbinder, and his grand and baroquely theatrical girl-on-girl melodrama *The Bitter Tears of Petra von Kant* (1972) reminds us that the delirious enslavement of women is not just a man's game, or a heterosexual one. Also in Germany, Volkor Schlöndorff and wife Margarethe von Trotta were making films about contemporary women who come to see and wrestle with the chains of tradition that bind them. In *A Free Woman* (1972), a divorced woman struggles to find fulfillment in a male-dominated society, and *The Lost Honor of Katharina Blum* (1975) tells the story of a young woman whose life is turned upside down by a terrorist lover.

For Ingmar Bergman, whose TV series *Scenes from a Marriage* came out as a film in 1974, men and women still want and need each other. But in the long anguished husband-and-wife duet enacted by Liv Ullmann and Erland Josephson, the marital landscape can no longer maintain its old familiar contours. *Familiar* as in *family*, for it is the family itself, as defined by spiritual and temporal law at least since the Industrial Revolution, that is under the microscope. Movies like *The Rain People*, *Wanda*, and *Diary of a Mad Housewife* look more interesting today precisely because they are so open-ended, so unresolved, so incapable of finding a satisfying conclusion to rough-edged stop-and-start encounters, stabs at love and lust that leave people more bruised and embarrassed than fulfilled. It's as if, like Carol Kane's immigrant in *Hester Street*, they're all in a foreign country whose language and gestural cues they haven't yet mastered. Moreover, the sense of estrangement is compounded for women as they try to find their bearings on the new continent of "Self Determination," whose geography and laws have been laid out by men. Picaresque quests have always been the male province, flight never an equal-opportunity fantasy. Hitting the road is almost invariably a bromance—two guys in a car in *Two-Lane Blacktop*, and all those cowboy dudes in stories of Tom McGuane, Jim Harrison, et al. It's men who walk out on their lives, you see it and read about it: husband (and father) goes out to buy cigarettes and disappears—into another identity, another country. So it's refreshing to see women hit the road, shrug off lives and identities and husbands in an attempt to start over. In *The Rain People* and *Wanda* women flee, and throw the world into a tailspin. Women are meant to be the anchor, the responsible ones. The rebellion of the housewife-heroines terrifies their "near and dear" because it radically upends the order of things, requires some as yet unknown reorientation of their own lives.

By custom, women were not the solo fliers; indeed, not fliers at all, but mediators and peacekeepers. Between her bickering men, Burstyn's Alice is the solicitous (and unavailing) seeker of harmony between two equally repellent poles—crude overbearing husband and smart-aleck show-off son. So bifurcated is she that the image of living uncoupled arouses the idea, as she confesses to her best friend, of a solitary life. They are talking of marriage, the friend confiding she couldn't live without a man, while Alice imagines she could—unless well, let's say, Robert Redford walked through the door. Radical solitude, as we suspect, will not be her fate, and the "reality" that awaits her in the form of the kindly but virile rancher played by Kris Kristofferson is hardly less fantastical. When trucker husband conveniently dies in a road accident, Alice wastes little time mourning. She gives the ivories a workout, singing her signature song, "Where or When" ("It ain't Peggy Lee," she says ruefully) before hitting the road with son Tommy to seek her fortune as a singer.

Martin Scorsese, who had scored with art house audiences for his nervy, electric portraits of Italian Americans in *Mean Streets* with Robert De Niro as a punk hustler and Harvey Keitel as his sometimes pal and protector, and a documentary, *Italianamerican*, hadn't yet made a studio picture and wanted to. He was the ideal director to "rough up" the Robert Getchell script, but in other ways it was an odd fit: he was basically urban—and the movie would take place in the Southwest: a bleak New Mexico exurbia and a hardly more welcoming Arizona of motels and dives. Nor was he the ideal choice for a "woman's" director. He would make only one other woman-centered movie in his entire career, an adaptation of Edith Wharton's *The Age of Innocence*—a sort of challenge to the genteel Merchant-Ivory and the Masterpiece Theatre aesthetic.

Yet of all the Young Turks who were plugged into the new European cinema, he was the one with the strongest links to old Hollywood. He had grown up watching studio movies on television, gradually discerning differences in style, and had a fine appreciation for Warner Bros. musicals, and a fan's crush on tough show-biz dames like Ida Lupino. Moreover, as a keen observer, he developed a real feeling for the Southwestern landscape, seen through Kent L. Wakeford's cinematography, for the tawdry natural lighting of a bar by day, the impersonal seediness of motels, hovering loneliness and despair. He discovered that a road-stop café could provide an arena for verbal roughhousing and insult duets as dynamic as any dive in Little Italy. Alice wasn't much of a stretch as she might seem. A loose cannon, given to outbursts, she was as cut adrift as the De Niro of *Mean Streets* and Scorsese's next film, *Taxi Driver*. Further jolts would be provided by a jazzed-up misogynist played by Harvey Keitel.

Any shortage of physical violence is made up for by the verbal warfare waged by the movie's three deliriously foul-mouthed satellites—the waitress played by Diane Ladd and the preteen terrors Alfred Lutter and Jodie Foster. In the fusillade of obscenities that emerge from their mouths like demons in an exorcism, they seem to be competing for Trash Talker of the Month. In the staccato bursts of Scorsese-style volleys, they could give the denizens of Little Italy a run for their money.

Indeed the sordid is always just off center, threatening to encroach but held at bay by the figure of Burstyn's Alice, preternaturally sweet, endlessly optimistic, and protected from the grimy and venal by a kind of, well, Doris Day sheen! No matter what obstacles she encounters, she displays a fresh-faced hopefulness that she'll make a go of it in the face of awesome odds to the contrary. Her Academy Award–winning portrayal is less of a fully dimensional character than a series of discrete star turns. Could this blushing ingénue really be the mother of this pint-size Lenny Bruce? Naïveté and knowingness (the wisecracks) coalesce uneasily: Alice as traditional "Yes, dear," wife; Alice wittily mocking her husband at the dinner table. As preparation for the rigors of waitressing—not to mention those of a single mom with superbrat child—she might have been better off watching *Mildred Pierce* instead of Betty Grable and Alice Faye musicals—though it's unlikely she'd have learned any more from the experience than her Warner Bros. predecessor did. Like that outwardly hardbitten heroine, she's putty in the hands of her son, more child than mother, given to pleading with him rather than disciplining him, and when Kristofferson gives the brat a much-deserved spanking, Alice flies into a rage. That the rancher would continue to pursue Alice, even knowing he'll have to take on the kid as well, is a testimonial to a happily-ever-after fantasy alive and well.

In a sense, like so many of the neo-woman's films, the tension between old romantic values and the emerging spirit of independence gives rise to what sometimes seems like hopeless chaos and confusion and at other times as improvisational genius—and occasionally both at once. And so it is that Alice, baffled by her feelings, wavers in the consoling companionship of Ladd, her new best friend. I always wanted a man to dominate, Alice says. But she also knows she wants to play out her childhood dream, return to Monterey and become a singer. "If I knew what I wanted, I wouldn't be in the bathroom with you, sobbing," she says, half laughing. Ladd urges her to stand strong,

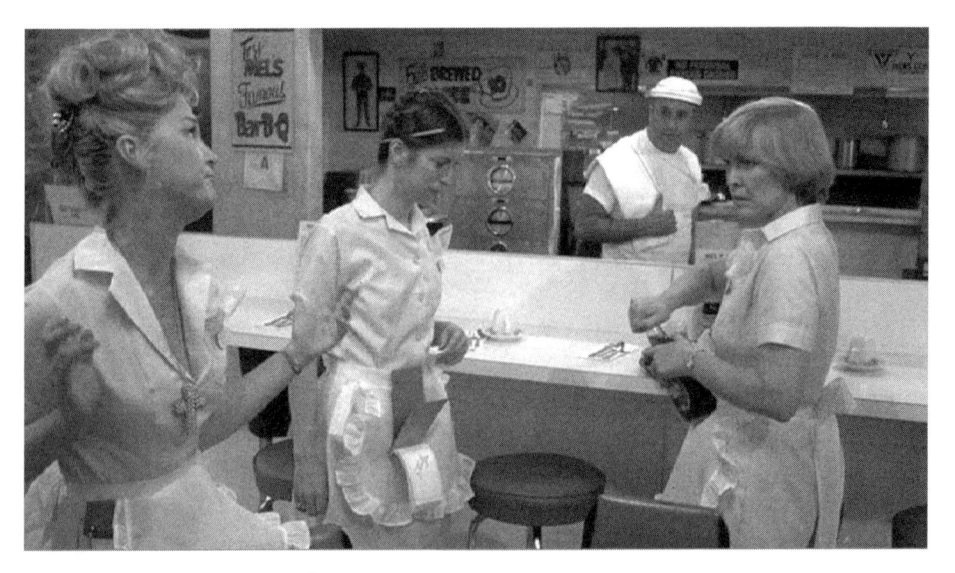

Fig. 3. Ellen Burstyn (far right) hired Martin Scorsese to direct *Alice Doesn't Live Here Anymore* (1974, Warner Bros.).

to follow her dream to become a singer. When she emerges and Kristofferson, understandably bewildered, asks her what she wants, she repeats her dream. "But you were a *child* in Monterey!" he protests, before caving in.

The dream of becoming an artist is more often doomed than not under the best of circumstances, and nothing could better express both the absurdity of this late-life decision and, in Alice's near-heroic determination, the reality-resistant nature of the fantasy. And this desire for a new sense of self may or may not accord with the other equally persistent dream of romantic love. (In Scorsese's *New York, New York*, De Niro's jazz saxophonist finally acknowledges to singer-wife Liza Minnelli that two "stars" can't make a go of it as a couple.)

As Alice's musings suggest, a lot of the ambivalence springs from women's lingering desire for an old-fashioned take-charge male, solid, masculine, dominant—caveman in leopard skin, wielding club—while also yearning for a new feminist-compatible guy, sensitive and supportive. And a lot of the clash is between conscious, politically approved wishes: an equal relationship with this designer male, and the unconscious forbidden fantasies in all of us, say, for example, for a man who will overwhelm us, removing "responsibility" for sexual choice. Hence, in this new world we don't know quite where we are with each other; we are left to negotiate as best we can without the old protective proprieties. Movies deal more frankly with sex, but without guidelines, reflecting a culture where the word no sometimes means yes, sometimes means no, and sometimes means maybe. Thus the violent misunderstanding at the heart of *Blume in Love*, and George Segal's rape of his ex-wife Susan Anspach. Blume is so sure if he loves her this passionately she must love him back with equal fervor. She doesn't.

How do we read each other? The news, on campuses and elsewhere, is filled with the casualties of miscommunication, predation and assault. Perhaps there were always missteps and missed cues, yet there was what felt like a universal language of courtship—some of its lexicon provided by movies—guidelines toward the stages in a dance of intimacy. Women didn't always mean no when they said it, they didn't want to initiate sex but wanted to be seduced, "persuaded" into it. Just what form that persuasion might be remained and remains a murky affair, with neither party exactly sure, and any step likely to misfire. I published an essay in *Ms. Magazine* exploring women's so-called rape fantasies: women, I said, didn't want to be attacked in a dark alley.[3] Rather, they wanted to find themselves in a voluptuous "bind" where Robert Redford (or Rhett Butler; or Hugh Grant; or Colin Firth; or fill in the blank) wouldn't take no for an answer.

Both *Klute* and *Alice* offer a have-your-cake-and-eat-it-too denouement: old-fashioned, even gently paternalistic, males who nevertheless seem ready to acquiesce to the conditions set by their strong lady loves. Far from the pseudo-hip world of Mazursky's characters or Richard Benjamin's smarmy arriviste, Klute is a small-town investigator with irreproachable integrity, a man of few words. Ditto Kris Kristofferson, a farmer who speaks haltingly, but does things with his hands. They look at their women not with lust but with True Love. At the more realistic end are the lascivious barfly males in *Wanda*, and the practiced womanizer played by Frank Langella in *Diary of a Mad Housewife*. In the latter, the performances of Snodgress and Langella are quite stunning, not to mention incredibly erotic, partly because of the cross-purposes at which they find themselves. Langella, beautiful then, the androgynous, self-loving seducer-writer, so knowing, and the lovely Snodgress, whom he thinks to pin down as a type. She smiles wryly, she *is* the type (good Upper East Side girl, Ivy League college, etc.), but she's also something a great deal more, something his defensive ego is incapable of dealing with.

The seventies and eighties weren't particularly good for women, with barely enough performances to fill the Best Actress and Supporting Actress slots come Oscar time, but television began to take up the slack. The stories of women negotiating love and work, home and career, went from the realm of possibility to the baseline situation in every genre from police procedurals to rom-coms. Whether they play detectives, nurses, doctors, or babes in the city seeking Mr. Big, Mr. Right, and bridal gowns, actresses flourish in offbeat series where characters can live, breathe, and even grow organically. For women, the need to please continually wages war with a desire to go against the grain of sympathy, and in the more adventurous realm of television, the latter often wins. As it seems to be doing with a vengeance in recent series television, which has brought us a veritable bonanza of antiheroines ranging from not nice to cringe making: stalkers and narcissists, anorexics and drug addicts, sociopaths and murderers. To name a few, Laura Dern (daughter of sassy *Alice*-friend Diane Ladd) in *Enlightened*, Kathryn Hahn in *I Love Dick*, Edie Falco in *Nurse Jackie*, Laurie Metcalf in *Getting On*. In the accumulated tics and features of a persona lived over time, they've established the kind of audience rapport that the stars of classic Hollywood achieved in their own very different way. Even the double standard of aging shifted ever so slightly to allow actresses like Helen Mirren, Jessica Lange, Meryl Streep, Annette Bening, and Charlotte Rampling to thrive and grow old with refreshing honesty and brio.

Speaking of which: as I was writing this essay, a film opened that was like the neo-woman's film of my dreams, Mike Mills's *20th Century Women*, starring a beautiful, aging Annette Bening. More accurately and movingly than anything I've seen, Mills's great time-skipping movie captures the turmoil of women in the seventies. The movie contains the DNA of those earlier films but is able to look back to the period with hindsight. The year is 1979, a time of "malaise," as Jimmy Carter described the national mood in his "Crisis of Confidence" speech.

In a rambling Victorian house, Bening's Dorothea is a single mom, trying to figure out how to raise her son Jamie (Lucas Jade Zumann), a task for which she enlists the help of her two lodgers—Greta Gerwig as a punk photographer and Billy Crudup as a handyman hippie (shades of Kris Kristofferson's man who works with his hands), along with their neighbor, a luminous Elle Fanning, as Jamie's beloved playmate now suddenly sexual light years ahead of the pubescent boy. Feminism is in the air, Jamie reads *Our Bodies, Ourselves* and tries (to the horror of his male friends) to understand the female orgasm. The sense of family, real and surrogate, permeates this ensemble piece about women (and men) thrashing out the gender roles and obligations in a time of turmoil, when expectations seem to be changing as quickly and confusingly as the rise and flameout of music groups. Mills has acknowledged this as an exploration of his own mother, reserved like most of her generation, a woman with untapped yearnings.

The movie is a series of privileged moments as the chronicle moves back and forth in time, and characters become, arrive, look back. Dorothea tries to see Jamie not as her son, but as a man in the world. He tries, also unsuccessfully, to see his mother's inner life. It is only in later years that we can come close to seeing our parents and children as human beings in their own right, just as it has taken decades for the seeds of feminist cinema to grow and nourish such wisdom as this. By the same principle, it is perhaps only now that we can assess the films of the early seventies, in the light of "what happened next," can see more clearly the aftermath of freedoms unleashed.

Mills's *20th Century Women* is a love story, but unlike *Alice Doesn't Live Here Anymore*, it doesn't have to answer to John Calley, and Dorothea doesn't go off with the hippie who's good with his hands. It's a mother-son love story, but it's also a love story that radiates in multiple directions. Instead of the sacrosanct soul-mate couple (Dorothea's fantasy touchstone is *Casablanca*), the love is spread and dispersed among a group of odd but congenial individuals who form their own community, not apart from the world but within it, arguing, inspiring, consoling one another, dealing with feminism both as an idea and as a fact of life. As he flashes back and forward, Mills gives us a window onto Dorothea's yearnings through the years, her longing to be a pilot during the war years, her romantic fantasies centering on Humphrey Bogart. We are granted, finally and most gloriously, a glimpse of the future: Dorothea after Jamie has grown and has his own family, Dorothea with a man she loves, and Dorothea realizing her childhood dream: climbing into an aircraft as a licensed pilot . . . Dorothea flying alone!

CHAPTER 2

ANTONIONI'S AMERICA
Blow-Up, Zabriskie Point, and the Making of a New Hollywood

Jon Lewis

In December 1966, when the Production Code Administration (PCA) denied MGM a production seal for its planned American release of Michelangelo Antonioni's *Blow-Up*, it was a verdict executives at the studio had surely seen coming. At issue was a single nonnarrative and in the censors' view nonessential sequence in which two female fashion models strip out of their clothes and playfully wrestle with a male photographer at his studio. The scene, which featured full frontal female nudity, would, they were told by the censors, have to be cut in its entirety before resubmission.

MGM's contract with the film's producer Carlo Ponti and the British production company Bridge Films stipulated that the film could not be cut without Antonioni's permission. That MGM contracted for the film's release anyway set the stage for a confrontation between the studio and the Motion Picture Association of America (MPAA) and its censorship apparatus (the PCA) that would hurry the arrival of a new American cinema.

Blow-Up was a fully international production: directed and produced by Italian filmmakers (Antonioni and his producer, Ponti); based on a novel written by Julio Cortázar, an Argentine; shot on location in London for a British production company (Bridge Films); with a cast comprising a who's who of the current swinging London scene—the actors David Hemmings and Vanessa Redgrave, the model and actress Jane Birkin, the British rhythm and blues band the Yardbirds, and the Russian-born supermodel Veruschka. The film evinced a keen interest in the emerging sixties' counterculture, a phenomenon the auteur observed with anthropological fascination.

Before the release of *Blow-Up*, Antonioni had a reputation for a very different sort of effete and intellectual cinema—films that focused on a lost generation of postwar misfits and spoiled brats. His visual style was characterized by static long takes of dramatic landscapes and carefully staged and set interiors. The stories he chose to tell—and "stories" may not be the right word here—were stripped of motivation and consequence. Handsome actors cast as the idle rich wandered through the director's meticulous compositions as if in a trance, not so much as people or players but as signifiers of some unfathomable postwar European ennui.

Antonioni became an important figure on the international scene in 1960 when his film *L'avventura* was showcased at Cannes. The film was met with open derision by audiences and then won the Jury Prize despite (or because) of the film's frustrated reception. *L'avventura* reached American screens in the spring of 1961 along with an even more impactful Italian import, Federico Fellini's *La dolce vita*—a box office sensation that grossed nearly $20 million. A film culture assembled pinned on an appreciation for these two films, which were at once not Hollywood and anti-Hollywood.[1]

L'avventura is a difficult, inaccessible picture—a curious starting point for a trend in American moviegoing. The title is ironic, even misleading; the film depicts the search for a missing person, but there is precious little that happens over its 143 minutes that could be described as "an adventure." The *avventura* in the title refers as well, in colloquial Italian, to a love affair, but the wordplay was lost on most American filmgoers. Here too Antonioni's characters seem too bored for romance, too narcissistic to feel much of anything for anyone else. The film ends with an ambiguous gesture between former lovers in a setting (and in a filmic composition) so breathtaking the problems of these puny mortals are quite clearly inconsequential. That American audiences—that young, well-educated American moviegoers—connected to such a difficult and, in the many ways the term might be applied, *foreign* film said a lot about how disconnected they were from the sorts of pictures made in Hollywood at the time.

The critical response to *L'avventura* in the United States was rapturous. The *Village Voice*'s Andrew Sarris dubbed the film "a sensation,"[2] and Stanley Kaufmann in the *New Republic* described its influence on film language and history as revolutionary: "Antonioni is trying to exploit the unique powers of film as distinct from the theater. . . . He attempts to get from film the same utility of the medium itself as a novelist whose point is not story but mood and character and for whom the texture of the prose works as much as what he says in the prose."[3] Among the influential New York critics, only Pauline Kael registered so much as ambivalence, but she too affirmed the film's and the director's undeniable importance. Kael fell into and then out of love with the film, championing *L'avventura* upon its initial release as the work of singular and obstinate genius, and then later disparaging the film because it set in motion a new wave of disaffected European pictures, which she colorfully dubbed "the come dressed as the sick soul of Europe party."[4]

The film's global impact was considerable. When a panel of international reviewers was asked by the British film journal *Sight and Sound* in 1962 to assemble a list of the Top Ten Best Films of all time, *L'avventura* was ranked at number two, behind *Citizen Kane*.[5]

Blow-Up seemed upon its release a point of departure for its director, suited to a wider American release, and not only because it was set in London and performed in English. The plot roughly fits the American thriller template; quite by accident a fashion photographer captures on a roll of film what looks like a murder, and those implicated in that crime endeavor to silence him. Meanwhile, the characters are diverted by a trendy and enviable lifestyle, a culture at the time associated with the Beatles, Carnaby Street, and Mary Quant.

Blow-Up was as well recognizably foreign in sensibility—a good thing, given the moribund American movie industry at the time. In 1966 no American filmmaker would have dared to so casually depict a subculture so characterized by casual sex. Film censorship in the United States after 1934 and the advent of Production Code enforcement by the PCA was built upon a gentlemen's agreement among the studios that no one film was bigger than the industry as a whole, that sacrificing free expression—cutting a scene or line of dialogue here and there—was the price the studios collectively and collusively paid to maintain the necessary fiction of social responsibility.[6] So, when MGM decided to purchase domestic distribution rights to *Blow-Up* and then went ahead and released the film without a production seal, they did so appreciating the message they were sending to the other studios . . . the agreements, policies, and procedures they were defying.

To avoid a public relations backlash and in order to avoid an MPAA fine and sanction for distributing a noncompliant picture, MGM released *Blow-Up* under the banner of a newly formed non-MPAA subsidiary, Premier Films. *Blow-Up* thus reached the market as a quasi-independent, a convenient fiction in the scheme of things. Executives at MGM did not know how management at the other studios would react or, in the future, how, as a consequence of their decision to subvert PCA authority, other MGM films might be judged by the censorship board. The calculated risk of the Premier Films release involved as well the challenge of contracting with exhibitors.

The risk paid off. *Blow-Up* opened to terrific reviews, and long-struggling theater owners proved altogether willing to book the film. When the film posted strong box office numbers in its full winter/spring 1967 release, it was the MPAA (and not MGM) that had a problem on its hands. Under a March 22, 1967, headline, "'Blow-Up' B.O. Comforts Metro," *Variety* staff writers acknowledged the studio's short-term success in defying the MPAA and PCA.[7] Anticipating other studios following suit with noncompliant titles, the MPAA president, Jack Valenti, posted a press release in the same issue, strategically laid out by the magazine on the same page, announcing his plan to test the feasibility of an age-based, exhibitor-enforced classification system—what would in eighteen months become the MPAA's Voluntary Movie Rating System.

In addition to age-based "variable censorship" criteria, Valenti supported the creation of "other qualifying lines," to differentiate between, for example, foreign-made prestige/art films with adult content like *Blow-Up* and domestically produced soft-core exploitation pictures, designations that might "genuinely inform parents about the content of films."[8] The significance of Antonioni's film in the development and adoption of this new system should not be underestimated.

Learning to Love the European Art Film

In an interview published in the September 18, 1968, issue of *Variety*, Valenti voiced his and by extension the Hollywood industry's concern about the growing *value* of foreign-made pictures in the American film marketplace. Impolitic as it would have been for an MPAA president to blame homegrown filmmakers for what had by then become a generation-long box office slump (the steady slide began in 1947), Valenti instead reproached American film reviewers, who, he contended, had failed to support Hollywood movies and had become instead "hung up on foreign film directors whose names end with 'o' or 'i.'"[9]

First and foremost on Valenti's mind at the time was Antonioni and *Blow-Up*, which premiered in the United States in December 1966 and enjoyed over a successful first run the following year profits exceeding ten times its production budget. Antonioni's film went on to win the Palme d'Or at Cannes and earn Oscar nominations for Best Picture and Best Writing, Story, and Screenplay.

Valenti's remarks about foreign-made films were, to be fair, a subtext to a larger argument about content regulation. He used the *Variety* interview to remind movie reviewers and the readers of the trade journal that foreign auteurs had at the time an unfair advantage, that filmmakers like Antonioni, Bernardo Bertolucci, and Federico Fellini—to name just three directors whose names end with *i*—made their films under comparatively lax regimes of content regulation. The new classification system that Valenti was in the process of developing promised freer and fairer competition in the US market. Once the playing field was leveled, Valenti contended, these same reviewers would need to see past this prejudice against the domestic product or risk being left behind by the popular audience and an inevitable new Hollywood.

Valenti's bold, nativist enthusiasm for a forthcoming American moviemaking revolution begged an obvious question: who currently working for the major studios was prepared to make the sorts of films that might exploit the freedom provided by a new regime of censorship? And moreover, who working for the studios might be prepared to make movies that would capture the interest of the many American moviegoers who, like the reviewers on Valenti's mind in September 1968, had rather fallen for the European art film? Valenti had a ready answer. He boldly announced in *Variety* that "the future of the film business lies on the [college] campus."[10] The prediction proved prescient, as a new generation of film-school students, *would-be* auteurs later dubbed "the movie brats," rose to prominence in the early 1970s. In an irony likely lost on the MPAA president, these young auteurs were themselves enamored with and influenced by the films of foreign directors whose names ended in *o* or *i*.

Just as MGM had contracted to release *Blow-Up* in the United States, Valenti introduced a first and cautious step toward a more competitive film censorship/classification system, a new "M"—"suggested for mature audiences"—rating. The M rating was applied to six new films: *Deadlier Than the Male*, *A Funny Thing Happened on the Way to the Forum*, *Georgy Girl*, *The Long Ride Home*, *Rage*, and *Welcome to Hard Times*. A seventh film, *Who's Afraid of Virginia Woolf?*, got its own designation; on all advertising for the picture, an MPAA legend read, in all-capital letters, "No person under 18 admitted unless accompanied by a parent."

The annual MPAA report for 1967 highlighted another trend: a growing studio reliance on international "negative pickups"—that is, the contracting for U.S. distribution of complete foreign-made and financed films like *Casino Royale*, *The Dirty Dozen*, *For a Few Dollars More*, *A Man and a Woman*, *The Night of the Generals*, *You Only Live Twice*, and *The Good, the Bad and the Ugly*. While these films were not exactly foreign art features like *Blow-Up*, they nonetheless signaled a shift in the studio's business model away from producing films "in house," emphasizing instead distribution.

Six of the top ten box office films for 1967—in order, *The Dirty Dozen*, *You Only Live Twice*, *Casino Royale*, *A Man for All Seasons* (which won the Oscar in 1967 for Best Picture), *Georgy Girl*, and *To Sir, with Love*—were studio releases produced overseas. Of these six hit films, only one—*A Man for All Seasons*—had an easy time with the PCA. Adult or mature content, which played a part in the success at the box office of these films, came to be associated in filmgoers' minds with foreign-made movies.

Though he had by then added the M rating, in January 1967, under the *Variety* headline "Valenti Won't 'Blow-Up' Prod. Code for Status Films; No Church Push," the MPAA president lent his support to then PCA chief Geoffrey Shurlock's decision to deny *Blow-Up* a production seal.[11] (The "no church push" in the headline referred to the National Catholic Office of Motion Pictures or NCOMP, which had issued *Blow-Up* its "condemned" rating.)

Fig. 4. Vanessa Redgrave and David Hemmings in the swinging London-set thriller *Blow-Up* (Michelangelo Antonioni, 1966, Premier Productions / MGM).

The film was for the censorship board simply too much, too soon. But just a few months later, when it became clear that neither the denial of a production seal nor the local activism from NCOMP had adversely affected the film's astonishing first run, American studio executives could no longer ignore the appeal of the less rigorously censored European art film, epitomized by *Blow-Up*. And they began to dream about and plan for a new American cinema in which American filmmakers might enjoy a similar degree of artistic freedom.

Antonioni, a director formerly known for esoteric, inaccessible art films about modern Europe, became after the release of *Blow-Up* in the United States an unlikely but indisputable hot Hollywood property. As part of the agreement securing distribution rights to *Blow-Up*, executives at MGM offered Antonioni a three-picture deal.[12] Antonioni signed the contract, which set the stage for disaster; there was, finally, no meeting of such different minds. The studio entered into the agreement risking a lot on a noncompliant release of *Blow-Up*, banking as well on an American follow-up to the film, figuring Antonioni would produce another stylish thriller. What they got instead was an American *L'avventura*—a languid, plotless, road picture called *Zabriskie Point* (1970).

In retrospect we can see as well how the MGM contract with Antonioni foregrounded and foreshadowed the auteur contracts that would a few years later become a business model in the new Hollywood—a business model that would make possible the American auteur renaissance: films directed by Coppola,

Scorsese, Altman, and Peter Bogdanovich. The business model would as well make inevitable the bloated auteur disaster *Heaven's Gate* (Michael Cimino, 1980), a film Antonioni's *Zabriskie Point* would eerily presage.

The three-picture contract came at a crossroads moment for MGM and the other MPAA studios. Valenti indulged a cockeyed optimism; observing the ruins of the American film market, he implausibly announced in the industry trades: "What's cheering me up is that the new leadership coming up recognizes the problems. . . . I can't tell you when these dinosauric vestiges of the old Hollywood are going to disappear, but I know it's going to happen."[13] Many of the nation's movie reviewers were, as late as 1969, most decidedly not on the same page. The *Time* magazine film reviewer Stefan Kanfer, for example, vented a widely shared pessimism about the state of Hollywood in his 1969 year-end review: "1969 may have been to the movies what 1955 was to Detroit."[14] Kael, writing for the *New Yorker*, made similar use of an auto-industry metaphor: "The movie companies keep bringing out these 'Edsels.'"[15] The irascible *New Yorker* reviewer was hardly in the mood to mince her words; studio Hollywood had, in her view, devolved into "a rotting system in which mediocrity and skyrocketing costs work together to turn out films that would have had a hard time making money even if they were good."[16]

Filmmakers in Europe were up to something different, Kanfer and Kael pointed out, something leaner, smarter, more modern. It was a matter, then, for the studios to catch up, and to do so they would need to do more than just import European talent. (Roman Polanski's *Rosemary's Baby* was released by Paramount in June 1968 to critical and box office success. And just as Paramount was contracting with Polanski, the screenwriter Robert Benton was meeting with François Truffaut and Jean-Luc Godard to discuss directing *Bonnie and Clyde*.)

A quick survey of the National Society of Film Critics Awards for 1969 betrays the extent of the critics' preference for the European auteur cinema. The critics selected *Z*—a political thriller directed by the Greek filmmaker Costa-Gavras and financed and supervised by a French production company—for Best Picture. The two runners-up were films made by veterans of the French New Wave: *Stolen Kisses*, directed by Truffaut, and Claude Chabrol's *La femme infidel*. Only one American-born director made the short-list of the year's best: Sam Peckinpah, for his ultraviolent western, *The Wild Bunch*.

The programmers for the 1969 New York Film Festival opened their annual event with a controversial gesture to a post-rating-system Hollywood, a screening of the very un-festival-like feature *Bob & Carol & Ted & Alice*, directed by Paul Mazursky. But after opening night, the festival program fell back upon a decided preference for the European art film: Robert Bresson's *Une femme douce*, Godard's *Le gai savoir*, Éric Rohmer's *My Night at Maud's*,

Agnès Varda's *Lion's Love*, Pier Paolo Pasolini's *Pigpen*, and Bo Widerberg's *Ådalen 31*.

The following year marked a significant transition as the 1970 program featured new American films directed by Martin Scorsese, Peter Bogdanovich, Robert Altman, Robert Benton, and Bob Rafelson on a program that continued to feature Bertolucci, Godard, Truffaut, Bresson, Chabrol, and Luis Buñuel. In 1970, a significant reevaluation of the American product was under way overseas as well, as Altman's *MASH* won the Grand Prix du Festival at Cannes. An American film would win the top prize at Cannes again in 1973 (Jerry Schatzberg's *Scarecrow*), 1974 (Coppola's *The Conversation*), and 1976 (Scorsese's *Taxi Driver*).[17]

Viewed in retrospect, Antonioni's *Blow-Up* was just ahead of this curve—the right film at the right time, merging the French and British postwar New Waves with something undeniably and, to American filmgoers, recognizably hip. Its successful first US run anticipated by a few months the release of two successful American-made accommodations of the same influences and impulses: *The Graduate* (Mike Nichols) and *Bonnie and Clyde* (Arthur Penn). All to say, in 1970, with auteur American films drawing from and evolving out from the styles and sensibilities of the European art film, the market seemed primed for Antonioni and MGM to further explore and expand a new American cinema built upon the postwar European New Waves. The stage was thusly set for *Zabriskie Point*.

Antonioni's America

When MGM purchased the US rights to *Blow-Up*, it had already seen the finished product, financed from development through postproduction by Ponti et al. With *Zabriskie Point*, Antonioni was, so to speak, playing with the studios' money from start to finish. The negative pickup model had limited MGM's risk on *Blow-Up*, but it had limited as well the studio's stake in the film's profits, which were substantial. The risk-to-reward ratio was steeper on *Zabriskie Point*—with more complete ownership came an increased potential payoff . . . or, as well, increased exposure at the back end.

During preproduction, Antonioni showed executives at MGM a brief outline penned by the American playwright Sam Shepard about real estate speculators and wilderness exploitation in the desert Southwest. Antonioni would soon abandon Shepard's scenario, opting instead to tell the story of two young lovers. To better understand the American counterculture from which these characters emerge, Antonioni conducted interviews with student radicals and employed as an adviser and later as an on-screen extra Kathleen Cleaver, whose husband, the Black Panther leader Eldridge Cleaver, was in 1969 one of the FBI's ten most wanted fugitives.[18] To state the obvious here, the development process was not exactly what the studio expected or wanted.

Five writers earned screenplay credit for *Zabriskie Point*: Shepard, Antonioni, the veteran Italian screenwriter Tonino Guerra (who had worked with Antonioni on *L'avventura*), the journalist and left-wing political organizer Fred Gardner, and Clare Peploe, Antonioni's girlfriend at the time. Their various contributions, whether sequential or more directly collaborative, are hard to figure in retrospect, as the film comprises long stretches of on-set improvisation. Many scenes are characterized not by dialogue or scripted exposition but instead by long periods of silence.

Antonioni prepared for the shoot by taking a long sojourn across the United States, during which he proposed to divine the *feeling* of young Americans. The trip had a profound effect on him, significantly impacting what would become, conceptually, a work of American neorealism: nonprofessional actors captured in a quasi-documentary style. A similar vibe and style would come to characterize another road picture shot just a few months earlier, *Easy Rider* (Dennis Hopper, 1969); but the differences in execution and in subsequent popularity and profitability between the two films are remarkable.

Hopper and Peter Fonda (who coproduced and costar in *Easy Rider*) comfortably embodied their characters; both emerge as archetypes of a new American youth culture searching for an alternative to the conservative "establishment" of their parents' generation. It is never clear in Antonioni's film what his actors Daria Halprin and Mark Frechette are up to . . . and not just because neither was an experienced or instinctive actor. They appear throughout at once beautiful and baffled—metaphors for some larger *feeling*

Fig. 5. The American Southwest dominates the characters in *Zabriskie Point* (Antonioni, 1970, MGM).

the director hoped would emerge organically from their movement through the gorgeous Southwest landscape. MGM had wanted an American *Blow-Up*. Then, after the director opted to make a road picture about two young Americans, they maybe fantasized that he might make for them an art-house *Easy Rider*. What they got instead was a desert Southwest *L'avventura*, a road trip to Death Valley and the continent's geographic low point, Zabriskie Point . . . a road trip, if we embrace the metaphor, to nowhere.

In an interview with the film reviewer Roger Ebert, Antonioni spoke about the power and allure of the film's emptied landscape as quite distinct from Hopper's very American celebration of the open road: "The desert is nothing. It's an enormous area of nothing. We do not have spaces like that in Europe. . . . The existence of these great spaces so close to the city says something to me about America."[19]

In the same interview, Antonioni reflected upon the film that had first attracted MGM, characterizing the success of *Blow-Up* as a fluke. The international audience had misread *Blow-Up*, Antonioni mused; the film was not at all "about a certain lifestyle in London." Instead, the film "expressed a feeling about [a] style" that emerged organically out of what he and his crew captured daily on the set, a feeling that "[he] wouldn't want to put . . . into words." *Blow-Up*, the director argued, was not a movie about a crime and the mystery surrounding it—that is, it was not the film MGM executives rather liked—but instead "the story of a photographer." The photographs that set the narrative in motion were not for Antonioni plot points, but instead "things that happened to [the character] . . . in the course of being a professional photographer. . . . Anything could have happened to him; he was a person living in that world with that personality."[20]

With *Zabriskie Point*, Antonioni focused again on producing "a feeling about a style." It was a moviemaking method MGM executives never understood or appreciated at all. Antonioni's dailies seemed to them incomprehensible, occasionally pornographic. A moment of truth was reached in the unhappy collaboration between director and studio when Death Valley National Park rangers objected to Antonioni's use of the park to shoot an explicit sex scene and briefly blocked his access to the site. The studio quietly declined to intercede, hoping Antonioni would abandon his plans and move on. But the passive-aggressive strategy failed, as an organized group of environmental activists, believing Shepard's anti-developer script was still being used, intervened. The environmentalists successfully persuaded Park Service officials in Washington, DC, to force the local rangers to allow Antonioni to shoot his scene.

The Death Valley shoot proved to be the film's signature moment: an eight-minute widescreen tableau set to a guitar duet depicting dozens of naked couples making love in the sand, becoming in some physical and spiritual way part of the landscape of the continent's geographic nadir: Zabriskie Point. Executives at MGM would look back on this scene with a mix of disgust and frustration. Antonioni had produced a very long sex scene with no dialogue and no apparent connection to the story that would make an R rating impossible to get. After the rangers backed off, MGM dutifully helped Antonioni shoot the scene; per the director's request, the studio arranged for the delivery of a massive amount of finer-grain sand so the actors and extras might more comfortably cavort under the desert sun.

The rangers acceded to pressure from DC. But they did not go quietly, sending letters of complaint to executives at MGM, to the press, and, most effectively, to law enforcement, which brought the production to the attention of the FBI. Kathleen Cleaver's presence on the set rather maintained their interest.

Antonioni's perceived leftist/communist politics caused problems as well with the politically conservative craftsmen hired by MGM to work on the film. And in solidarity, the Teamsters organized a series of slowdowns and sickouts. According to Beverly Walker, a publicist hired by "Antonioni's people" to do damage control during the production, the crew openly referred to the director, who throughout the shoot communicated with them through an interpreter, as "a pinko dago pornographer." The craftsmen and the Teamsters' reaction was a sign of the times; it may have been the Age of Aquarius, but it was as well two years into President Richard Nixon's first term, a regime built upon a conservative coalition dubbed "the silent majority" that included the very sort of hourly workers hired for the location shoot.

Less than a month after principal photography was completed and just as the film was being prepared for release, in April 1969 Antonioni's problems

Fig. 6. The Death Valley orgy scene in *Zabriskie Point* (Michelangelo Antonioni, 1970, MGM)

with federal law enforcement came to a head as several among the major players in the production company and at the studio were named in a bizarre criminal action. The US Attorney's office alleged that the extras who were bused in to appear in the Death Valley scene were ostensibly transported across state lines for immoral purposes in violation of the 1910 Mann Act—a law meant to combat turn-of-the-twentieth-century white slavery.[21] When several members of the crew came forward to testify against Antonioni, the film's evolving backstory took on much the same tenor as the political inquisition in Hollywood two decades earlier . . . so much so that, in a wonderfully ironic turn, the *Hollywood Reporter*, a politically conservative trade journal that had played a significant role enforcing the blacklist, weighed in on Antonioni's behalf, calling the federal investigation "politically inspired" and condemning the government's "attempt to thwart the release of the picture, which is said to be anti-American."[22]

By the time the US Department of Justice got involved, MGM was already doing all it could to distance itself from the film and its director. And Antonioni was learning on the fly about making a movie for and doing business with a Hollywood studio: that securing production financing was one thing—influencing a film's playoff in theaters quite another. Antonioni's contract assured him reasonable production finances and a salary as the film's director. But once the film was complete, the marketing of "his" film was left to a studio disinclined to promote the picture.

In the latter half of 1969, as *Zabriskie Point* was being prepared for release, MGM ostensibly walked away from what they discerned to be a bad investment. The director went public with his frustration: "[MGM] asks me why the film is so expensive, but that's what I'm going to ask them. I'm seeing such a waste of money. It seems almost immoral. . . . They are consumers. They are used to wasting."[23] MGM countered in the trades and popular press, characterizing Antonioni as a profligate and a charlatan and the film as a neo-Marxist, neorealist, art picture without a coherent plot, without professional performances.

After just one film, Antonioni's American career was over. And most everyone involved in the making of *Zabriskie Point* was suitably relieved that they would never have to work together again.

Antonioni, American Cinema, and the Counterculture

The corporate raider Kirk Kerkorian and his right-hand man James Aubrey took control of MGM in 1969, inheriting *Zabriskie Point* and the many problems that came with it. New regimes in Hollywood routinely shortchange their predecessors' projects. It's not enough to succeed in the movie business; it's necessary as well for those you might be compared to to fail.

Kerkorian and Aubrey delayed the release of *Zabriskie Point* for over a year. The limited play-off signaled their lack of interest, and the film as a consequence grossed an embarrassing $900,000 off a $7 million production budget. The critics, many of them former fans of the director, panned the film. Charles Champlin of the *Los Angeles Times* described *Zabriskie Point* as "shallow and obvious . . . unusefully oblique."[24] Ebert, writing for the *Chicago Sun-Times*, was similarly dismissive: "[*Zabriskie Point*] is such a silly and stupid movie."[25] In the *New York Times*, Vincent Canby remarked on the film's "stunning superficiality."[26]

Looking back at *Zabriskie Point* today, free from the bad press that attended its release, we can more fairly acknowledge Antonioni's success in capturing the feeling of what it was like to be young, to be blissed out, and then a moment later pissed off as the sixties wound down.[27] And we can see why he decided to cast Halprin and Frechette, even though they couldn't act. For Antonioni, it was only important that they looked the part, that they embodied the feeling of what it was like to be young in America at the time.

Antonioni cast Halprin after seeing her in *Revolution* (Jack O'Connell), a 1968 documentary on hippies in San Francisco. Quite by accident, a casting director "discovered" Frechette engaged in a heated and pointless argument at a bus station in Boston. Halprin had, according to Antonioni, a "bratty, free, earth-child quality." She thus ably attended to the blissed-out angle. When the casting director stumbled upon Frechette, he rattled off a telegram to Antonioni stating simply: "He's twenty and he hates." When Antonioni finally met

Fig. 7. Mark Frechette and Daria Halprin, in Michelangelo Antonioni's eccentric road picture *Zabriskie Point* (1970, MGM)

Frechette, he perceived "the elegance of an aristocrat . . . there was something mystical about him."[28] No screen tests were deemed necessary, as Halprin and Frechette were not so much people or characters as archetypes.

Casting nonprofessional actors was for the director a matter of principle as well as design. His goal, elaborated in the interview with Ebert, was "to make a film about youth in America by taking two American young people and making a film about them." It is hard to dispute that he accomplished that goal. But in doing so—accomplishing that goal, that is—Antonioni embraced a fundamental un- if not anti-American concept of moviemaking, in which plot is subsumed to design, in which character motivation is subsumed to something more vague like instinct, or just being. For Antonioni it was not that life imitates art. It was more that life *is* art.

The confluence of life and art persisted after the production wrapped. As if carrying on with his role as pissed-off Mark, Frechette smugly refused to promote the film.[29] He appeared with Halprin on *The Dick Cavett Show*. Seated alongside the comedy writer and filmmaker Mel Brooks and the *New York Post* film reviewer Rex Reed, Frechette remained in character. In a feature about the film's director, Frechette told Ebert he planned to quit acting to go back to carpentry; he had lately seen several of Antonioni's previous films and didn't much like any of them. As to *Zabriskie Point*, the actor's candid remarks echoed the nation's critical establishment: "Nothing happens, man; it's just a lot of young people going nowhere." Antonioni, interviewed for the same article, deigned to agree: "What happens to [Daria and Mark] is not important. I could have them do one thing, or another thing. People think that the events in a film are what the film is about. Not true."[30]

During and then briefly after the production, Halprin and Frechette, like their screen counterparts, fell into and then out of love. Like her screen surrogate, Halprin escaped intact and alive, first into the arms of the Hollywood rebel Dennis Hopper (whom she married in 1972 and divorced four years later) and then into dance therapy, cofounding (with her mother, Anna Halprin) the Tamalpa Institute in California, which she continues to run today. Frechette settled, with Halprin at first, at the Fort Hill Community, a Boston commune founded by a charismatic and deeply crazy former harp player named Mel Lyman. The *Rolling Stone*'s David Felton described the organization of the commune as "acid fascism" and dubbed its leader, Lyman, "the East Coast Charles Manson."[31]

As Antonioni remarked to Ebert, *Zabriskie Point*, like all his previous films, is about loneliness. His characters look "for personal relationships that will absorb them," but instead "find little to sustain them." In the final analysis, "they are [all just] looking for a home."[32] The real-life Mark Frechette turned his back on Hollywood and in the aftermath of *Zabriskie Point* resumed looking for a home. Lyman gave him a way out, a counterculture lifestyle far from Hollywood.

In 1973 Frechette robbed a bank, acting, he claimed, on behalf of Lyman, who may or may not have known in advance about the crime. Frechette claimed the robbery was performed as a political act—a protest against Watergate. He was caught, arrested, tried, and incarcerated, and then, in 1975, he was discovered dead in a prison exercise room with his throat crushed under a barbell. His death by misadventure was altogether cinematic, but it was not the sort of scene Antonioni would have ever staged or shot. It lacked restraint.[33]

Frechette's unhappy demise rather suited his post-Hollywood sojourn, offering a fitting coda to the lives of the real Mark Frechette and the loosely fictional Mark in *Zabriskie Point*. It offered as well an apt conclusion to and commentary upon Antonioni's brief and disappointing Hollywood career.

CHAPTER 3

"JASON'S NO BUSINESSMAN... I THINK HE'S AN ARTIST"
BBS and the New Hollywood Dream

Jonathan Kirshner

The six-picture deal between Columbia Pictures and the production company BBS was the big brass ring of the New Hollywood. It all came down to this: if the films came in under their modest-but-sufficient budgets of $1 million each, the studio would have no say over content, which would be left entirely to the discretion of partners Bob Rafelson, Bert Schneider, and Steve Blauner. Producer Schneider was essentially the house paterfamilias; in addition to producing, Rafelson would also write and direct; Blauner's portfolio left him responsible for distribution. With good friend, fellow traveler, and triple threat (writer, director, and actor) Jack Nicholson along for the ride, BBS set out to fulfill the dream of an American New Wave: to make personal, ambitious, commercially viable films influenced by the European art house cinema of the late 1950s and early 1960s. And the BBS deal would indeed result in some of the landmarks of the New American Cinema, including *Five Easy Pieces*, *The Last Picture Show*, and *The King of Marvin Gardens*. But that success would not be long sustained, nor would it prove easy to duplicate.

Bob Rafelson studied philosophy at Dartmouth (where he counted among his friends Buck Henry, who would also play an important role in the New Hollywood, principally as a writer).[1] The restless, peripatetic Rafelson was drafted into the army and stationed in Japan, where he worked as a free-form disc jockey (shades of *Marvin Gardens*) and where he had the good fortune to be exposed to the cinema of Yasujurō Ozu, whose signature style of a motionless, observing camera would inform the future director's exterior compositions. Rafelson decamped to Hollywood in 1962, and in 1965 he met Bert Schneider when both were working for Screen Gems, the television production arm of Columbia Pictures. The politically radical, troublemaking Schneider had been kicked out of Cornell University, but he had good Hollywood connections (his father served as president of Columbia Pictures). The two men quickly hit it off and in short order formed a partnership, Raybert Productions, where they would enjoy a runaway success by creating and producing the television show *The Monkees*. (The improbable lark also accounted for their first feature, *Head*, directed by Rafelson and produced by Schneider.)

Flush with cash from *The Monkees*, Raybert was able to finance Dennis Hopper and Peter Fonda's low-budget biker picture (then a common youth-market subgenre) *Easy Rider*, and secured a distribution deal for the film from Columbia after the movie was a sensation at the Cannes Film Festival. The wildly unexpected commercial success of *Easy Rider* that followed convinced the anxious suits at a then-struggling Columbia Pictures to take a relatively inexpensive chance on the youth market—thus the legendary six-picture deal. By that time Schneider's childhood friend Steve Blauner, another veteran of Screen Gems (and onetime manager of Bobby Darin) had joined the partnership, and Raybert became BBS.[2]

Jack Nicholson, then a journeyman actor, who, failing to break out after ten-plus years of effort, was transitioning toward what he expected would be a largely behind-the-camera career as a writer and a director, was a virtual fourth partner at BBS. Fittingly for that "heroic age of film-going," he first met Rafelson at a mid-sixties underground LA art house film screening. Another close friendship was forged, and Nicholson would cowrite *Head* with Rafelson and was a coproducer of the film. It was in that context that Nicholson was attached to *Easy Rider*—assigned by Schneider essentially to keep an eye on the picture, he stepped into the career-making role of George Hanson only after Rip Torn left the production.[3]

Nicholson is to some extent the fulcrum of the BBS story, because he came to the company having been among the many young and aspiring talents who essentially apprenticed in the business at American International Pictures (AIP). The participants in Corman's low-budget, all-hands-on-deck AIP productions were almost all affiliates-of-Jack in one way or another. And it was Nicholson who suggested that Hopper and Fonda bring *Easy Rider* to Raybert after Corman, wary of market saturation—he had directed Fonda in *The Wild Angels* (1966) and was alert to the recent success of the (Nicholson-starring) *Hell's Angels on Wheels* (1967)—turned down yet another biker picture.

Many of Nicholson's friendships could be traced to the acting classes of the blacklisted Jeff Corey; whether via Corman's assembly-line or Corey's workshops (or both), these relationships deepened the talent pool that BBS would eventually draw from. Prominent among these affiliates were writers

Robert Towne and Carole Eastman, cinematographer László Kovács (he shot *Hell's Angels on Wheels*, and Nicholson recommended him for *Easy Rider*), director Monte Hellman, and a large cohort of actors that included Bruce Dern and Dean Stockwell. Dern, Stockwell, and Nicholson had lead roles in *Psych-Out* (1968), which followed on the hallucinogenic heels of Corman's *The Trip* (1967), written by Nicholson and featuring Dern, Fonda, and Hopper. These were heady times for young, aspiring filmmakers. Hellman and Nicholson would haunt screenings of European films and talk about them into the night—the influences of these films and the conversations that followed were visible in two micro-budget westerns they would shoot on Corman's dime, *The Shooting* (1966), written by Eastman, and *Ride in the Whirlwind* (1966), written by Nicholson.[4] "We wanted to have film that reflected our lives . . . the cultural changes that we were all products of," BBS affiliate Henry Jaglom would recall years later.

A New American Cinema

BBS's debut effort was also its most archetypical, in both form and content. *Five Easy Pieces* was shot in late 1969 and released in 1970, and like all the company's productions, in both text and especially subtext, it reflected the demoralizing legacies of recent history. Nineteen sixty-seven was the year of *Sgt. Pepper* and the Summer of Love—anything seemed possible. But in 1968 everything came crashing down, from the Tet Offensive through the assassinations of Martin Luther King Jr. and Robert Kennedy to the police riot at the Democratic National Convention in Chicago. "On to Chicago, and let's win there," were the final public words of a triumphant Bobby, moments before the end of everything; five months later, Nixon was narrowly elected president—1969 was the first year of the new administration. The scheming, seething, hopelessly square Nixon was the antithesis of the New Hollywood. Assuming office, Nixon would expand the Vietnam War abroad and promised "law and order" at home. In 1969 Bobby Seale would be bound and gagged at the trial of the Chicago Seven, and the American public would first learn of the My Lai Massacre. These were dispiriting times, to say the least, and they contributed to an elegiac pessimism that informed many New Hollywood films.

Rafelson, who would direct, developed the story for *Five Easy Pieces* with Carole Eastman, with Nicholson in mind for the lead. Eastman (under the shield of her pseudonym Adrien Joyce) wrote the screenplay, revising in response to the director's suggestions (neither Rafelson nor Nicholson, for example, found Eastman's original ending, in which Jack's character would perish in a car crash, satisfactory). This would be the most fertile period of

Eastman's career; she had just contributed dialogue to Jacques Demy's first American film, *Model Shop* (1969) and would next turn to the screenplay for Jerry Schatzberg's Faye Dunaway vehicle, *Puzzle of a Downfall Child* (1970).[5]

Working closely with cinematographer László Kovács, Rafelson, channeling his inner Ozu, settled on a visual style that emphasized long shots and long takes, with exteriors invariably featuring fixed camera positions. According to Kovacs, they both saw the film "as kind of a Chekhovian play," which informed these choices.[6] Another key participant in the film was Karen Black, who had appeared in Francis Ford Coppola's *You're a Big Boy Now* (1966), as well as briefly in *Easy Rider*. Seen as too intelligent for her character, Black promised Rafelson, "Bob, when you call 'action,' I will stop thinking." The results are on-screen—when *Five Easy Pieces* won the New York Film Critics Circle awards for best picture and best director, Black took home the award for best supporting actress (in what was really a leading role).[7]

In the popular imagination, *Five Easy Pieces* is most commonly remembered for its least representative scene. At a restaurant on the long road trip that connects the two disparate parts of the film, Bobby (Nicholson) has an ugly confrontation with a waitress, as he cleverly if rudely explains how she can serve him toast without violating "the rules"—a broadly cheered, (relatively) youthful rebellion against the absurdity of the thoughtless, conformist, older establishment. But Bobby is no rebel (and, as he points out, despite his theatrics and his ability to see through the game, he actually didn't get his toast). The two other eruptions of his temper—strikingly parallel episodes, first among the working-class oil riggers of Southern California and later with the ascetic intellectuals of remote Washington—are not so much rejections of those groups as they are expressions of frustration at his inability to feel at home in either setting. In each instance, Bobby's outburst is associated with him fleeing the scene, ultimately for good. Flight is his one defense mechanism, and he does it instinctively, shedding one skin and seeking rebirth elsewhere. The ritual has a subconscious element to it. Twice before Bobby's shocking, final escape at the gas station, he is seen in a trance-like state, first at the bowling alley (and note the foreshadowing service station in the background in the conversation that follows) and later, in a quite explicitly analogous episode, looking in the bathroom mirror at home. But it was not quite time; the urge was not yet overwhelming, though in that second episode he makes it all the way to his car before reluctantly doubling back to collect Rayette (Black).

Bobby's problem is not with society; it is with himself. As Stephen Farber emphasized, in *Easy Rider* the problem is *external* (murderous rednecks, intolerant America); here the problem is found *within*, which is why Farber considers *Five Easy Pieces* to be "a more mature and honest work" and one that is thus able to interrogate "American myths in a more thoughtful and coherent way."[8]

And Bobby's troubles are indeed internal. Whether because of the weight of oppressive paternal expectations (the perspective favored by Eastman, and even more explicit in earlier drafts), or the result of a more general inability to make emotional connections with others (the interpretation favored by Rafelson), Bobby has a serious Jackson Browne problem on his hands: "I've been up and down this highway / Far as my eyes can see; No matter how fast I run / I can never seem to get away from me."[9]

It is not just this "inward turn" that situates *Five Easy Pieces* as a seventies film; equally important, at least, is its deeply flawed, ultimately irretrievable protagonist. Swimming upstream against Nicholson's formidable charisma is the cold fact that our protagonist is not simply unheroic—he is not a nice guy. And more seventies still is that the movie beats the hell out of him. His pursuit of Catherine (Susan Anspach) is first emasculating and finally shattering. Catherine has the better of him in their verbal exchanges, and is often presented in ways suggestive of her relative strength, as when she returns from horseback riding (an earlier version of that scene had her just back from a swim, which would have changed the power dynamics of that conversation). Bobby is repeatedly, with some effort, seeking her out; his final such search culminates in the bizarre fight with Spicer (the "male nurse"), which is plainly choreographed as sexual act that places Bobby in the submissive role and ends with him collapsing, dropped on the floor.

But that was nothing compared to what Catherine would lay on him immediately afterward, in a devastating indictment of everything Bobby had become: "If a person has no love of himself, no respect, no love for his work, family, friends, something . . . how can he ask for love in return?" That settles that, and from there Bobby finally has his "conversation" with his mute, stricken father (Nicholson wrote much of this monologue), in which the mask comes off, and Bobby tries to make some sense of his life: "I move around a lot . . . not because I'm looking for anything. . . . I'm getting away from things that get bad if I stay."

And with that, Bobby sets off to leave home again—and, reverting to form, without saying goodbye, as his sister notes with chastising dismay, catching him in the act by chance. But how many lives Bobby has left is unclear. Stripping away every possession in that final gas station restroom, he bums a ride on a truck, heading north, without even a jacket, to a place that will be "colder than hell," while the camera lingers, observing impassively from a distance the departing Bobby and an uncertain, abandoned Rayette. Roger Ebert, who saw *Five Easy Pieces* when it premiered at the New York Film Festival, recalled "the stunned attention as the final shot seemed to continue forever, and then the ovation." They knew what they had seen: "We'd had a revelation. This was the direction American movies could take."[10]

Jack of All Trades

The second BBS effort was Nicholson's directorial debut, *Drive, He Said*. With *Five Easy Pieces*, these two projects were the "couple of things" Nicholson anticipated working on as the production company was taking shape—as noted, at that time he was then envisioning a turn away from acting. But with the sensation of *Pieces* following on the heels of *Easy Rider*, Nicholson would soon be in demand as a movie star. That formidable incentive, coupled with the largely hostile reception to *Drive, He Said*, pushed him back in front of the camera, where he would largely remain, for decades to come, as an international sensation. This yielded an impressive body of work that included many important performances, but the road not taken is interesting to contemplate, because *Drive* shows considerable promise. Vincent Canby concluded it was "not a great film, but it is an often intelligent one, and . . . so much better than all the rest of the campus junk Hollywood has manufactured in the last couple of years." And Nicholson's handling of actors was widely praised. Bruce Dern, who delivers the best performance in the film, and one of the finest in his long career—Ebert called it "a small masterpiece of accurate observation"—lauded both the specific suggestions and the space provided by his first-time director, who "gave me the opportunity to be really good" and "encouraged me to push the envelope all the time." But the film had a disastrous premiere at Cannes, where it was met with catcalls, whistles, and even some who "got to their feet and waved indignant fists."[11]

Contemporary viewers are likely to look past two attributes of the film that were potentially offputting to audiences in 1971. Most problematically then, given the politics of the moment and the core audience to which the film would have to appeal, *Drive* paints a somewhat skeptical picture of the counterculture—Nicholson goes as far as to describe the film as "very critical of youth," which of course stood in marked contrast with the rebellious characters he was known for as an actor, and thus the expectations (and preferences) of viewers at that time. Others might have been left slightly uneasy by the film's then somewhat raw presentation of nudity and sex.[12]

Seen today, the film sheds those handicaps. *Drive, He Said* is a campus-based story centered on two friends, Hector (William Tepper), an NBA-ready basketball star with mixed feelings about signing up for what all that would entail, and his roommate Gabriel (Michael Margotta), flirting with both collegiate radicalism and mental illness as he attempts to evade the military draft. Robert Towne, who polished his own dialogue to impressive effect, has a fine turn as Richard, a local professor married to Olive (Karen Black), with whom Hector is having an affair that he (Richard) is not quite ready to confront. Dern, as the basketball coach, has the best role in the film; Henry Jaglom also

Fig. 8. Karen Black in *Drive, He Said* (Jack Nicholson, 1971, Columbia)

makes an appearance. The narrative is driven, loosely and episodically, by the crises faced by the protagonists: Hector's fraying relationship with Olive and his ambivalence about turning pro, and Gabriel's increasingly tenuous grip on his sanity.

Drive, with a screenplay by Nicholson and Jeremy Larner, was based on the latter's debut novel. Written in 1961 and published in 1964, the book often feels dated, a result of the enormous social-cultural changes that had taken place in the years between novel and film. But Nicholson was taken with the source material, and had been developing the project from as early as 1967. Larner, then a hot, hip young writer, would become a speechwriter for Eugene McCarthy during his 1968 presidential campaign and would go on to win an Academy Award for writing the cautionary political tale *The Candidate* (1972) starring Robert Redford and Peter Boyle and best and properly remembered for its killer ("now what?") denouement.[13]

The screenplay for *Drive* is virtually unrecognizable from its source material—as Canby noted in his review, "reading the novel might mislead." Only two passages are closely identifiable with the book: chapter 2, which lingers on the locker-room/shower scene (this almost certainly piqued Nicholson's original interest), and, near the end, with the cross-cutting of the "big game" and Gabriel's assault on Olive. The considerable changes from book to film over successive drafts were invariably for the better—that assault, for example, ended in murder in the novel, and was initially limited to rape and then, quite wisely, to attempted rape, revisions without which any audience sympathy for Gabriel (a much more disturbed and disagreeable character in the book than in the film) would have been lost. Still, despite successful efforts to tone down specific aspects of Gabriel's most unpleasant behavior, both Larner and producer Bert Schneider thought the finished film was too critical of campus radicalism more generally.[14]

Inventively shot by cinematographer Bill Butler[15]—key moments include the early faux-terrorists-in-the-darkness sequence, the long zoom that shifts from Coach Bullion running to Hector shooting hoops (which speaks volumes), as well as capably handled documentary-style moments and hand-held work—*Drive, He Said* nevertheless has its limitations. New Hollywood films gloriously reject the feel-good notions of happy or tidy endings, but Gabriel is insufficiently charismatic for his disturbing and ultimately final descent into madness to carry adequate emotional weight. More generally, the fact that the supporting parts are more compellingly drawn than the principals leaves the audience most curious about what is taking place at the margins of the story and even off-screen. Characteristically a great strength, one drawback of the BBS policy of deference whenever possible to the vision of its filmmakers was that mistakes were sometimes left uncorrected. Thus although Schneider had considerable reservations about the casting of both Hector and Gabriel (Nicholson toyed with playing the latter part himself, and invested the character with some of his own personality quirks), Nicholson held firm, and was especially enthusiastic about Tepper, whose impassive performance makes it difficult for viewers to become invested in Hector's struggles. Nevertheless, *Drive, He Said* merits close attention. Concerning his director, Schneider lamented in 1975 that it was "unfortunate that his acting career has been so successful," because Nicholson "is one of the most interesting directors I know."[16]

Life in Black and White

Schneider's support of his directors, however, was what made the best BBS productions possible. When Peter Bogdanovich—at the persistent urging of Orson Welles—told his producer that he wanted to shoot *The Last Picture Show* in black and white, Schneider was skeptical.[17] It was unlikely that a major studio would have approved such a decision—the recent switch of television to color broadcasting decimated the tolerance of an always-fearful-of-TV Hollywood for new film productions in black and white—but as was his wont, Schneider acceded to Bogdanovich's request, and Columbia was not asked for its opinion on the matter.

Bogdanovich took a rather European path to filmmaking, starting out initially as a film critic and historian. Precocious and confident, he bluffed his way first into film classes and then a job organizing retrospectives of his favorite directors at the Museum of Modern Art; once established, he would place essays in high-profile outlets, interview legendary filmmakers, publish monographs on John Ford and Fritz Lang, and program films for the New Yorker Theater.[18]

In 1965 he met Roger Corman, inevitably at the movies—a screening of Jacques Demy's *Bay of Angels*. The following year Corman invited him to work on *The Wild Angels*, at which time he did what many Corman hands did, that is, a little bit of everything: working as an assistant and second unit director, rewriting much of the script, and even cutting some of his own footage in the editing room, responsibilities all pretty much learned on the job. Corman was pleased with the results and backed Bogdanovich's first feature, *Targets* (1968), which garnered critical acclaim and earned a tidy profit. The most cinephilic of them all, even in this crowd of movie lovers, Bogdanovich could not only talk of the funeral scene in *Picture Show* as obviously including a "Ford Shot" (many critics thought the film was indebted to the cinema of John Ford and Howard Hawks), but also add in the same breath that he presented the scene first in a series of close-ups, holding back the final long shot, "something I learned from Hitchcock."[19]

Bogdanovich and his wife Polly Platt met Schneider through their mutual friend Henry Jaglom, and when Schneider asked what project the director might be interested in pursuing, Platt suggested *The Last Picture Show*; she had been given Larry McMurtry's novel by the actor Sal Mineo and thought its treatment of small-town 1950s sexual politics was promising source material. Platt, who had been Nancy Sinatra's stunt double on *Wild Angels*, would serve as production designer on *Picture Show*, though in addition to that formal credit most accounts emphasize her role as an essential partner to Bogdanovich in almost every aspect of the production. (Platt, who would have a distinguished career as a production designer and a producer, worked on Bogdanovich's next two films, *What's Up, Doc?* (1972) and *Paper Moon* (1973), despite the fact that the couple would separate in the wake of Bogdanovich's relationship with Cybill Shepherd that emerged during the *Picture Show* shoot.)[20]

Unlike *Drive, He Said*, Bogdanovich's film tracks fairly closely the trajectory of its source material, and much of the novel's fine dialogue is retained verbatim. But Welles, and even McMurtry, urged that the film avoid being "too faithful" to the book, which was wise advice—the movie is tough and unflinching; the book is routinely crude and unpleasant, and gratuitously tawdry. Bogdanovich also thought Jeff Bridges's natural charisma took some of the edge off Duane's character, noting that if you only read the screenplay, you would conclude "the guy is not very nice." Bridges's boyish charm notwithstanding, every omission and revision by screenwriters Bogdanovich and McMurtry left

Fig. 9. Mother and daughter (Ellen Burstyn and Cybill Shepherd) in *The Last Picture Show* (Peter Bogdanovich, 1971, Columbia)

the film far superior to the novel, most notably (but in no way limited to) the marvelous, wistful monologue by Sam the Lion (Ben Johnson).[21]

Nominally the story of Duane and Sonny (Timothy Bottoms), two friends facing uncertain futures in an undistinguished, past-its-prime Texas town (the "last picture show" refers to the closing of its only movie house), as Heather Hendershot has observed, the film is remarkably "thoughtful about the female perspective." There are in fact four substantial female parts, and the film is arguably more about their narratives, which reflect the prospects and possibilities for the women of their time and place, than those of the two boys; these characters have greater depth than do the ostensible male protagonists. Ellen Burstyn read for three of the roles, and Bogdanovich let her have her pick. She chose Lois, who married well and unhappily, and hopes her daughter Jacy (Shepherd) might avoid the mistakes she made; Eileen Brennan plays the working-class Genevieve; Cloris Leachman the tragic Ruth Popper, who delivers a spellbinding monologue near the very end of the film. (Leachman and Ben Johnson would each win Academy Awards for their performances.) Likely with some exaggeration, Bogdanovich once stated "I made the picture only so I could have that scene in it."[22]

With its classical compositions and impeccable framing, *The Last Picture Show* had a very different look from "typical" New Hollywood productions, which tended to feature washed-out colors, murky soundtracks, and edgy camera work.[23] But one of the first rules of the New Hollywood was that there were no rules, other than a commitment to an unflinching, determinedly antiromantic interrogation of the American experience, and one that followed the credo of the French New Wave: that "Truth . . . was positioned morally above the Good and aesthetically above the Beautiful." The bleak, downbeat *Picture Show*, which also shared, as J. Hoberman put it, "that now trademark BBS sense of failure," had all of that, in spades.[24]

They Can't All Be Hits

BBS (and Bogdanovich) hit pay dirt with *The Last Picture Show*. A small-budget film that grossed millions, the picture was also showered with positive reviews—*Newsweek* not only declared it "a masterpiece" but went on to crown it as "the most impressive work by a young American director since *Citizen Kane*."[25]

But they can't all be hits—and that's OK—that's the nature of the business, and the art. Released a week after *Picture Show*, Henry Jaglom's *A Safe Place* is as undisciplined as Bogdanovich's film is painstakingly crafted. In fact, *Safe Place* is so far out there that it is very hard to get a confident hold of it. Jaglom, a childhood friend of Schneider's, was another BBS intimate. There from before the beginning, he was a charter member of the watch-foreign-films-and-talk-about-them-into-the-wee-small-hours club with Nicholson and others; he also participated in the heroic editing effort led by Rafelson and Schneider to cut Dennis Hopper's sprawling three-hour work print of *Easy Rider* down to its release time of ninety-four minutes. Given carte blanche on *Safe Place*, Jaglom also initially developed what would become his second feature, *Tracks*, as a BBS production, with its railway location suggested by Rafelson and originally written with Nicholson in mind. But Rafelson ultimately passed on the picture, which was eventually released in 1977 with Dennis Hopper in the lead role.[26]

A Safe Place, accurately described as "essentially non-narrative," resists straightforward summary. Based on his play, the autobiographically inspired *The Uncommon Denominator* that Jaglom staged at the Actors Studio (with Karen Black in the leading role), Jaglom sought to broaden the action for the movie version, shot tons of film, and encouraged improvisation.[27] In the film, Tuesday Weld steps into the role that originated with Black; other players included Nicholson, Gwen Welles (who would go on to appear in Robert Altman's *California Split* and *Nashville*), and, however improbably, Orson Welles, with whom Jaglom would forge a lasting friendship. An impressive roster: Weld, whose talents were never fully utilized by Hollywood, was in the midst of a strong run, coming off John Frankenheimer's *I Walk the Line* (1970) opposite Gregory Peck; she would follow Jaglom's film with *Play It as It Lays* (1972), Joan Didion's adaptation of her own novel about the mental

Fig. 10. Orson Welles and Tuesday Weld in *A Safe Place* (Henry Jaglom, 1971, Columbia)

breakdown of an actress, directed by Frank Perry. (Anthony Perkins also stars in *Play It as It Lays*; in 1968 he and Weld both appeared in the intriguing *Pretty Poison*.) Nicholson was reliable, as always; and Orson Welles, was, well, delightfully Wellesian. Cast as a magician, according to Jaglom he performed all his own tricks.

What it all adds up to, however, remains an open question. One could observe that it is about Tuesday Weld's character, her boyfriends old (Nicholson) and new (Phil Proctor), a magician who may or may not actually exist, two apartments (one crowded flat populated by hippies, one more exclusively spacious Central Park West), and lots of action attractively shot in Central Park. But because, apparently, the entire film is supposed to take place in Weld's mind in a few fleeting moments—and as such is intended as a rumination on memory, imagination, and childhood fantasy—anything can happen, and pretty much anything does. Defenders of the film link this fracturing of time to the cinema of Alain Resnais, which is generous. (And the go-to New Hollywood Resnais-inspired film remains John Boorman's *Point Blank*.) The film does have its champions. Anaïs Nin offered this in her diary: "I went to see *A Safe Place* by Henry Jaglom. It made me weep." She wrote a positive review of the film, met Jaglom, and went to considerable personal effort to promote—and present—the film. "I believe in his talent," she explained.[28] Nevertheless, *A Safe Place* failed to find much of an audience. Most viewers (then and since) were likely puzzled, and more than a bit restless. But it is certainly a film that would not have been possible without the support of BBS—and it is necessarily the case that when you swing for the fences, sometimes you will miss.

The King of Marvin Gardens

But sometimes you knock it out of the park. *The King of Marvin Gardens* was, loosely speaking, a follow-up to *Five Easy Pieces*, reuniting writer-director Rafelson with Jack Nicholson and cinematographer László Kovács. It was an intensely personal project for Rafelson, who drew on some of his own experiences, and, even more than that, his "despairing mind-set" in developing the story. The director was also keen to make a movie that focused on a relationship between brothers, an element of *Pieces* that he thought was underdeveloped in that film. Working with critic and essayist Jacob Brackman on the screenplay, Rafelson crafted an uncompromisingly bleak assessment of America adrift in the fading wake of its twentieth-century achievements.[29] The film was shot on location in Philadelphia and, more pointedly, Atlantic City in the winter of 1971–72. The setting matched the mood, as that once-bustling resort community had fallen on hard times by the 1970s. (Brackman, who hailed from Atlantic City, also drew on some of his own experiences to fill in characters' backstories.) The locations were essential: Philadelphia, like most of the great cities of the Northeast, had seen better days; and in his first meeting with Kovács to discuss the movie, Rafelson talked for hours about Atlantic City before even touching on the elements of the screenplay. Those discussions left their mark—in the film, looking up from the beach and past dilapidated boardwalks, Kovács's camera captured the last days of soon-to-be-razed, once-palatial hotels like the Traymore and the Marlborough-Blenheim (where most of the picture's interior scenes were shot).[30]

In an inspired choice, the lead actors were cast against type. Bruce Dern, a case study in self-control in *Drive, He Said*, in *Marvin Gardens*, as Jason Staebler, gesticulates wildly and fills every room with his exuberant voice; Nicholson plays his awkward, introverted sibling David, who is so sensitive to disorder than in an early scene he can't resist properly setting right the tangled telephone cords strewn on a desk in a stranger's house. When loudly reminded of the few months his brother once served in a Cincinnati jail, David, no stranger to intuitions, responds with a quiet, meaningful, "We've all done our time, Jason." Ellen Burstyn landed the crucial female lead. She had previously read for the part of Rayette in *Pieces* (the Karen Black role) and was not of a mood to be turned down a second time. In reference to Rafelson, Burstyn wrote in her diary at the time (shades of the screenplay?) "Either I play Sally or he dies."[31]

The film, both structurally and visually, is more ambitious than *Five Easy Pieces*; as critic Jay Cocks observed in *Time*, the earlier film might have been more successful, but *Marvin Gardens* "in many ways . . . is more interesting and certainly more daring."[32] Once again Rafelson and Kovács keep the camera still for the exteriors, but here the colors are washed out, and in the interiors, shot on location, the camera glides effortlessly in long takes through under-lit settings, occasionally yielding to the vibrant colors associated with Jason and the enthusiasm of his wild plans (and which contrast with David's inevitable white shirt and black tie). Kovács's work here and throughout is exceptional, and he can also be credited with providing the film's "black blacks," that is, its deeply saturated darkness. But the contributions of Toby Carr Rafelson (then the director's wife) were also significant. Credited as the film's art director, she was influential in setting color schemes and choosing locations.[33]

"*The King of Marvin Gardens* is Monopoly minus the reassurance of toy money," wrote David Thomson, an early champion of the film. "The movie conjures with the prospect of Hawaii, but delivers nothing more than an air-mail blue shirt that will be stained with blood."[34] A requiem for the American dream, the action is initiated when Jason summons David to Atlantic City to include him in the grand scheme of building a resort on a postage stamp of an island that is part of the Hawaiian archipelago. But that long shot seems unlikely to pay off. Upon his arrival, David is promptly confronted with two formidable barriers: getting backing for the scheme, which seems increasingly doubtful given Jason's deteriorating relationship with his boss, Lewis (Scatman Crothers), a local mobster whose blessing would be essential, and the emerging crisis in Jason's ménage à trois, as Jessica (Julia Anne Robinson) begins to eclipse her stepmother Sally (Burstyn) as the principal object of Jason's affections.

On a first viewing, *Marvin Gardens* might appear undisciplined, especially as advances in the (slow to become apparent) plot are occasionally interrupted by small pieces of business (like a mock Miss America pageant) that border on the surreal. But in fact the film is quite purposeful, and unusually symmetrical: it both opens and closes with David's riveting monologues (single-take shots—Nicholson contributed to his monologues here and at other moments), visits to his home, train trips to and from each city, and decisive conversations with Jason and Lewis. The first five-part sequence, ending with Lewis, accounts for the film's initial twenty-two minutes; the mirror image, starting with David's second conversation with Lewis eighty-eight minutes in ("you're the philosopher"), puts the movie on track to its conclusion.

Moreover, every scene, no matter how much it might appear to stray from what came immediately before, relates directly to at least one of the film's two underlying narrative threads: Jason's increasingly desperate efforts to keep his Hawaiian scheme afloat (which requires him to secure Lewis's financial support and David's willingness to believe in the project), and, perhaps more pressing, the escalating tensions in his ménage, which threaten to spiral out of control. These two threads come together in the bizarre lobster dinner Jason hosts for two would-be Japanese investors, during which Jessica snuggles with Jason, while Sally sits, fuming, trapped between the two guests. The meal marks a crucial turning point in the threesome—and presents a crisis for the must-be-pushing-forty Sally. Barely one movie minute before dinner, at that mock Miss America pageant, Sally (described as "last year's queen") had presided over the ceremony that crowned Jessica as her successor. Immediately following dinner, an increasingly confident and uncharacteristically defiant Jessica is clearly slipping beyond the reach of her stepmother's authority. The next morning, Sally gathers a bucketful of her beauty products and sets them ablaze at a beachfront bonfire while taking a scissors to her long hair—for real.[35]

Things are coming apart. David, as he would recount later (as with *Five Easy Pieces*, Nicholson's character offers an emotional, final confession to an audience that cannot respond, in this instance to his radio audience),[36] would like to have stayed "in the funhouse" forever. But he is ever the realist, and his final meeting with Lewis establishes once and for all what ought to have been obvious: there will be no financial backing for the Hawaiian escapade. Lewis, unintentionally equating the brothers, explains that Jason is no businessman; "he's an artist"—a designation that previously had been invariably associated with David. And Jason can be seen as an artist, in a way, with the expression of his fantastic schemes the flip side of David's introspective tales. But Jason's affairs are unraveling, twin crises that come to a head in a riveting six-minute scene back at the hotel, as the movie heads toward its surprising (if in retrospect inevitable) climax.

Fig. 11. Brothers at odds: Jack Nicholson and Bruce Dern in *The King of Marvin Gardens* (Bob Rafelson, 1972, Columbia)

Marvin Gardens represented everything to which the New Hollywood might aspire. But even in the much more welcoming time of 1972, despite having a few defenders, the film was met with a shower of negative reviews. Andrew Sarris, then the dean of American film criticism, complained that the movie leaves its audience "stranded on a lonely sandbar of alienation."[37] As if that was somehow a bad thing. Nevertheless, the BBS window was closing.

All Things Must Pass

A testament to the remarkable independence of the BBS deal—as well as to Bert Schneider's not-kidding-around political passions—its sixth (and final) film would be a documentary. And *Hearts and Minds* (1974) was not just a documentary (a genre with extremely limited box-office prospects), but a controversial Vietnam War exposé—the kind of fare that most studios wouldn't touch, for fear of lawsuits and boycotts from angry consumer groups. (In fact, Columbia Pictures, under new management, wanted no part of it.)

Hearts and Minds is a film of extraordinary power. It hoists with their own petards crucial figures in the war such as American military commander William Westmorland (whose reputation cannot survive a viewing of this film) and LBJ national security adviser W. W. Rostow (who unsuccessfully sought to block the documentary's release). Harrowing footage from Vietnam, including of the Tet Offensive, is interspersed with moving passages of the social conflicts on the home front (one interlude, with grieving parents who look like they just stepped out of a Norman Rockwell painting, struggling to articulate the sacrifice of their son, lingers in the mind). At its most ambitious, *Hearts and Minds* aspires to dig deep into the American cultural psyche, suggesting that elements of the country's righteous self-confidence can generate an unthinking and dangerous militarism. Undeniably effective, the film is somewhat undercut by its overwhelming one-sidedness—this is, unambiguously, a piece of propaganda, even if largely correct—a fundamental unsubtlety that invites skepticism. It is also necessary to acknowledge the naïveté of *Hearts and Minds* with regard to the ruthlessness and brutality of Vietcong fighters and their North Vietnamese affiliates, who are typically presented in the film in a benign light.

Producer-director Peter Davis, then best known for his TV documentary *The Selling of the Pentagon* (1971), had originally been approached by Schneider with the idea of making a documentary about the Pentagon Papers trial. When legal complications rendered that project impractical, Davis shifted his attention to the war more generally, shooting in South Vietnam for seven weeks in the autumn of 1972. Two hundred hours of film produced first a ten-hour work print, and then a five-hour cut that was screened for Schneider and a party of favorites on Christmas Eve, 1973. The producer declared it "incredible" but also "a mess." Cut down to 112 minutes, *Hearts and Minds* looked good to go, and set to premiere at the Cannes Film Festival, when things got complicated.[38]

In 1973 a once-again struggling Columbia Pictures handed over its leadership to super-agent David Begelman, tasked with reviving the fortunes of the studio. Begelman had little love for BBS and even less for *Hearts and Minds*, and withdrew the studio's support to bring the film to Cannes. (Begelman was later fired from Columbia in the wake on an embezzlement scandal.)[39] Schneider and Davis brought the film to Cannes anyway, where it was met with enormous enthusiasm. But the film remained controversial—the *New York Daily News* killed Rex Reed's rave review of the movie, and Columbia refused to distribute it. But the studio did ultimately agree to sell the film to Rainbow Pictures, the production company formed by Henry Jaglom; Warner Bros., under the guidance of the New Hollywood–friendly John Calley, agreed to provide distribution.[40]

Hearts and Minds would win the 1975 Academy Award for best documentary. Schneider took the opportunity to speak of a Vietnam "about to be liberated" and shared a message of "greetings and friendship to all the American People" from Ambassador Dinh Ba Thi. Much of Old Hollywood promptly freaked out, and Frank Sinatra was soon reading a disclaimer that had been written by one of his cohosts, Bob Hope: "We are not responsible for any political utterances made on this program tonight, and we are sorry they were made." On camera, Warren Beatty expressed a different perspective, chastising Sinatra with a "Why, you old Republican"; sharper words were exchanged backstage as participants chose sides in the brouhaha.[41]

With this one final triumph, BBS could go out on a high note. But it was going out. Its six pictures were up, and Columbia was clearly moving in a different direction. As were, it should be noted, the BBS principals. Schneider's commitment to politics only deepened, diverting his attention from the movie business (as did the unexpected death of his brother Harold, who produced *Three Days of the Condor*). Schneider, who had been under close FBI surveillance since 1971, helped Black Panther Huey Newton escape to Cuba in 1974. He would complete his labor-of-love Charlie Chaplin biopic *The Gentleman Tramp* in 1976, but after that would have a hand in only three more films. Rafelson would struggle to find traction for his projects without the protections afforded by BBS; his next picture would be *Stay Hungry* (1976), and five more years would pass until his subsequent effort, a remake of *The Postman Always Rings Twice* (1981). Nicholson would star in several more essential seventies films, including *The Last Detail* (1973), *Chinatown* (1974), and *The*

Passenger (1975), but he was increasingly pricing himself out of low-budget productions.[42]

The BBS model also proved difficult to duplicate elsewhere. Universal set up something of a rival unit, under the direction of Ned Tannen, with a similar "low budgets, no interference" philosophy. Tannen's unit also yielded some notable New Hollywood films, including Peter Fonda's directorial debut, *The Hired Hand* (1971), written by Alan Sharp and shot by Vilmos Zsigmond; Monte Hellman's *Two-Lane Blacktop* (1971); and Czech New Waver Miloš Forman's first American film, *Taking Off* (1971), featuring Buck Henry. But the effort was ultimately short-lived, barely surviving into 1973. Another promising venture was the Directors Company, an arrangement between Peter Bogdanovich, Francis Ford Coppola, and William Friedkin under the auspices of Paramount Pictures. The deal was very BBS: the principals were given a free hand, without even showing a script, to direct any picture that came in under $3 million—and even to produce pictures by others that cost less than $1.5 million. The Directors Company was responsible for Coppola's masterpiece *The Conversation* (1974) and Bogdanovich's *Paper Moon* (1973), which was also well received and turned a profit. But Bogdanovich's next film, *Daisy Miller* (1974), was a flop, and Friedkin, who found *The Conversation* arty and pretentious, became suspicious of the enterprise, and, with at least one eye fixed on hopes for a big commercial hit, never delivered a picture for the partnership.[43] The New Hollywood in general would prove fleeting, as the studios ultimately regained their footing, American culture turned more cautious, and the flood of money, drugs, and ego took its toll. But BBS left before the party was over, as Schneider, Rafelson, and Nicholson went their own ways—abandoning us like Rayette, alone at the Gulf station, to wonder about the films that might have been.

CHAPTER 4

ROBERT ALTMAN
Documentaries, Dreamscapes, and Dialogic Cinema

David Sterritt

Deploying an unprecedented mix of multilayered soundtracks, restlessly moving cameras, exploratory zooms, sinuous narrative structures, and irreverent themes, Robert Altman helped define New Hollywood cinema with the savagely comic *MASH* in 1970 and helped close out the era with the surrealistic *3 Women* in 1977. All of which is surprising, since New Hollywood auteurs often have sophisticated film-school backgrounds, while Altman was a forty-something autodidact when he made his first important marks. His origins notwithstanding, Altman became a major trendsetter, and no movies better exemplify this than three he made during New Hollywood's heyday: the 1971 western *McCabe & Mrs. Miller*, which builds strong emotional power while radically revising both the myth of the frontier and a primary Hollywood genre; the 1975 musical *Nashville*, a portrait of American celebrity, politics, and popular culture; and the oneiric *3 Women*, a dreamscape marking the outer limits of New Hollywood iconoclasm.

The unpredictability, spontaneity, and elusiveness of Altman's films are such that no one critical stance provides a firm grasp on them. An eclectic outlook is called for, and I find three different but complementary approaches useful here. Two hail from Mikhail Bakhtin: dialogic theory, which holds that "the word [and by extension the image] is not a material thing but rather [an] eternally mobile, eternally fickle medium of . . . interaction," and carnival theory, which envisions healthy social interaction as "one great communal performance" that draws "the world maximally close to a person and . . . one person maximally close to another."[1] The third is the schizoanalytic theory set forth by Gilles Deleuze and Félix Guattari, for whom the individual has "no fixed identity" but is "forever decentered, *defined* by the states through which it passes."[2] The point here is not to pin Altman down with poststructuralist theory but to see his films as gateways to new understandings of the creative "chaos, 'wild' connections, immersive overload of the senses, ambiguity, confusion and affect" that schizoanalytic thinker Patricia Pisters accurately sees at the heart of contemporary culture.[3]

Altman's work lends itself particularly well to theoretical consideration, since each of his major films is a kind of thought experiment, an aesthetic laboratory test carried out by means of technique, intuition, and collaboration with creative partners. As always with laboratory trials, some of Altman's came to naught, as the theatrical adaptations *Streamers* (1983) and *Beyond Therapy* (1987) and the teen rom-com *O.C. and Stiggs* (1985) attest. But most of them, including films that succeed in limited, specialized ways—as when *Quintet* (1979) finds swells of chthonic resonance amid the bleakness of the Arctic, or *Ready to Wear* (1994) teases out fleeting visual pearls in the high-fashion milieu—are rewarding as tests of particular ideas regarding narrative form, character psychology, audiovisual expression, and self-reflexive rumination. Elements from such neighboring disciplines as painting, music, design, and drama are also in the petri dish, and the large-canvas experiments with the most exciting outcomes—including *Nashville*, *A Wedding* (1978), *The Player* (1992), and *Short Cuts* (1993)—come within hailing distance of the *Gesamtkunstwerk*, the "fusion of all the arts into one work" constituting a unified and unifying whole.[4] Reaching this goal is a matter of aspiration, not achievement, but the impulse to fuse image, word, performance, and music is present in all of Altman's most ambitious works.

The Improbable Candidate

First some history, since the contexts of Altman's artistic development cast light on his mature accomplishments. A number of transformational New Hollywood movies—including Arthur Penn's *Bonnie and Clyde*, Mike Nichols's *The Graduate* (both 1967), Dennis Hopper's *Easy Rider*, and John Schlesinger's *Midnight Cowboy* (both 1969)—premiered before Altman made his first major impact with *MASH*, and they helped to prime audiences for the novel qualities that made his war movie different from any before it. In additional to its financial success, *MASH* won the Palme d'Or at the Cannes International Film Festival and garnered five Academy Award nominations. Altman was definitively launched, but until that point he seemed an improbable New Hollywood prospect. Penn, Sidney Lumet, John Frankenheimer, and Sam Peckinpah had honed their skills in live television, whereas Altman entered TV after

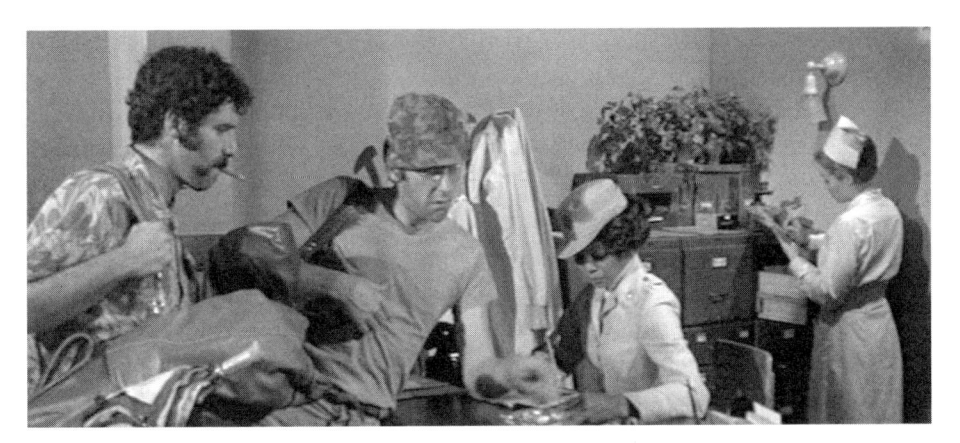

Fig. 12. Elliot Gould and Donald Sutherland in *MASH* (Robert Altman, 1970, Twentieth Century Fox)

live broadcasting had waned, and "movie brats" like Martin Scorsese, Steven Spielberg, George Lucas, and Brian De Palma cultivated their craft in film schools. Altman learned the basics during long years in the industrial-documentary business.

Far from being an extra added attraction in his career, however, his documentary experience percolated into his creative personality. After failing to get a foothold in show business as a young man, Altman had returned to his hometown of Kansas City, Missouri, in 1950 and taken a job with the Calvin Company, which specialized in training films, educational movies, commercials, and the like. There he underwent a brief apprenticeship in screenwriting and film editing, graduated to the director's chair, and filled various roles on more than sixty productions with utilitarian titles like *Modern Football* (1951), *How to Run a Filling Station* (1953), and *The Builders* (1954). Still hoping for a big-league career, he created a short-lived television series for an independent network in 1953 and 1954; cowrote an hour-long movie in 1955; and directed a TV episode for Desilu Productions in 1956. But mainly he worked at Calvin.

Persuasively arguing that Calvin was not merely a training ground but a hands-on workshop where Altman could experiment with diverse methods, Mark Minett identifies two techniques—camera movement and multiple-camera cinematography—that Altman tested and refined there. He pushed continually for camera mobility, which provided "a three-dimensional effect" that he found aesthetically pleasing and emotionally engaging. And he worked with a Calvin cinematographer to devise a lighting system compatible with multiple-camera shooting, which facilitated a natural, off-the-cuff feeling by cutting down the time needed for changes from one setup to another, and by allowing one camera to concentrate on the overall action of a scene while another served "as a sort of roving eye," seeking out meaningful details.[5]

Altman further developed these methods—and others, including the expressive zooms that became a trademark—when television became his chief proving ground, first at Republic Studios and then at all three major TV networks, where he built a reputation as a hardworking professional whose intermittent bursts of originality and eccentricity were generally tolerated if not exactly welcomed by the eminently pragmatic industry. Directing more than one hundred episodes in the five years from 1959 to 1964, some for half-hour shows and others for hour-long programs, Altman honed his technical and creative skills while immersing himself in many of the genres—the western, the war story, the private-eye yarn—that he would later revisit and revise in prototypical New Hollywood fashion; critical sleuths can now seek the roots of *The Long Goodbye* (1973) and *Thieves Like Us* (1974) in his 1958 episodes of *M Squad* (NBC, 1957–60) and *Peter Gunn* (NBC/ABC, 1958–61) or look for the seeds of *McCabe & Mrs. Miller* and *Buffalo Bill and the Indians, or Sitting Bull's History Lesson* (1976) in his 1960–61 episodes of *Bonanza* (NBC, 1959–73) and his 1959–60 installments of *Sugarfoot* (ABC, 1957–61). Although his predilection for long takes and camera movement was apparent in his Calvin films, the standard three-camera setup of 1950s-era TV allowed him to further explore the possibilities of these techniques, and the frequent presence of important female characters in his TV episodes presaged the woman-centered stories of features as different as *3 Women* and *Come Back to the 5 & Dime, Jimmy Dean, Jimmy Dean* (1982). In sum, Altman's television work built on the foundations of his Calvin films, and his early features built on both of those formative stages in his career.

The device for which Altman is perhaps best known is multilayered voice recording, a rarity in classical Hollywood filmmaking. With a few privileged exceptions—films by Orson Welles and Howard Hawks are obvious instances, of which Altman was very aware—almost invariably in mainstream Hollywood films, clearly recorded alternating dialogue replaces truer-to-life overlapping dialogue. "I think that films became too closely connected with theatre," Altman said, "and theatre is about words and a way of presenting them to an audience in an unrealistic situation. If everybody projected like that at somebody's house, you'd leave the party."[6] Pursuing the goal of realistic dialogue caused trouble with TV producers, and Altman was fired shortly before the completion of his first studio production, *Countdown* (1967), because a Warner Bros. executive saw footage and complained, "That fool has actors talking at the same time."[7] Altman refined the technique by putting individual microphones on performers, obtaining a clarity and flexibility suited to both the artistic and pragmatic needs of a production.[8] Few filmmakers apart from his protégé Alan Rudolph have deployed the device as frequently or successfully as Altman has.

Altman himself felt his Calvin years were important to his formation as an artist. "I think that beginning probably helped me a great deal," he remarked. "As I'd never worked in any other film job, I'd not seen what other directors did, and I'm sure all that separated me in a funny way."[9] A flair for on-location shooting, a readiness to alter scripts as circumstances demand, and a disdain for niceties of classical Hollywood scene construction are additional legacies of that period. And working for a company with a regular staff surely fostered Altman's lifelong commitment to filmmaking as a collegial, process-oriented activity in which the input of the collective is as important as the decision-making function of the director.

Observing that collaboration is a key concept in artistic modernism, Jonathan Rosenbaum describes Altman as one of the rare filmmakers—others are Jacques Rivette and Jacques Tati, both more radical in this regard—who believe "that the experience of making [a work] is in some way coterminous (if far from identical) to the experience of hearing, seeing or reading it."[10] Altman said much the same: "To me the fun of all these movies I've made has been taking your mates and creating something like a stock company."[11] These writers, designers, cinematographers, and other mates were not just fun people to work with; they were participants whose contributions Altman oversaw and distilled but did not dictate and control. Actors had a special position in the creative process, because more than almost any director this side of Rivette, Altman invited them to inject their own personalities and imaginations into the creation and evolution of the characters they played. This practice made Altman a tremendous favorite with actors, as witness the army of celebrities who volunteered for cameos and walk-ons in *The Player* (1992), his most pointed attack on the Hollywood establishment.

McCabe & Mrs. Miller

Altman's habit of challenging technological, audiovisual, organizational, and aesthetic norms first reached the public in *MASH*, and since the art of theatrical filmmaking can never be separated from the commerce thereof, it bears mentioning that the financial success of *MASH* was essential to the leap in aesthetic derring-do that Altman then took, making the unbroken string of bold, idiosyncratic works that extended from *Brewster McCloud* in 1970 through *Quintet* in 1979. The first of these ranks with *Images*, *3 Women*, and *Quintet* as a work of markedly experimental purpose, and although Altman always named it as a personal favorite among his works—in a sort of ugly-duckling sense, more out of loyalty than full belief in its excellence—its tepid reception made him more cautious about throwing narrative expectations entirely out the window. His next film and first indisputable masterpiece, *McCabe &*

Mrs. Miller, is an odd and moody western, fashioned by a director who disliked westerns, but definitely a western nonetheless, following too many genre rules and delivering too many genre ingredients—good guys, bad guys, shootouts, gunplay, gamblers, prostitutes, rowdy saloons, galloping horses, the building of a town in the American wilderness—to merit the "anti-western" label often hung on it. Acknowledging and even welcoming the familiarity of the basic plot and characters, Altman thought of them as an "anchor" that the audience could cling to while he concentrated on the "background."[12]

That background is essential to the film, which relies less on propulsive narrative than on its setting and its look. Shot in rain-drenched British Columbia, the action is dank and wintry throughout, and cinematographer Vilmos Zsigmond enhanced the effect by "flashing" the film stock, altering the emulsion to heighten detail in dark areas and using filters to darken the image during photography. Combined with Altman's camera movements and zooms, the grainy, gray-tinged negative fosters a subtly disorienting sense that time has somehow stopped, allowing viewers to scrutinize the premises and inspect the innumerable fine details in the painstakingly crafted mise-en-scène. The buildings of the town are not flat facades but three-dimensional buildings with solid walls and roofs—the film was shot in sequence, as the town was built—and costuming has unusual importance in the ambience. "I wanted it to be as if I were making an immigration film," Altman remarked. "Almost nobody who conquered the west was American; they were first-generation immigrants from Italy, Ireland, France, England, Holland, most of the northern [European] countries."[13] Chinese laborers and an African American couple round out the mix.

Naming both a man and a woman in its title, *McCabe & Mrs. Miller* follows the western tradition of focusing on a male protagonist, but extends

Fig. 13. Warren Beatty in *McCabe & Mrs. Miller* (Robert Altman, 1971, Warner Bros.)

the tradition by giving nearly equal emphasis to the main female character. John McCabe (Warren Beatty) has traveled to the crude mining town paradoxically called Presbyterian Church to set up a brothel, staffed by a handful of "chippies" purchased in a nearby community. Running the business is difficult, so McCabe is receptive when Constance Miller (Julie Christie) comes to town and proposes a partnership. An energetic Englishwoman who knows the brothel business from the inside, she joins him in building a proper bordello with decent health and hygiene standards. McCabe then develops tender feelings toward Mrs. Miller, whose addiction to opium has not yet caught his attention, and the story acquires new contours when a mining company sends representatives to buy them out. McCabe does not realize that the high-powered capitalists are—to borrow the idiom of Francis Ford Coppola's *The Godfather*, released the following year—making him an offer he cannot refuse. Before long the businesslike emissaries are gone, and a trio of thugs are in their place. McCabe kills them but meets his own death in the process, perishing in the drifts of a snowstorm as townspeople struggle with a conflagration in the church and Mrs. Miller finds transitory quietude in an opium den. The last scenes are shrouded in fumes, fire, and ice.

While some of Altman's films (e.g., 1969's *That Cold Day in the Park*, 1985's *Fool for Love*, 1998's *The Gingerbread Man*) have relatively straightforward stories with relatively linear structures, *McCabe & Mrs. Miller* marks his second venture into the sort of ensemble structure that *MASH* had introduced. Pursuing the experiment farther than before, he leads a great many characters through a rambling yet coherent story in which even secondary figures—a saloonkeeper (René Auberjonois), an amiable cowboy (Keith Carradine), the sociopathic thugs—have crisply sketched personalities and meaningful narrative functions. Here is the first full flowering of Altman's *rhizomatic* style, in the sense adduced by Deleuze and Guattari, who contrast the freely exfoliating rhizome with the firmly rooted "arborescence" of phenomena, artworks included, that burrow into stability instead of branching into discovery. "The rhizome operates by variation, expansion, conquest, capture, offshoots," the philosophers write, adding that its map "is always detachable, connectable, reversible, modifiable, and has multiple entryways and exits and its own lines of flight." A rhizome thrives "in the middle, between things, interbeing, *intermezzo*," and its nature is not the "either/or" of ordinary discourse but rather "the conjunction, 'and . . . and . . . and . . .'"[14] This is a fair description of the twisting, interlacing configurations of Altman films as different as *McCabe & Mrs. Miller*, *Nashville*, *Images* (1972), *Ready to Wear* (1994), and *The Company* (2003). These flowing, rhizomatic forms extend their shoots and tentacles beyond their own borders, into one another and into Altman's filmography as a whole.

Looking at *McCabe & Mrs. Miller* through a Bakhtinian lens, it abounds in dialogic interplays of realism and artificiality. The potent naturalism of the profilmic elements (details of architecture, wardrobe, makeup, set decoration, and so on) are simultaneously enhanced and offset by the crafted nature of the roving camerawork, the chiaroscuro lighting, and the blending of foreground and background sound, including source music by a country fiddler and Leonard Cohen's non-diegetic songs. Altman's cinematic interventions are as calculated and fabricated as the narrative ingredients are illusionistic and "real," and the dance of artifice and actuality reaches its zenith when the film concludes with intercut images of Mrs. Miller's face and the random knickknack on which her half-unfocused eyes are fixed. Her reverie is depicted as both a lifelike mental state *and* a flight of filmic abstraction that anticipates the hallucinations in *Images* (1972) and the otherworldly paintings in *3 Women*. Altman's steady drive toward contrast, combination, and assemblage is at once richly dialogic and keenly attuned to rhizomatic form. The ability to swing between the concrete and the conceptual dates from his earliest career—as at the Calvin Company, he starts with the tangible and wrangles it into the configurations he wants it to have—and its employment here confirms the 1971 western as a major step in his development.

As already mentioned, *McCabe & Mrs. Miller* modestly reworks the gender patterns of the western. In her book on American film and social change, Elaine M. Bapis makes a balanced case for this, arguing that Mrs. Miller champions equality for women and has "a pragmatic resourcefulness typically reserved for men," but that she also subverts female liberation and fosters "typical male/female division" by acting as an agent for prostitution, which is both a "means to independence" and "a form of dependence" for women.[15] In his book on Altman's westerns, Stephen Teo similarly finds Mrs. Miller to be a "practical and hardnosed woman [with] a pragmatic and business-minded outlook" that aligns her with values presumably held by the town's industrious and entrepreneurial Chinese immigrants. But although I agree with Teo that these traits set "the prostitute with the heart of gold" apart from "the gambler who only has a gold tooth," I don't share Teo's suggestion that opium provides a positive link between Mrs. Miller and the "alternative . . . possibilities and dreams" represented by the immigrants, or that she therefore "embodies the *spiritual* essence of the antihero," by contrast with McCabe, who can be seen as quasiheroic (he is not cowardly and follows a code of honor) despite his many failings.[16] *McCabe & Mrs. Miller* closes with the juxtaposition of McCabe's frozen corpse and Mrs. Miller's narcotized body, and while Mrs. Miller is clearly the surviving member of the ill-starred partnership, her final image in the film—her body recumbent, her eyes fixed somnolently on whatever happens to be in front of them, her mind floating in some blissed-out netherworld—hints less at evolutionary change than at the sense of human vulnerability to mortality and fate that underlies the most haunting moments in Altman's cinema.

Nashville

Altman worked on commercials at the Calvin Company, and *Nashville* begins with one—an advertisement for the film itself, and also a parody of such an ad, since anyone seeing it (in the days before home video, at least) has already bought a ticket to the movie and settled in for the show. In another echo of the Calvin years, *Nashville* is something of a documentary, locating its lightly stitched-together story in real Nashville settings and illustrating how a pop-cultural product—country music in this case—is brought into being by the efforts of many people, possessing many degrees of talent but all committed to securing their own livelihoods and having a good time along the way. The film's most effective nonfiction aspect adorns the soundtrack, where Altman accompanies his famous multilayered dialogue with a wealth of songs written by the same actors who perform them (as opposed to professional composers and lyricists) and recorded on the set while the camera rolled, breaking emphatically with the time-honored Hollywood imperative of recording diegetic music under studio conditions and then post-synching it with the image.

Although music is important to every Altman film, *Nashville* is the first to use music as a foundational source of narrative logic and psychological context, drawing on feelings dating from the director's early life. Listening to radio music as a child, he recalled, "kind of half in a half-dream state, half asleep, half awake, I'd hear that music. I'd make up stories to go along with [it]. These stories had no beginning or ending . . . but they [were] impressions. . . . I guess my ideal film would be a painting with music."[17] *Nashville* is also a textbook instance of self-reflexive film, investigating a segment of the cultural scene in ways that look forward to Altman's journeys through the late-nineteenth-century art world in *Vincent & Theo* (1990) and Hollywood in *The Player*.

Like most Altman movies, *Nashville* defies easy synopsis. It has twenty-four characters, a fact eagerly disseminated in its publicity, although some—such as the Tricycle Man (Jeff Goldblum), who does magic tricks, and Glenn Kelly (Scott Glenn), a low-ranking military man—are largely ciphers, playing little part in the narrative. With its teeming population, multilayered soundtrack, and interpenetrating story lines, *Nashville* is an intensely dialogic film, bearing out Bakhtin's view that meaningful communication "never gravitates toward a single consciousness or a single voice [but] is contained in its transfer from one mouth to another, from one context to another context, from one social collective to another, from one generation to another generation. . . . Every thought, feeling, experience must be refracted through the medium of someone else's discourse, someone else's style, someone else's manner, with which it cannot immediately be merged without reservation, without distance, without refraction." It is also a highly carnivalistic film, portraying "the *life of the carnival square*, free and unrestricted, full of ambivalent laughter" and allowing "familiar contact with everyone and everything."[18]

Carnivalistic worldviews need not be frivolous or flippant, and the ligaments that hold the sprawling narrative of *Nashville* together have strong political edges. This is mildly surprising from a filmmaker who generally puts more weight on personality than ideology, but the politics of *Nashville* are so closely imbricated with pop culture that the distinctions between them are hard to make out; think of Haven Hamilton (Henry Gibson) declaiming his song "200 Years," a paean to American exceptionalism that's as unexceptional and self-righteous as Hamilton himself. Two specifically political elements stand out. One is an assassination plan being brooded over by Kenny Fraiser (David Hayward), an otherwise minor character; perhaps too diffuse and demented to qualify as an actual scheme, it festers on the edges of the story until it bursts crazily and chaotically into view. The other is a presidential campaign waged from a loudspeaker van by Hal Phillip Walker (Thomas Hal Phillips) of the Replacement Party, an organization whose name is an inspired Altman touch, anticipating by a full two decades the nebulous moniker of the Reform Party founded by H. Ross Perot in 1995. Although we never lay eyes on Walker, we hear a good deal of his spiel from his peripatetic sound truck, as for instance, "When you pay more for an automobile than it cost for Columbus to make his

Fig. 14. Henry Gibson in *Nashville* (Robert Altman, 1975, Paramount Pictures)

first voyage to America, that's politics." To which one might respond, "When you pretend such a nonsensical sentence means something, *that's* politics."

In this movie as in life, most people pay only superficial attention to the people who aim to run their country. Walker's words make little impression on anyone, apparently including Kenny, the shadowy young assassin whose murderous design is the scarlet thread that ultimately unifies the tragicomic narrative. Kenny seems bland and innocuous through most of the film, but this changes abruptly in the climactic concert scene. The crowd has come to see the comeback of the psychologically unstable singer Barbara Jean (Ronee Blakely), and the proceedings go smoothly until she reaches the end of her solo number. Kenny then removes a handgun from the violin case he's been carrying and shoots her, wounding her gravely, and hits Haven as well, wounding him slightly.

Why does Kenny aim his weapon at a couple of country singers and not at Walker, the politician whose messages have surely reached his ears from the speakers on the sound van? According to the film historian Virginia Wright Wexman, Joan Tewkesbury, the film's credited screenwriter, added the political motif and made Barbara Jean the target, in line with Altman's notion that assassins are usually motivated by cravings for attention "more than political ideals."[19] This being a film about Nashville, it makes sense that the attention-hungry assassin would target a country singer, but it does not necessarily follow that a female singer would end up in the gun sights, and here Altman's characteristic gender discourse again comes into play. Kenny's selection of Barbara Jean is by far the most vicious instance of antagonism against women in the film, but it is not the only one; some female characters are relatively strong and sympathetic, as Linnea Reese (Lily Tomlin) is throughout and Albuquerque (Barbara Harris) is at the end, but Barbara Jean has an on-camera breakdown, Sueleen Gay (Gwen Welles) is coerced into doing a humiliating striptease, and L.A. Joan (Shelley Duvall) and Opal (Geraldine Chaplin) are made to seem ridiculous. Although most Altman films "challenge the dominance of masculinity in American culture," as the film historian Robert T. Self correctly notes, this does not obviate Altman's own susceptibility to gender bias. The best defense of Altman lies in Self's observation that some films (he names *Ready to Wear*, but the point applies to *Nashville* as well) show how "a complex mix of glamour, seduction and politics" exerts diverse influences on "the social nature of gender roles";[20] but while Altman indeed critiques the false consciousness of socially constructed gender behaviors, his self-awareness is in this area is incomplete.

Looking at Kenny's act of violence from another direction, it bears comparison with the notorious mayhem that erupts in Martin Scorsese's *Taxi Driver*, released a year after *Nashville*. In that film the unhinged Travis Bickle

(Robert De Niro) intends to kill presidential candidate Charles Palantine (Leonard Harris) until a combination of chance events and obsessive thinking redirects his rage to the lair of a degenerate pimp. Kenny's lack of motive is arguably more chilling than Travis's twisted motive, because while the *Taxi Driver* shooter is not too particular about his target as long as he perceives it as evil—to him, a politician and a pimp are pretty much the same—the *Nashville* shooter is completely *unparticular* about his target, since *all* privileged people and celebrities are pretty much the same. It is also interesting that these two films resolve their narratives in similar ways, depicting public responses to gun violence that utterly misrecognize the degree of public menace represented by the shootings. One need not posit a direct connection between the Altman and Scorsese films to see both as near-synchronous manifestations of concern with the increasingly shaky ethical climate of America in the Vietnam era.

The denouement of *Nashville* extends the implications of the climax in less melodramatic terms. In the confusion that follows Kenny's gunshots, the concert microphone lands in the hand of Albuquerque, a wannabe country singer who seizes the moment and pours her heart into a song with a desperately revealing refrain: "You may say that I'm not free / But it don't worry me." Here the twin sociocultural commentaries embedded in *Nashville*—the negative one censuring American apathy, the positive one celebrating American resilience—reach their dialectical apex. And the commentary goes even deeper if we draw a parallel with one more movie from the New Hollywood era, George Roy Hill's putative anti-western *Butch Cassidy and the Sundance Kid*, the most commercially successful American picture of the 1960s.[21] In this 1969 release, which also ends with the gunning down of two key characters, B. J. Thomas sings the Burt Bacharach–Hal David song "Raindrops Keep Fallin' on My Head," with its own lackadaisical refrain: "I'm never gonna stop the rain by complainin' / Because I'm free / Nothing's worrying me." Hill's film is very different from Altman's in most respects, but their similarities are instructive products of the same American moment.

Film critic Molly Haskell deemed *Nashville* a canonical New Hollywood film, calling it "the crowing glory of a journey toward greater and greater freedom from conventional narrative cinema, a journey on which [Altman had] brought his audience."[22] Altman made other large-canvas films in succeeding years—the best and most underrated of them, *A Wedding*, has forty-eight characters—and he returned to politics on occasion, notably in the Richard Nixon monodrama *Secret Honor* (1984) and the TV miniseries *Tanner '88* (1988). But *Nashville* is his most striking fusion of musical expression, political context, and sociocultural commentary. It is also his most effective experiment in fusing the aurality of music with the visuality of painting, as Self recognizes when he writes that each of the film's many characters is "a colour whose meaning resides in its proximity to adjacent colours and its various intensities within the figure the film makes."[23] *Nashville* is a movie about music, but like other Altman films it also takes inspiration from art. Even in a film where the Grand Ole Opry seems supreme, shades of the *Gesamtkunstwerk* hover nearby.

3 Women

Altman commenced *3 Women* without a finished screenplay, declaring his intention of making the movie without one. This unusual plan suited the unusual origin of the film's concept, which had come to Altman in a dream during an insomnia-plagued night when his wife was hospitalized with a serious illness. He did not dream the content of the movie, but rather the vision of what the movie should be: a drama called *3 Women*, set in the California desert, starring Sissy Spacek and Shelley Duvall, and centering on the theft of someone's personality.

Eager to commence the moment he awoke, Altman worked up a fifty-page treatment with writer Patricia Resnick—then a neophyte, although she worked on *A Wedding* and *Quintet* soon after—and successfully enlisted support from Twentieth Century Fox, which had backed *MASH* and hoped the maverick director might serve up another out-of-the-blue hit. Spacek, Duvall, and Janice Rule agreed to play the title characters, and shooting took place in the California desert. The goal was to bypass ordinary narrative in favor of a semi-linear mood piece that would be concrete in its details, circuitous in its psychology, and multivalent in its meaning.

Its all-embracing ambiguity notwithstanding, *3 Women* has compelling characters, an intriguing story, and dialogue (some of it improvised) that glides between dramatic and comic modes. Duvall plays Millie Lammoreaux, a permanent adolescent and perpetual flirt too self-absorbed to notice how men disdain her. Spacek plays her new friend Pinky Rose, a naïf who has traded the sun and dust of Texas for the sun and dust of California, clueless about nearly everything but willing to learn, up to a point. Millie and Pinky become roommates and work as physical therapists at the Desert Springs Rehabilitation Center, a facility for seniors. Rule plays Willie Hart, a pregnant artist who paints bizarre frescoes on swimming pools while waiting for her child to be born. In the film's one important male role, Robert Fortier plays Willie's husband, Edgar Hart, a macho womanizer whose pastimes are beer drinking and target shooting. The personality theft is perpetrated by Pinky, who steals Millie's clothing, diary, and Social Security number and starts insisting that Mildred is her real name. At one point an elderly pair show up and claim to be Pinky's parents, but she says she never saw them before. Willie eventually gives birth to a stillborn baby boy, attended by Millie, who is helpless to save the situation. The final scene follows: Edgar is dead, and the women now comprise a strange new ménage unto themselves.

Altman held that no single interpretation can explain the film, although he sometimes tossed out reasonable-sounding hints—the water in the therapy pool might stand for amniotic fluid, Edgar might be buried under scrap automobile tires at the end—and likened it to Ingmar Bergman's magisterial *Persona* (1966), another film about women whose identities blur, split, and merge. Literal meanings are not the point of *3 Women*, which comes as close as any New Hollywood movie to being what Alfred Hitchcock referred to as "pure cinema."

The film announces its disposition at the outset. The first image is an unfocused shot of Willie at work on a pool, seen through a vague mist unmotivated by the setting or the weather. Her images were painted for the film by Bodhi Wind, a young California artist whose drawing of "simian grotesques" had caught Altman's eye. The critic Jennifer Dunning aptly describes the swimming-pool frescoes in *3 Women* as "paintings of reptilian figures. . . . Erotic and mythological beasts, their eyes stare and their mouths open in screams. The male is a figure of antagonistic sexuality. The females, one of whom is pregnant, have lethally erect nipples." After giving Wind a general idea of what he needed, Altman left him largely to his own devices, although Wind said he never had a clear idea of what the movie was about.[24]

These monstrous, alluring figures set the tenor of the film, but like the haze through which the camera first views them, their unfathomable nature steers away from narrative meaning in favor of purposefully diffuse qualities that are schizoanalytically indeterminate rather than psychoanalytically

Fig. 15. Sissy Spacek in *3 Women* (Robert Altman, 1977, Twentieth Century Fox)

comprehensible. These are qualities of atmosphere, tone, and what Martin Heidegger calls mood or *Stimmung*, one form of which is "the mood of loss and lack one may call normal nihilism," produced when one becomes aware of "the self-concealing, technological character of our ordinary practices" in dehumanized modernity.[25] Altman's film is steeped in ordinary practices of a kind we rarely pay much attention to until they go awry: social habits of speech, dress, domestic work, making a living, recreation, and profoundly ingrained habits of simple bodily movement, foregrounded in the rehabilitation center where Millie and Pinky put near-decrepit clients through endless repeated therapeutic paces.

Immersion in such routines is an uncertain shield against the encroachment of normal nihilism, and the film's three women are thrown into crisis when unmanageable factors—Millie's neediness, Pinky's deceitfulness, Willie's failed effort to bring life into the world—knock their illusions to pieces and throw their lives into bewilderment. Their experiences are gloomy offshoots of the Bakhtinian carnivalesque, which incorporates "debasings and bringings down to earth" as well as "*mésalliances*" and "obscenities linked with the reproductive power of the earth and the body." The carnivalesque is ultimately liberating, however, giving access to "life drawn out of its *usual rut*" and "the reverse side of the world."[26] That life and that world are what the three women may finally have at the end of their film, when they have "kicked the last male off [the] rock" and formed a household that echoes and inverts the ordinary world in which they have never been at home.[27]

Altman's *3 Women* is a self-reflexive film, although a subtler one than *Nashville* and *The Player*, which take cultural production as their theme; its reflexive tropes are closer to those of the earlier split-personality drama *Images*, in which photographic equipment is a frequent presence. Reflexivity is embedded in the opening moments, which show an image maker (Willie) making images, and in the first episode at the rehabilitation center, when a slow pan around the pool arrives at Pinky looking on with a gaze as steady as that of the camera. Pinky seems to mirror the camera at this early moment, and the metaphor persists in other ways as she peers into private things like some kind of privileged snooper. This motif reaches its fullest form at the climax, when Willie goes into labor, Millie desperately tries to help her, and Pinky, told to run for assistance, instead backs away into the darkness outside, again staring as fixedly as the camera is staring at her. The camera zooms gradually toward Willie's bed as she and Millie grapple with pain and panic, whereupon Altman cuts to a close-up of Pinky's face, now accompanied by the same thin, luminescent mist that was seen in the film's first moments, looking like strands of ectoplasm in some nineteenth-century séance. The next shot of the bed is partially obscured by haze and soft focus, as if seen through a mass of water, echoing the earlier time when pregnant Willie walked into a pool to rescue Pinky from a suicide attempt. Millie slaps and berates Pinky for failing to act, but Pinky shows no reaction, still gazing with the emotionless affect of a movie camera. Her motivations are inscrutable, as is the episode as a whole. Yet the final scene—the most dreamlike of all, showing the three women in their strange new domestic sphere—is photographically distinct and sharp, bringing the narrative to a conclusion that is also a new start. Altman likened *3 Women* to a painting with no clear beginning, middle, or end. "The only end I know of," he said, "is death."[28]

Building emotional and even spiritual truth from the play of what New Hollywood historian Robert Kolker calls "radical surfaces" and Self calls "subliminal reality," *3 Women* can be understood only by "reading between the lines, excavating the silences," and pondering, again in Self's well-chosen words, "leaps across chasms of causality and relation [that] reveal meanings unspoken, half glimpsed, suppressed, intuited."[29] The film is not just a dream project but a dream of cinema, filtering its imagery through a Delphic succession of physical veils (water, mirrors), metaphysical veils (the ungraspable nature of what it is to be human), and stylistic veils reflecting Altman's wish to traffic in allusion and indirection rather than mere items, objects, and facts caught with the camera's supposedly objective eye.[30]

Altman likened the essence of a good movie to that of a good painting, finding linear narrative and character psychology less compelling than the moment-to-moment immediacy of images and sounds. He was nonetheless a storyteller, *New* in his techniques and sensibilities yet *Hollywood* in his aspiration to popular appeal and his attachment to such key elements of mainstream cinema as genre-based narrative, expressive acting, and audience-friendly balances of drama and comedy. But unlike many of his New Hollywood peers, he moved from one unorthodox venture to another without pausing for clearly commercial projects on the order of Coppola's *The Godfather* or Scorsese's *Alice Doesn't Live Here Anymore* (1974) or De Palma's *Carrie* (1976), and partly for that reason his reputation remains somewhat wobbly to this day. "How can it be that this most canonical of New Hollywood directors may not . . . make singularly good films upon which there is sustainable agreement?" asks Hamish Ford in a post on the website "Senses of Cinema." Ford sees in this conundrum an aspect of Altman's perennial charm: "The enjoyment of Altman's work is that, the more you look at the films and think them through, the more they transcend the question of whether a particular scene, shot, or film is good, almost embarrassing, or swinging wildly in between."[31] To watch an Altman film with due attention is to experience a sense of creative edginess and aesthetic surprise that few directors this side of outright experimentalists like Terrence Malick and David Lynch have so effectively produced.

Neither critical opinion nor box-office statistics have consistently registered in Altman's favor over the years, and even his strongest partisans have been hard pressed to defend items as intractable as the glacial *Quintet* and post–New Hollywood misfires like *HealtH* (1980) and *Beyond Therapy*. But he embodied the exploratory spirit of New Hollywood more steadily than almost any of his peers, and the best of his richly textured, bravely idiosyncratic works are enduring capstones of that adventurous era.

CHAPTER 5

CITY OF LOSERS, LOSING CITY

Pacino, New York, and the New Hollywood Cinema

Heather Hendershot

In 1965, John Lindsay beat out Abraham Beame and William F. Buckley Jr. to be elected mayor of New York City. It was perhaps the worst job in America. The city was spiraling down economically, crime rates were on the rise, the unions were angry, and ghetto residents were angrier. That same year, only two major films were shot on location in New York. This was, in a way, a blessing, because what did NYC have to show off to the rest of America? Garbage pileups and peep shows? To put it bluntly, the city was a dump, and there was little incentive to shoot films there. Few Hollywood directors had the stamina to brave not only the tough city streets but also the labyrinthine permit system, not to mention the bribes required by the cops and the Teamsters. Just two years later, in 1967, the streets were no cleaner, but forty-two features were shot in the city. There was one straightforward explanation: Lindsay had created the Mayor's Office of Film, Theatre and Broadcasting in 1966, and shooting a movie now required acquiring only a single permit.[1] The idea was to bring business to New York. Lindsay famously said he wanted to make the city "fun."

A few of the movies made in the wake of the creation of the office did show a fun version of New York (*The Producers*, Mel Brooks, 1967) or at least a nostalgic version (*The Godfather*, Francis Ford Coppola, 1972), and there is no denying that Lindsay's office created new business. But the vast majority of films enabled by the office conveyed a city of despair and decrepitude: the New Hollywood showed New York as a place not for jaunty, singing sailors (*On the Town*, Stanley Donen, 1949) but for pitiful, sweaty no-goodniks (*Midnight Cowboy*, John Schlesinger, 1969). The figure of the loser would quickly come to dominate American filmmaking, and many of the biggest and best losers

Fig. 16. Documenting pollution in 1973, this Environmental Protection Agency photograph shows a Forty-Second Street infused with not only poor air quality but also dirty films. (National Archives and Records Administration, #554297)

were based in New York City, with a handful of actors coming to prominence via these roles. Dustin Hoffman as Ratso (Rico) Rizzo in *Midnight Cowboy* fully embodied the new vision of New York City on film. But following this film, Hoffman would take on a wide range of parts—dramatic and comic, gritty and goofy—shot in a range of locations. No one would have pegged him specifically as an iconic New York City actor.

If any single actor did embody the new vision of the city, it was Al Pacino. By engaging with Pacino's films of this era—spanning from *The Panic in Needle Park* (Jerry Schatzberg, 1971) to *Cruising* (William Friedkin, 1980), with *Dog Day Afternoon* (Sidney Lumet, 1975) as centerpiece—we can see how New York City, which came to symbolize all that was wrong with America in the troubled 1970s, functioned as a driving narrative force, a character in and of itself, in the films of the New Hollywood years. If the old Hollywood had been based in the City of Angels, New York would become the City of Losers, symbol of the shattered fallout remaining in the wake of Attica, Vietnam, Mayor Daley, Nixon, and Watergate. Early on, Pacino—as hero, antihero, or just plain lost soul—emerged as the preeminent tour guide of Mayor Lindsay's "fun" town.

Pacino's first leading role was in *The Panic in Needle Park*, a bleak and depressing affair that a cranky *Village Voice* reviewer described as both "an

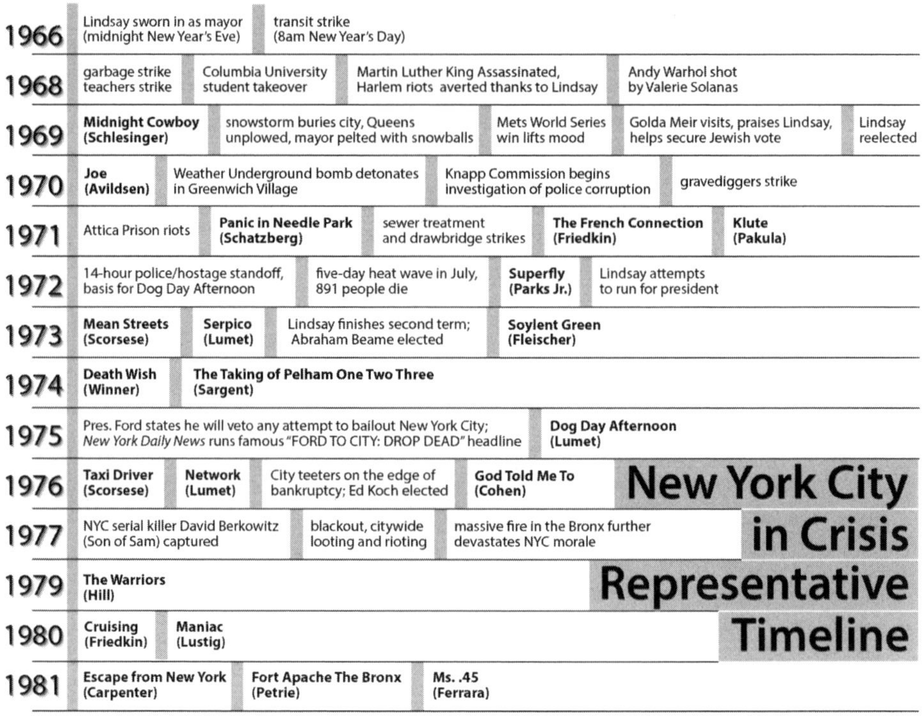

1966	Lindsay sworn in as mayor (midnight New Year's Eve)	transit strike (8am New Year's Day)		
1968	garbage strike teachers strike	Columbia University student takeover	Martin Luther King Assassinated, Harlem riots averted thanks to Lindsay	Andy Warhol shot by Valerie Solanas
1969	Midnight Cowboy (Schlesinger)	snowstorm buries city, Queens unplowed, mayor pelted with snowballs	Mets World Series win lifts mood	Golda Meir visits, praises Lindsay, helps secure Jewish vote	Lindsay reelected
1970	Joe (Avildsen)	Weather Underground bomb detonates in Greenwich Village	Knapp Commission begins investigation of police corruption	gravediggers strike
1971	Attica Prison riots	Panic in Needle Park (Schatzberg)	sewer treatment and drawbridge strikes	The French Connection (Friedkin)	Klute (Pakula)
1972	14-hour police/hostage standoff, basis for Dog Day Afternoon	five-day heat wave in July, 891 people die	Superfly (Parks Jr.)	Lindsay attempts to run for president
1973	Mean Streets (Scorsese)	Serpico (Lumet)	Lindsay finishes second term; Abraham Beame elected	Soylent Green (Fleischer)
1974	Death Wish (Winner)	The Taking of Pelham One Two Three (Sargent)		
1975	Pres. Ford states he will veto any attempt to bailout New York City; New York Daily News runs famous "FORD TO CITY: DROP DEAD" headline	Dog Day Afternoon (Lumet)		
1976	Taxi Driver (Scorsese)	Network (Lumet)	City teeters on the edge of bankruptcy; Ed Koch elected	God Told Me To (Cohen)
1977	NYC serial killer David Berkowitz (Son of Sam) captured	blackout, citywide looting and rioting	massive fire in the Bronx further devastates NYC morale	
1979	The Warriors (Hill)			
1980	Cruising (Friedkin)	Maniac (Lustig)		
1981	Escape from New York (Carpenter)	Fort Apache The Bronx (Petrie)	Ms. .45 (Ferrara)	

New York City in Crisis Representative Timeline

Fig. 17. New York City from Lindsay to Koch: crisis in the streets and on the screen

expensive remake of *Trash* with all the traces of humor removed" and "a tacky remake of *Love Story* with all traces of fantasy removed."[2] These jabs are not altogether incorrect, although they miss three key points. First, with a script coauthored by Joan Didion and John Gregory Dunne, the film was relentlessly relationship and character driven; within the opening moments one can predict that the lead characters, Helen and Bobby, will descend into heroin addiction and prostitution, but one also grasps that the plot is not really the point. This is an *actor's* movie, focused on strong performances and the revelation of interpersonal relationships.

Second, and relatedly, there is a gentle poignancy to Helen's ultimate pitiful subservience to Bobby. This is a finely crafted and sympathetic female character, and that is more the exception than the rule in the New Hollywood, which for all its strengths was underpinned by a relentlessly masculinist drive. Molly Haskell's attack on the buddy films of this era for their "homophile impulse" was disturbing, but she was spot-on in her lament that meaty roles for women were few and far between in the breakthrough films of the New Hollywood.[3] While one could hardly describe *Panic* as feminist, it offers a real woman with real struggles.

And third, this is a film that more than teeters on the edge of documentary. It is not only about Helen and Bobby but also about New York City itself, a filthy and impoverished place that can only inspire its underdog residents to turn to the needle for relief.[4] The scenes of junkies on benches at the film's eponymous home base (now the tidy and hygienic "Sherman Square") are grueling, and I do not think that anyone could convince me that all of the "extras" in the film are simply "playing" heroin addicts.[5] If neorealist films like *Germany: Year Zero* (Roberto Rossellini, 1948) are gripping in large part precisely because they show real bombed-out cities, not sets, the same must be said of films like *Needle Park* and even *Super Fly* (Gordon Parks Jr., 1972), with its grueling images of the rats and rubble of Harlem—a film that most would characterize as "blaxploitation" rather than "New Hollywood," but which must rank high on any list of "Burnt-Out New York City Movies."

Pacino's performance in *Needle Park* was strong enough to impress Francis Ford Coppola, and Pacino's very next film role was in *The Godfather*, a rather stunning feat for a virtual unknown. The rest, as they say, is history. After Michael Corleone, Pacino would play the lead in *Serpico* (Lumet, 1973), a film that patently nods to *The Godfather*'s success by milking an overwrought Italian orchestral theme, though, of course, it is aggressively contemporary, not a period piece, and it is overtly about New York City, whereas *The Godfather* takes place mostly in postwar New York but thematically is more generally about America. After *Scarecrow* (Schatzberg, 1973) and *Godfather II* (Coppola, 1974), neither of which is a New York City film, Pacino would make *Dog Day Afternoon*, to which I will turn shortly.

First a pause, though, to consider why on earth an essay on Pacino's New York would center more on *Dog Day* than *Serpico*. At first glance, *Serpico* offers more probing commentary on the city. It is, after all, about Gotham's intransigent political corruption. Serpico is an honest cop who wants to do his job and fight crime instead of spending all day picking up tribute money from criminals. He ends up as a whistle-blower exposing the NYPD. For his trouble, Serpico is shot in the face. Lumet's film is based on Peter Maas's best-selling book, which dutifully conveys the tedious details of bureaucratic corruption and intransigence. The movie repeats the book's key plot points but ups the ante by showing in graphic detail crumbling police stations, rotting hospitals, and garbage-strewn neighborhoods.[6] Certainly, *Serpico* is more directly "about" New York than *Dog Day*, offering a clear history lesson on the city's corruption. This pedagogical drive makes it one of the most *informative* of all the New Hollywood films.[7]

In short, *Serpico* offers a crash course in John Lindsay's city and how the police profited from the downward spiral rather than doing their best to pull in the opposite direction. It is unique for its focus on police corruption, but also typical for its moment—there was really no question that any film made in the 1970s about New York City cops would not be about corruption. These were the Watergate years, when disillusioned American moviegoers took it for granted that absolute power corrupted absolutely. Friendly cops would appear only in bland TV sitcoms and live-action Disney family films.

What viewers learn from many New York City–based New Hollywood films, like the aforementioned *Midnight Cowboy*, is that New York is a city of drugs and orgies and hustlers and hookers, but they won't learn exactly how it got that way. The grimy films of the era show us a dying city, but, with a few notable exceptions like *Serpico*, they convey a "structure of feeling" more than a direct factual or historical explanation of political realities.[8] *Dog Day* conveys the feeling of the era, and of New York City, particularly well, and this makes it ultimately a more gripping, compelling, and even optimistic film than *Serpico*. It may sound a bit ridiculous to describe a film about hapless, failed bank robbers—one a burnt-out Vietnam vet who is shot in the head at point-blank range, the other a bigamist done in by his inability to keep his first family off welfare and to fund his second wife's sex-change operation—as "optimistic." But the film has within it a deeply moving humanist core: the authorities cannot be trusted in this world, but maybe regular people can be.[9]

The city of *Serpico*, by contrast, is definitively doomed, its bureaucratic machinery immune to reform. Lindsay only set up the Knapp Commission to investigate Serpico's revelations because Serpico went to the *New York Times*: the mayor was exposed and had no choice. There's no sense that the Knapp Commission can save New York from itself. The opposite is true of *Dog Day*: it conveys a city where things go awry, and some people are cruel, and the law is a force of coercive violence, but where people can still care about each other—or at least can try damn hard to care. This is signaled from the very beginning, in an opening that represents a complicated ecosystem of neighborhoods and class barriers but ultimately favors the proverbial "little guy."

Dog Day begins with a montage sequence that sets a very specific tone: we'll get to the story eventually, but first we are meant to see that this is a film about New York City itself, a crowded and challenging place. The set piece opens with an overhead shot of a Circle Line boat pulling out into the Hudson, as the Elton John song "Amoreena" plays. Circle Line cruises are one-and-a-half- to four-and-a-half-hour affairs in which the island of Manhattan is circled as an announcer on a loudspeaker gives a long lesson in history and trivia. In my own experience, the cruise is designed not to sugarcoat the city but to convey a complicated metropolis that one should—or could, with an openness of spirit—come to love, warts and all.

The deck of the Circle Line boat in the opening shot of *Dog Day* is crowded, even though a title has already informed us that we are about to see a true story from August 22, 1971. Late August is no time to take a sightseeing cruise in New York City. We might here recall that when Lindsay's office finally acknowledged some of Serpico's complaints of police corruption, the administration told him in no uncertain terms that summer was riot season, exactly not the time when Lindsay had any intention of investigating or undermining the police force. Twenty-first-century viewers watching a film set on a hot day in New York City in 1971 must remind themselves that anyone viewing back in 1975 when *Dog Day* was released would *assume* the probability of violent conflict between police and citizens.

The film next cuts to a dog sifting through garbage on the streets, looking for food. She has a collar with tags, presumably belonging to someone, but at this moment she's on her own—and patently a she, given the nipples hanging from her underbelly. Life in New York City in the summer, it's a bitch. Tilt up, pan right to some middle-aged white gents with hands in trouser pockets, smoking, hanging out, one sitting on an old milk crate, not necessarily down on their luck, but not at the top of their game either. A black man sits forlornly by himself on a step ten feet away. Cut to the top of a luxury high rise, where lucky children find relief by jumping into a swimming pool. Then cut right back down to the blacktop, where hard hats are toiling with shovels and jackhammers. Note that the hard-hat riot had taken place fifteen months before this scene, when some two hundred construction workers chanting "Love it or leave it" and "All the way, USA" had beaten college students demonstrating against Vietnam.[10] (One counterdemonstrator held up a sign saying "Only America could have produced a champ like Nixon and a chump like Lindsay.") *Dog Day* viewers in 1975, New Yorkers or not, might well have recalled the right-wing construction workers hurling invective at the students and telling the "Commie" mayor exactly where he could shove his liberalism. John Avildsen's *Joe* (1970), centering on a bigoted hard hat, and released just two months after the riot, had patently cashed in on this. *Joe* was an indictment of white working-class men. But in *Dog Day* what we see is simply hardworking men trying to get through the day.

Cut next to the brick row houses of Queens, where middle-class people have tiny rectangular front yards. A man waters his with a garden hose. The next cut—a neat match on the hoses—takes us to a man hosing down a sidewalk in front of a store labeled simply "Chairs Tables Stools." Then cut back to the blistering asphalt, as cars pass through tollbooths. The following shot carries us to an outdoor public tennis court, with oversize tufts of grass poking through the ill-tended sidewalk outside the chain-link fence. It is not only those with fancy rooftop swimming pools who engage in recreation on a hot day.

But not everyone can play. The next shot take us back to more construction workers, now attempting to maneuver a gigantic girder that is still earthbound and doesn't look like it is going anywhere. The next three shots transport the viewer to Coney Island, where regular folks who don't have time or money to take off for the Hamptons sit on the boardwalk or beneath umbrellas on a beach strewn with bottle caps and cigarette butts. Back in midtown Manhattan, a large fountain is for show, not relief, as a New Yorker improbably suns herself nearby with a reflector. Cut to a man also "lounging," passed out on a sidewalk. Then cut to squinting businessmen in suits caught on a macadam crosswalk. In the next shot, a fleshy woman, in a dress just one notch above "housecoat," walks beneath a movie theater marquee, yanking a child in each hand. (This is the protagonist Sonny's wife Angie, but here she seems just like one of the crowd.) Cut to a shot of bumper-to-bumper cars on the highway, haze and heat distortion making the air around the traffic menacing. Next, we are back on the city streets, where garbagemen empty cans, but they make no attempt to keep up with the effluvia floating in curbside puddles. The camera tracks toward the men, and then we cut to a left-to-right tracking shot of black and Latino street merchants with fruit. Then it's right back to the beach, the camera still tracking right as two speedboats race by.

Finally, we make our way to Brooklyn, where balding men powwow on sidewalks in lawn chairs, a yogurt delivery truck drives past a bank, and a gigantic cemetery is set against the Manhattan skyline—as if to say, "don't forget, New Yorkers, you'll be here someday!" A Kent cigarette billboard not only flaunts the product's dubious "micronite filter" but also informs us via digital panel that it is now 2:57. Cut back to that bank from before, and Al Pacino's name appears, and then the film's title. Ah-ha, the movie is starting! But, of course, it started two and a half minutes earlier, with its relentless back and forth between wet and dry, hot and hotter, work and leisure, kipple and more kipple. This is Lindsay's New York, somehow captured at a moment between garbage strikes, teacher strikes, transit strikes, and (no kidding) gravedigger strikes. People are muddling through a hot day without rioting or fighting, going about their business. New York is capable of equilibrium, but for how long?

Three men enter the Brooklyn bank at closing time. One of them, Sonny, carries a large flower box tied up in ribbons, the kind of box that non-florists see most often not in real life but in heist movies. Obviously, it can only contain a gun, in the same way that suspicious men in trench coats do not keep violins in violin cases. Sonny's partner Sal comes in and sits at the manager's desk, quietly holding a gun on him. A third would-be criminal is on the scene as well. We notice immediately that he is in a short-sleeved casual shirt, the way sensible men *should* dress on a hot day, but that the other criminals are wearing suits with ties to look "normal." It seems that back in 1971, white middle-class men still wore suits in New York everyday, and not just on Wall Street.

Sonny awkwardly wrenches the gun out of the box, flummoxed by the ribbons, and we have our first clue that this film is *sort of* a comedy. Our shortsleever is not up to the task. He tells Sonny he can't take it, and Sonny orders the security guard to let him out before the heist continues. We now deduce that Sonny's team is not slick. This may be a smart heist movie, but it is not going to be a classy heist movie. If *Le cercle rouge* (Jean-Pierre Melville, 1970) is the filmic equivalent of Tiffany's, with a new shipment of Fabergé eggs just in, *Dog Day* is Filene's bargain basement, and today vinyl handbags are 75 percent off.

Sonny has once worked in a bank, and he is showing off that he knows what he's doing. He knows where the trick alarms are and which bills are marked. He spray paints over the security camera lenses. But he has screwed up already: he probably should have gone for the security cameras first thing, and unbeknownst to him, the vault money had been picked up earlier in the day, so that only a little over a thousand dollars remains. Sonny burns the daily register in a trash can, for no clear reason. He tries to put the tellers in the vault, but one of them has to go to the bathroom, and he never considers the possibility of ignoring her request. Though he's high-strung, he seems like a nice young man. But he's a total wash as a criminal. The smoke from the trash can has come out the exterior vents, raising suspicions across the street. Before you know it, the "half hour job" has escalated into a hostage situation, with Sonny in charge of negotiations, and Sal brooding, itchy trigger-finger at the ready, intimating that he is just as open to wiping out the hostages as he is to blowing his own brains out.

At the same time, Sal is the ultimate straight man, staring with empty eyes as Sonny tries to get through to him. At one point, Sonny asks what country he'd like to go to in the airplane they are trying to squeeze out of the police. Sonny earnestly responds "Wyoming," and Sonny has to explain that Wyoming is not a country. It feels like a twisted George Burns–Gracie Allen routine.[11] It's worth adding that Sal is played by John Cazale, who also played Fredo Corleone; Sonny's efforts to take care of Sal are all the more poignant when we recall Fredo's unhappy end in *Godfather II*.

Meanwhile, the hostages are scared, excited, and looking out for each other. The head teller bosses Sonny around and tells him to watch his language— "we've got girls here!" Offered a chance to escape with the cop leading the negotiations, the teller wrests her arm loose from him to go back inside and take care of her girls. The manager has a health crisis that offers him an opportunity to leave, but he chooses to stay with his team because it is the right thing to do. When the air conditioning shuts off, the ladies loosen their blouses and fan each other. A crazy guy starts phoning in and telling Sonny to kill everyone, and Sonny hands the phone off to a gum-chomping teller, who freaks the caller out by retorting with a heavy breathing routine. (This is at a moment when the prank-calling heavy breather was a running joke in American popular culture.) As day drags into night, the tellers goof around, dancing, and at one point the gum-chomper is holding Sonny's gun showing him how to do a drum majorette routine . . . but then we realize that it's probably the reverse, with him teaching her his Vietnam drill training. Amping up the black comedy another notch, Moretti, the negotiating head cop, is trying hard to manipulate Sonny into releasing hostages, but he teeters between blustery and apoplectic, unable to control his own heavily armed men.[12] When an older hostage having a severe asthma attack is released, the cops immediately pin him down and cuff him (he's black, and therefore assumed to be one of the robbers), as Moretti helplessly screams to let him go. Sonny tells the manager, "They'll shoot you, you know, the cops. They don't give a fuck about your bank insurance. See what they did at Attica? Forty-two people they killed. The innocent with the guilty."

On the one hand, Moretti is just a guy trying to do his job, rescue hostages, and keep his gun-crazy men from wreaking havoc. On the other hand, when he falsely accuses Sonny's wife Leon of being an accomplice in order to manipulate her—she is mentally ill, doped up by Bellevue doctors, and clearly scared of Sonny—we are likely to lose sympathy for him, though, to Moretti's credit, while his men crudely laugh at the transgender Leon, Moretti conveys no signs of disrespect. Moretti is paunchy, loud, and sweaty. When he uses a bullhorn, the assembled civilian crowd mocks him by repeating his words. At one point we spot him haplessly looking on at the crowd scene while eating spaghetti from an aluminum takeout container.

In sum, we have utter mayhem, with one exception. Sheldon the FBI man arrives early on, standing expressionless behind the hapless Moretti, patiently awaiting his opportunity to take over. Sheldon has the look of a soulless contract killer. His double-cold assistant Murphy stands behind him, silent until the end, when he will be ordered into action. Notably, Sheldon is played by James Broderick, who was the train operator in *The Taking of Pelham One Two Three* (Joseph Sargent, 1974), a heist movie with substantially more competent criminals. He also appeared as a somewhat ludicrous bohemian type in *Alice's Restaurant* (Arthur Penn, 1969). In 1969, he was traipsing about in overalls, considering starting up a commune. In 1975, he is in a suit and tie, impossibly devoid of both sweat and emotion, staging the point-blank murder of a maladjusted bank robber. If Broderick represents the counterculture at its most silly in *Alice's Restaurant*, in *Dog Day* he is the Establishment at its most chilling.

Meanwhile, Sheldon's assistant Murphy is played by Lance Henriksen, who would later be known for *Aliens* (James Cameron, 1986) and *Alien3* (David Fincher, 1992), and also, on the lowbrow front, for the *Pumpkinhead* horror franchise. An accomplished character actor, Henriksen takes a modest role in *Dog Day* and makes it memorable. (He does the same thing in an uncredited cameo in Lumet's *Network* a year later.) Sheldon may appear the hit man throughout, but Murphy's the one who actually executes Sal at the end of the film without blinking an eye.

A crowd gathers outside the bank the moment the police are on the scene, and it only grows larger over the course of the film. With the crowds, of course, come the news media. On the surface, Sonny may appear to be a publicity hound. He is terribly excited when a TV anchorman calls him for a live interview. (Perceptive viewers might even note that the newsman on the tiny portable TV is played by William Bogert, a character actor best known at the time for his performance as the neurotic, anti-Goldwater chain smoker in the LBJ campaign ad "Confessions of a Republican.") And when he goes outside to confer with Moretti he begins to work the crowd's enthusiasm, leading them in chanting "Attica! Attica!" At this moment we are perhaps meant to realize that Sonny may be somewhat simpleminded, and that he has not really thought through what his actions mean as "protest," but that he intuits that media coverage is what validates resistance by virtue of making it visible.

Fig. 18. The *Dog Day* TV newsman is played by William Bogert, a character actor best known for his appearance in the anti-Goldwater ad "Confessions of a Republican."

The prisoners who led the 1971 revolt in Attica prison—where guards treated prisoners very poorly, medical care was abysmal, and prisoners were afforded one shower a week and one roll of toilet paper a month, among other indignities[13]—understood that they would simply be slaughtered for taking over the prison and taking hostages if they did not get the media immediately involved. They invited Tom Wicker of the *New York Times* onsite. Also, as Carol Wikarska explained in a review of the film *Attica* (Cinda Firestone, 1974), "two Black cameramen, Roland Barnes and Jay LaMarch, were allowed to film in the Yard; WGR-TV cameraman Terry Johnson's coverage was aired on the networks. The news of over one thousand inmates seizing thirty-one hostages (prison guards and employees) in the takeover of Attica began to reach the nation . . . one day after it happened. And the events at Attica were to be followed by the public via television and the front pages of the newspapers for days to come."[14] Things quickly got surreal as people showed up to see the tear gas canisters dropped, and "The Lion's Club set up a hamburger stand next to the prison's thirty-foot walls adding to what was called a *carnival* atmosphere."[15] As Wikarska concludes, the uprising "was a media event as much as it was a political event."[16]

So, in evoking Attica, Sonny taps into the crowd's sense of injustice but also into its awareness that it is on TV. One might cynically conclude that Sonny is a naïf and anything but a political operative. If he's enjoying the media, it's not because "the whole world is watching" unjust police brutality but because "the whole world is watching" his fifteen minutes of fame, as per Andy Warhol. The teller manager is also thrilled to be interviewed by a reporter dangling a microphone down off the roof. Even the pizza delivery boy who brings pies to the hostages is excited to be on camera, shouting exuberantly "I'm a fucking star!" The film simultaneously seems to be saying that to be excited about publicity in and of itself is hollow and foolish and, also, that the exuberance that Sonny and others feel about being on TV is genuine, perhaps the only way to feel "real" in the world.

This stance makes the film unique, for the films of the New Hollywood were inclined to vilify television as a shallow medium. In *Midnight Cowboy*, for example, a crazy rapid-fire montage of TV sounds and images is intercut with Joe Buck's first sexual encounter in the city, all designed to emphasize the tawdry, commercialized nature of the physical exchange. In *Joe*, the shallowness of the antihero and his wife is demonstrated by their earnest interest in a soap opera. And the whole point of *Network*, of course, is that TV is a base and dehumanizing medium. *Dog Day* accepts the notion that TV is shallow, but it does not by extension argue that ordinary people who engage with TV should be pitied or viewed as somehow deficient. If Sonny is excited about being on TV, it's because being a star, even briefly, feels better than being an anonymous nobody in a city determined to grind the life out of its residents.

The question that remains implicit in the film is, what exactly is Sonny revolting against? Is he a "prisoner" of America, or, more specifically, of New York City? I believe that the answer is both, but that what he feels is much narrower, the imprisonment of his own circumstances. He pays his parents' rent, his kids are on welfare, his first wife never stops talking, his other wife has mental troubles, his only friend may be a psychopath. How to "be a man" and fix all of this? Pauline Kael observes that Sonny "is trying to do the right thing by everybody. . . . In the sequence in which Sonny dictates his will, we can see that inside this ludicrous bungling robber there's a complicatedly unhappy man, operating out of sense of noblesse oblige."[17] Long before the bungled robbery, the pressure has been getting to him. He's been insulting his first wife, and he actually held a gun to the head of his second wife, we are told, which is particularly striking because he seems like an essentially gentle person. He can't get into a union, and he could not make ends meet as a bank teller. (The tellers nod in agreement when he tells this to the TV reporter.) The only way out is the bank robbery. Notably, he is upset not to have scored more money from the robbery, but after he pays the pizza delivery boy, he throws money into the crowd. They turn joyful, then almost dangerous, shouting "more, more!" Sonny has made a Robin Hood gesture, but has he made a political statement or simply an emotionally expressive one? Perhaps a little of both.

Their demands for a ride to the airport and for a jet apparently met, Sonny, Sal, and the hostages finally make their way out of the bank. The TV news had earlier revealed the details of Leon and Sonny's wedding, even showing a photo of Leon in a wedding gown, and as a result the crowd has now been joined by gay activists chanting "out of the closet and into the streets," their faces appearing more menacing than supportive. This tracking shot of the enraged gay libbers could be read as progressive on Lumet's part or simply as an attack on the mob mentality as purely negative. As the bus heads to JFK, drivers in other cars throw cans at Sonny, taunting him with "scumbag!" and "*maricón!*" He was a hero all afternoon, but now the people who would have gladly jumped and dived for free money dismiss him as a faggot. Is the city hateful, or simply fickle?

Arriving at the airport, Sonny realizes he hasn't eaten all day. Sheldon tells him there will be hamburgers on the plane. Murphy shoots Sal between the eyes, and Sonny is cuffed as he sadly watches the hostages disperse and medics cart away Sal's corpse. He offers no visible reaction as he is read his *Miranda* rights. End titles tell us that today (1975) Sonny is in jail, his wife is on welfare, and Leon has had the sex-change operation. That's one happy ending out of three possible ones. Roll credits.

Notably, the film ends much more succinctly than it began, with credits divided into three groups—the Law, the Family, and the Street—as if to say, well, this is what life is, these are the three things that we must deal with. The Street brings with it dogs, garbage, pizza delivery men, crowds that may become mobs, people looking for heroes, and people just trying to get by. Oddly, Lumet even includes the TV anchorman and TV reporter among his listing of the street folk. Like the chanting crowds, the media are trying to make sense of it all . . . and also like the crowds, they are trying to cash in.

The Family is also a troubled space. Sonny's father (Dominic Chianese, a Hyman Roth associate in *Godfather II* and much later Uncle Junior in *The Sopranos*) disowns him, but his mother attends his marriage to Leon. Upon arrival at the crime scene, she tries to save him by informing Sheldon what a good boy he is—a Vietnam vet who has always had good jobs and was even a Goldwater supporter in 1964. No wonder when Sonny spots her outside the bank he says, "Oh, shit, it's my mother!" As for family members Angie and Leon, Sonny tries to make peace with both of them over the phone, with uneven success. One of the beautiful things about the film is that even though one can imagine a comic intention behind the "big reveal" that one of Sonny's wives is "a woman trapped in a man's body," Sonny and Leon truly connect in their final conversation, even as they bicker.[18]

The Law is clearly the social grouping most immune to negotiation, reconciliation, or understanding. Even if Moretti may be a good enough cop to want to avoid an Attica-like situation, it is certainly the Law that the film represents as the most flawed of society's three-part structure. Sheldon and Murphy are soulless. They don't care about the life of the city, or of its citizens. And, of course, they are from the *Federal* Bureau of Investigation, which is to say, they are outsiders to the city from the get-go.

At the end of the day, New York City may be the real kidnapper in this film, holding all of its people hostage. If the bank tellers quickly fell into the Stockholm syndrome, coming to empathize with and root for their own kidnappers, the bigger picture is of people who manage to care for a city even as it constantly constrains them and lets them down.

Pacino would of course continue to make New York–set films, but after *Dog Day* the city is no longer felt so strongly as a central character in his work. William Friedkin's *Cruising* serves here as an interesting reference point. The film is a murder mystery set largely in the city's gay leather bars, with key scenes taking place in Central Park and Morningside Park. We see immediately that many of the cops are corrupt, harassing transvestites and forcing sexual favors from them. Or they are just plain lazy, refusing to pursue murder cases if they don't have to. One won't even concede to a coroner that a chopped-off arm must belong to a "murder" victim—he's already got too much paperwork to take the case on. Yet Paul Sorvino plays an ostensibly "good" cop determined to solve the gay murder mystery, and Pacino obediently goes undercover for him. Police corruption is not seen as systemic or endemic to the city. It simply *is*.

Further, Friedkin himself denies any political intention to the film, or any attempt to evaluate gay life in the city. He notes that he took a documentary approach, simply showing the leather bars as they were, with nonactors going about their lubing and fisting and dancing as always. He also claims that the ambiguity about who the killer is and even how many killers there might be is symbolic of our own ambiguity about our lives.[19] Now, clearly, this is a film that transcends such simplistic comments, and obviously Friedkin understands, as does the viewer, that much of the film's interest lies in the Pacino character's confused but unverbalized feelings about how turned on he may or may not be by all that he experiences undercover. For example, at first he can still get off with his girlfriend if he indulges in a bit of gay-bar fantasy, but by the film's third act he can't arouse any sexual feelings for her at all. They are reunited at the end, and while he freshens up in the bathroom, she puts on his sunglasses and leather cap and jacket, in a final moment of ambiguous transformation.

This is all quite compelling, but New York City does not emerge as a driving force as it had in *Dog Day*, or as a horribly flawed system, as in *Serpico*, or as the kind of petri dish that created a creep-loser like Popeye Doyle in Friedkin's *French Connection* (1971). Rather, New York serves as background.[20] The film could just as easily take place in San Francisco. Later Pacino films such as *Donny Brasco* (Mike Newell, 1997) and *Carlito's Way* (Brian De Palma, 1993) are similarly more invested in New York as background than as character. Obviously, by the 1990s the New Hollywood moment was long gone.

Still, New York does emerge one last time as central to Pacino's work, and that is in HBO's 2003 miniseries *Angels in America* (Mike Nichols), which is set in 1985, the moment of not only Ed Koch's New York but also Ronald Reagan's America. Throughout the series, we see a city that is slowly in recovery from the Lindsay years, but not because things are going great for residents. The AIDS epidemic is hitting NYC hard, and only the rich, like Roy Cohn (Pacino), have access to the drug AZT, which at that point is the only hope people with the virus seem to have. Lindsay had gotten the city into huge debt to cover the favorable contracts he struck with unions and to fund projects such as his City University of New York open admissions policy.[21] Koch tightened the city's belt, slashing programs. Then Reaganomics helped to further widen the gap between rich and poor. If *Dog Day* was a film of largely working-class people, *Angels in America* is a film of doctors and lawyers at the top, and homeless people at the bottom. When one character accidentally ends up in the Bronx, stumbling among the downtrodden warming themselves over trash cans, we pointedly feel that we are viewing a fallout zone left over from the Lindsay years. And yet this is no longer a world populated by the hopeful and deluded losers of the New Hollywood, the kinds of sad sacks who think that just one robbery, one last case, one road trip, one drug deal, one con job, one decapitation (!) is all they need to become winners.

As for Pacino, in *Angels in America* he delivers a devastating performance as the homosexual-hating, anticommunist, right-wing sodomite Roy Cohn. The amoral and wealthy Cohn had once said his objective was to die in tremendous debt, and he achieved this.[22] He also has one last chance, as he lies dying of AIDS, to deceive the ghost of Ethel Rosenberg (Meryl Streep), for whose execution he had been largely responsible thirty years before.

The New Hollywood was a distant memory by 2003, and New York City had lost all traction as a site of irresistible decrepitude, outside of a handful of low-budget exploitation films by directors like Abel Ferrara and Larry Cohen. But its actors lingered on, often giving strong performances. And so, in the classic style of the New Hollywood losers—like Gene Hackman in *Night Moves* (Arthur Penn, 1975), Dustin Hoffman in *Midnight Cowboy*, Warren Oates in *Bring Me the Head of Alfredo Garcia* (Sam Peckinpah, 1974)—Pacino as Cohn deceives Rosenberg and "wins" in *Angels in America*. And then he drops dead.

If the series had been shot in the true spirit of the New York of the 1970s, this death scene could only have cued a fade to black. Instead, *Angels* ends by showing the optimism and resilience of the surviving characters, jolting us to the realization that Pacino's caustic performance and inevitable death make us nostalgic for an earlier era of filmmaking. In *Alfredo Garcia*, Oates had pathetically asserted, "Nobody loses all the time," but in the context of the New Hollywood, this sort of declaration could never be more than wishful thinking. Nothing confirms this spirit of inevitable human failure more potently than Pacino's New York City films of that era.

CHAPTER 6

THE PARALLAX VIEW
Why Trust Anyone?

David Thomson

"Parallax" is a small displacement between reality and point of view: it comes from working with photographic lenses, yet it might also apply to whether that spasm in existence you felt a moment ago was God at play or just a shift in the light. Optics and philosophy may meet in infinity. Another displacement arises with Alan Pakula's *The Parallax View* (1974): what did it feel like when it was made, and how do we see it now?

So, we can look back on 1974 and marvel at how happy we were to be so uneasy then. That was a strange differential or inconsistency, but in those early seventies many new films were telling us to be suspicious and making us excited, too. Do you remember that vivid paranoia, and how thrilling it was to be alive in its shadow? The tattered strands of spirit still reckoned wrongs could be corrected. A word we used then was "justice," applied without irony. *The Parallax View* spoke to a kind of awe felt for malign conspiracy. The film was never close to perfect, but now it lingers in the mind like a dormant infection.

Pakula had been born in 1928 in the Bronx to Polish Jewish parents. He majored in drama at Yale and went into the film business. In just a few years he formed a partnership with Robert Mulligan (he produced and Mulligan directed), which made its name with the famous success of *To Kill a Mockingbird*, a grave portrait of troubles that still seemed confident about eventual triumph or reform. The two men worked steadily for several years and seven pictures. They were an unusually stable and productive team, but then Pakula determined to become a director himself. He began with *The Sterile Cuckoo*, a vehicle for the neurotic emotionalism of Liza Minnelli, before launching into insecurity and what would be known as his "paranoia trilogy"—*Klute, The*

Parallax View, and *All the President's Men*. These were thrillers bred by an age of conspiracy theory (or dread) and its close relative, conspiracy facts.

The Parallax View was the middle film in the trio, and the one of the three that missed commercial success, or an Academy Awards nomination. Like most people, I have fond memories of the other two, *Klute* and *All the President's Men*—terrific entertainments, both of them. But those films end more positively than they started. Their worlds rally—I mean from the old USA point of view, as in shouldn't we be rooting for LOVE, COUNTRY, and HOME? (More on those slogans later.)

In *Klute*, the dead-eyed detective (Donald Sutherland, without his usual edge or humor) and Bree Daniels (Jane Fonda) have solved the film's mystery (that's always a good feeling, for a few minutes), and it seems they are going to "be together" for a while in the way expected of movie couples then. But they aren't an ideal couple, so it's not easy to imagine where they are going to "go." Will they return to rural Pennsylvania, to John Klute's neck of the woods? Do we expect the volatile Bree to settle down there and be content to have Klute babies, bake pies for a rural community, and comfort her man when he remembers what he needs, and believes in it enough to ask?

Or will they hide out in some loft in lower Manhattan, with noises in the night to remind them of sleeplessness? Can Klute function as a private eye there, or will the city horrify him? Will Bree give up hooking and face the not dissimilar ordeal of going to open auditions for silly parts and being told she's a little too old, or tough, to be an appealing actress? Jane Fonda was lovely and sexy in *Klute*, but she was at an age (thirty-four) when audition production assistants don't always stop to look at you. Their brisk panning shot slides over your hard-earned experience. The public feeds on ingénues, or fresh meat.

More testing now is that upbeat ending to *All the President's Men* and its blithe assumption that a pair of boyish reporters and a swashbuckling editor like Ben Bradlee (Jason Robards Jr.) will guard the Constitution and keep us safe. The Bernstein-Woodward picture took pains to be "accurate," with its re-creation of the *Washington Post* newsroom, stressing the labor in reporting, and the small-part crookedness that made up "Watergate." But that realism now seems decoration, or even an evasion. The Constitution was endlessly vulnerable to our corruption and compromise. How could journalistic valor restrain those forces? How did the foreboding Pakula not see the perils in this situation? Well, he was a serious and distinct talent, and an interesting man, but no one ever accused him of being overloaded with irony. And he couldn't foresee the computer or the cell phone and what they would do to journalism.

Still, of the three Pakula films, *The Parallax View* is the one that asks, Hope? Are you kidding? It's clear from the outset that its leading character, Joe Frady, deserves to be alone—he resists being our hero. So don't kid yourself that this Frady guy in *Parallax* was Warren Beatty in the moment when he was most handsome and had a chance of helping us make it through the night.

Joe Frady *is* good-looking, and compliant with the sexual conquests that may come with that. Woodward and Bernstein, if you recall, have no private lives in their film, or no time for them; they are so resolved to file copy, nail down quotes, and save the nation. But Frady, far from being a dedicated seeker of truth out in the dangerous field, is having trouble with the law and inventing stories about a lost parrot to stay free. He may be charged with malicious mischief, vandalism. He's arrogant, abrasive, and superior. His weary editor, Rintels (Hume Cronyn), bails him out—again—and regards him as a pain in the neck who has a fatal urge to create news instead of just report it.

In the middle of the day, in his faded apartment, we find him fucking a young woman. It may be a pretty fair fuck, though the girl's face is not its best testimonial. It's more important that Joe is caught there by a prior lover, the anguished Lee Carter (Paula Prentiss). She has larger matters on her mind, but she comes in on Joe's latest lay with the bruised air of a woman who was herself betrayed by him in the past. A sensual indolence or self-regarding carelessness hangs over Joe and makes us wonder whether Frady isn't frayed, or afraid? Is he really stalwart hero material—a new Joe Friday? It's possible to realize that strong reporters can be weak men—we don't need to survey the journalists we have known—but it's significant that the movie takes a moment to characterize Joe in this way and to warn us against too many high hopes for him. He has Beatty's thick lips, with an air of self-love fighting alienation. When first seen in the film, Joe is lurking in the background, where an assassin might be.

Lee is herself a reporter, and she has a jittery story, about a shooting a few years ago that they both witnessed—a handsome senator was assassinated on July Fourth at the Seattle Space Needle; he was running for president. There was an earnest official inquiry, and it was determined by the credentialed panel of white men that a lone, unstable gunman had been responsible for the killing; this killer was acting "out of a psychotic desire for recognition." But Lee has never swallowed that explanation (she *is* called Lee). Her instincts tell her to be afraid—Prentiss is distraught in just a few moments—and as an actress and a person she was herself troubled. Lee tells Frady that half a dozen witnesses to the crime have died, or been removed, in just three years. She presents the case to Joe, her old Joe, fearful that she may herself be a target. He tells her not to be so imaginative, or paranoid. In his superior way he dismisses her approach. But then she is under a sheet in the morgue, which makes seven. Is seven out of the ordinary in the space of a few years, in a world where people are going to die anyway? Do we know enough about actuarial tables to be sure?

You may not have been born then, or understand how 1974 was a paradise for paranoia. In 1963, in Dealey Plaza, in Dallas, and then in the basement of

Fig. 19. Assassination at the Seattle Space Needle in *The Parallax View* (Alan Pakula, 1974, Paramount Pictures)

the police station, shots had been fired and an infernal struggle between fact and possibility set in. It has never ended.

A sensible, matter-of-fact estimate said the shots in Texas had been tragic, but random and unorganized. Lee Harvey Oswald and Jack Ruby were misfit loners with guns—that is an interpretation of American action that we still cling to at every modern shooting outrage, no matter that the shooters seem to feel there is a tradition, or a culture, to maintain (like FATHER, MOTHER, GOD). After a while, there may be so many disturbed solitaries that the concept of solitariness needs redefinition. There were some people in '63, and thereafter, who were no longer ready to take this obvious answer: Ruby being there, on police premises, ready to silence the most important witness—that was stretching a point; it was a door opening that we have never been able to close again.

Government and positive storytelling rose to the challenge. A commission was appointed, the Warren Commission, with impeccable membership: the chief justice of the Supreme Court, two senators, two representatives, a former head of the CIA, and a former head of the World Bank. (In the days when that meant impeccability.) Even without a woman, or a black—much less any kind of outsider—this commission was trusted to deliver twenty-six volumes of testimony and evidence. It resolved that our unlucky President Kennedy had been shot by a single gunman who might just as well have been crazy for all the chance anyone had of knowing why he had felt bound to do it. You could surmise he was crazy just because his rifle was hokey, and he didn't seem like a good shot. He had also lived in the Soviet Union once and then returned, without so much as a debriefing. Anyone who had done that would have been grilled, surely—unless he was crazy, or unless . . . ? And Jack Ruby? Just one more nut who had been so upset he felt he had to tidy up? So much bad stuff is done in the name of tidiness.

The Warren Report didn't hold. It stands now as a pioneering step in the larger process by which the state or its authorities will attempt to explain away awkwardness in a ponderous show of care and diligence that signifies very little—or even betrayal. By 1967, Mark Lane had published *Rush to Judgment*, a calm if not dull book about the haste, the errors, and even the ignominy of the Warren Commission. A year before, in the witty, subversive *Blow-Up*, Michelangelo Antonioni had glimpsed a gunman in the foliage of a London park, a nod to the unchecked fertile legend of the grassy knoll.

A cottage industry sprang up, speculating over what had occurred in Dallas, but a reactionary orthodoxy responded by saying take care, we leap at paranoia like a culture so addicted to storytelling that we may never trust "facts" again. Just because this view was cautious or conservative did not rule out its value. There was a growing sense how in a complicated world there were truths that were escaping us—and there went with that a fear that if we can't trust anything, then fact, history, and those handholds are up for grabs. We might all end up alone, untrusting and disturbed. Such is modernism.

But then in the era of Vietnam, Cambodia, and Watergate, those who feared the worst received an uncanny boost. If you were disposed to believe that government might be a front for dishonest, manipulative forces of merciless self-interest, then Watergate was your *À la recherche du temps perdu*. The material of that miniseries might seem sordid, criminal, and upsetting, but for paranoids the slow drip of revelation was daily bliss on television. Do you recall the thrill of discovering that these idiot scoundrels had recorded their own plotting? For a moment, it became not just tempting but delicious to believe that the best explanation of modern history was that any conspiracy theory was sound, and that SNAFU was the DNA of organized behavior.

So, check the dates: on June 14, 1974, *The Parallax View* was released; on July 27, the House Judiciary Committee passed three articles of impeachment against President Nixon; and on August 8 the president resigned. This looks like perfect timing, and it did leave some satisfaction of "mission accomplished," whatever the personal tragedy or revelation of malice and dishonor. It was widely claimed that just as the US could get itself into very bad messes, still it seemed to have the procedural means and the conscience to get out of them. So you might have imagined that *The Parallax View* was going to be a hit (like Pakula's *The Pelican Brief*, in which lone virtue defeats terrible intrigue), received in exultation by every fearful and righteous citizen.

That it didn't turn out that way speaks to the problematic virtues of the film. I am not calling *The Parallax View* an overlooked masterpiece, just the most interesting and least coherent of Pakula's three paranoid films. A central reason for that is the film's unwillingness to turn Joe Frady into a reliable guy. Instead, it leans toward a more ambivalent point of view: that our hero may actually have the misfit personality and the arrogance or alienation that could make him a lone, disturbed gunman. Joe is not a good guy, not reliable or likable—it was important that Beatty the narcissist couldn't look at himself without sneering.

The action of the film turns predictable: sooner or later our Joe gets the point of thinking Lee may be right, that there could be not just a Pulitzer Prize but a civic duty in uncovering the cavities in an investigation of the Seattle shooting. So Joe becomes a halfway regular fellow, doing the right thing, showing courage and ingenuity—just think of how he deals with the crisis of the bomb on the plane. The attraction of Woodward and Bernstein two years later was that they had been hardworking, right-minded Joes who got at the truth and sank a bad president like rookie detectives. Surely some possibility lurked in developing *The Parallax View* so that Joe Frady would come through, uncover the truth, get a prize, and go on to residency at the Columbia School of Journalism, while finding a woman he could Love and Settle Down With. You know that kind of comfortable ending.

But Pakula and the people who shaped the film were not content with cleaning up in that routine way. I'm sure this was a matter of the Loren Singer novel's dark forecast, of Pakula's own instincts, to say nothing of the approaches by screenwriters Lorenzo Semple and David Giler, star Warren Beatty, and another writer, Robert Towne (a third man?), who was slipped on board as the actor's private doctor.

Pause a moment, for that paragraph skims over a lot of fascinating detail. The New York publisher, Doubleday, had wanted to break into moviemaking. It bought the rights to the Singer novel, and hired Lorenzo Semple to do a script. He took only one idea from the book: that a sinister group existed ready to formulate a conspiracy theory that could suit many needs. The investigative protagonist was a cop. (The novel gets no credit in the film's titles.)

Alan Pakula was then hired to direct. He said he liked the Semple script, until he changed his mind and hired David Giler to do a rewrite that turned Frady into a journalist. A screenwriters' strike was then looming. Giler finished his script in time, but after the strike someone else came in and did a lot more work. Semple and Giler have the credit on the film, but neither of them felt it belonged to them. You could think of it as a kind of waiting to be taken in one direction or another. You can't trust anyone—but you were counting on that?

Whatever the credits say, the film owed a good deal to Warren Beatty's own uneasiness with playing a trusty hero and his enlisting Towne to write the script the way he wanted it to go—toward a dysfunctional egotist, a problematic fellow who might do damage in trying to save the nation. There's a deadpan irony in the picture that is its provocative virtue, for as Joe Frady pretends to be an ideal candidate for the Parallax Corporation, he is actually better suited to the job than he might care to admit.

Here is a disturbing truth: if you were close to the untrusting community of those who believed in conspiracy theories in the seventies—whatever the cause or the issue—then you encountered intense people, often young and highly educated, pale from the dark of scholarship and moviegoing, who believed the worst of their alleged masters and who had rooms of files, videotapes, and old newspapers that contained the secret truth, and who went into rages and hospitals if, say, their innocent girlfriend thought to please them by tidying up the house and throwing all the good stuff away. These secret agent guys might be as correct as they were depressed; they might be prescient in anticipating even greater furtive outrages from authority; they had the secret truth of the times in their troubled heads and their untidy pads. But they were people who were losing it—why not, they demanded to know, wasn't the whole culture losing it? Couldn't you be right *and* going mad at the same time?

To be more pointed about this: it isn't just the legendary hell houses like Russia and China that pick out their dissidents and send them away to the various Siberias they command, to isolation wards, pile-driving medication, or even brain surgery—"There, are you feeling better, comrade? Doesn't everything seem a little more cheerful now?" Countries closer to home also welcome their bipolar subjects into rehab or intensive care or the best quiet time money can buy, with benefit of medication, therapy, and every tranquilizing assurance that "yes, of course you're right. Every conspiracy theory is correct—now, how about a nap and forgetting?"

Fig. 20. Reporter Joe Frady (Warren Beatty) has a problem (*The Parallax View*, Alan Pakula, 1974, Paramount Pictures).

In other words, some of the people who "knew" the truth were a little unsettled by it—or deranged. And, you know how one can't rely on those who are deranged. You might even go so far as to ponder whether such people still have the right to possess forty-seven AK-47s in their own homes. Fascists and outlaws alike have shrugged off ordinary doubt.

Bree Daniels in *Klute* could easily end up an unstable woman no one would trust. But that film clings to hopes for her: she has not gone crazy or given herself over to drugs; she has not been physically damaged (though we hear she was beaten up); and even if she is a whore, she is still capable of delivering a loving lay to John Klute. But Joe Frady can't go home again, or back to that safe narrative territory. He is a danger to himself and those around him: wherever he goes, death follows. He may be the best hope of investigative journalism, but he may kill its chances. And he is such a loner that he has left no backup after he's gone, because he trusts no one.

But the film hesitates, as if at war with itself. It was set up to be the study of a loner (by contrast, *Klute* and *All the President's Men* are buddy films). Joe might have kept Lee in tow, a half-crazy woman, maybe, but intuitively discerning, and not just a companion, but someone to love. As soon as the editor, Rintels, emerges as a possible ally or companion—and he has been sourly critical of Frady—he is himself killed. Joe's only companions are Parallax agents. His ghost or his doppelganger is the Parallax profile that he is trying to live up to in order to infiltrate the malign organization. The ending is not just dismal and disappointing; it's anti-dramatic.

Beatty was an ambivalent actor. And his doubts shaped this picture. There was a side to him that actually resisted acting (he did so few films—twenty-three credits in fifty-five years) and flinched from trying to be attractive or likeable. At the same time, he was a commercial player, very interested in making successful films. In the mid-seventies, he was locked into playing unsound men—not just Frady, but McCabe in *McCabe & Mrs. Miller* and George, the Beverly Hills hairdresser, in *Shampoo*. It was as if he was drawn to dissecting the corpse of American attractiveness when the body looked like him. Yet he fell for the aloof image, too. There was a narcissist that wanted to be indulged in the vanity Carly Simon had scolded him for. He took pains to be "beautiful," and in *The Parallax View* there is that riveting, speculative moment where Joe goes along with the redneck who tries to intimidate him by treating him as a girl. In just a few years, the box-office Beatty would make *Heaven Can Wait*, a movie Joe Frady would have walked out on in disgust.

So the actor's stance is pulling in opposed directions, and yet the film, and Pakula, had to go along with Beatty's whims. (Since *Bonnie and Clyde*, he was hard to resist as a producer-like force.) The picture could have made Joe nicer—the guy who is looking after a semi-invalid Lee—or nastier: a man who is cold to others, chronically selfish, and closer in spirit to the alienated type, a guy who is beginning to be crazy. That much daring could have left the picture dead on arrival, but the film failed anyway and generally got mixed reviews. Or it could have been as disturbing as, say, *The Conversation*. Made in the same year, that film tracks another paranoid who senses an infinite realm of intrigue in which he has been a stooge. That Harry Caul (Gene Hackman) ends up isolated, destroying his own apartment because he thinks it has been compromised.

The life on the screen—the sheer presence of *The Parallax View*—is intriguing, but it's edgy and hard to penetrate: Beatty's Frady is passive, secretive, devious, self-obsessed, and unreliable. He so averse to sympathy you can feel the film shedding audience support. The fact that he has no one to talk to in a useful way makes him more isolated and suspicious. He has difficulty in joining with the world, so he becomes increasingly the victim of bizarre physical circumstances. The pursuit he undertakes is a series of semi-comic mishaps: the dam that fills up; the boat, the toy train; the bizarre unpopulated convention; and, of course, the plane that has to be stopped. And we don't even see it blow up!

These exigencies are as much his enemies as the shadowy Parallax agents who dog his steps. At the end of the film, Frady is destroyed less by human action than by an alluringly open doorway with a bright light beyond. He is handled impersonally, or like a mouse in an obstacle course. He gets no physical relief—and he has no Lee to make love to. What's a hero to do in an American adventure film unless he can fight and screw? At least Harry Caul is acclaimed "the best bugger on the West Coast," and he does have sex with the flaky blond whose task it is to betray him. By contrast, *The Parallax View* is a persistently frustrating film—as if it never believes Joe has a chance. That status is truer to American life than to the heroic movies we make. So it's hard to look at any film that old without entertaining thoughts of a remake. After all, the elements that may best be explained by conspiracy have not disappeared.

Pakula was a stealthy director (this was his strength and his limitation): he advanced with hushed care, in a mood that anticipated dismay. That is ably assisted here by the darkened color photography of Gordon Willis and the dripping menace in the musical score from Michael Small. Much of the film is composed visually in an unbalanced or oblique way. Action is photographed indirectly, thus depriving us of satisfaction or resolution or old movie excitement. Things happen, but in a way that begins to undermine actuality. These are the attributes of 1970s noir, but they can look studied now, like a kind of close carpeting that smothers vitality. If you watch *The Parallax View* more than forty years later, I think it cries out for more juice, jazz, and turmoil. The poker-faced comic potential within the story needs air and space. Instead of the stricken woe over this America, try an air of antic fun, and let a little more ineptness creep in at Parallax. How can any institution in America be so efficient? Ours is the country of *dis*organized crime—that may be our last hold on humanism.

Just because of adjacency in the career of Beatty, I wish for the humor that Robert Altman found in *McCabe & Mrs. Miller*. That is a sad story, made sadder by the Leonard Cohen songs that now feel like stones tossed on a coffin. But *McCabe* thrives on the foolishness of McCabe the hapless entrepreneur. He is forever talking to himself, imagining he has poetry in him, while making a disastrous hash of negotiations with those powerful outside interests disposed to buy him out of his cockamamie "business."

It's easier to believe in that haphazard way of life in the Northwest of 1900, and a raw township called Presbyterian Church, where homely whores make a trade and keep dumb men warm in winter, and where Mrs. Miller (Julie Christie) smiles wistfully at the idea that McCabe loves her. Beatty was freed by that film, whether he knew it or not. The stories say he and Altman were at odds on the production, but seen again today, his McCabe is as perky, silly, and charming as his bowler hat. Perhaps Frady needs more of that flighty, inadvertent silliness. Suppose that when he sits down to look at the test film that Parallax shows him, he is knocked out by it, bubbly with enthusiasm and a giddy sense of beauty. "That's so neat!" he sighed.

Suppose he wants to make test reels like that *himself* and has an unstoppable urge and a near complete lack of critical intelligence such as would thrive in advertising. Suppose he became a fully fledged spokesman for Parallax. Suppose, instead of exposing the organization, he found fulfillment in its enterprise. Hasn't his editor at the paper always said that Joe was a bundle of irresponsible whims and rebellions? Suppose our movie became a satire instead of a study in dread.

The Parallax test film—a rapid montage of American iconography and road-sign words—is (if you like, or are in a dismal enough mood) an indictment of Americana, advertising and consumer apocalypse, and a heavy-handed treatise on how vulnerable e pluribus unum can be to the riot of pluribus. (Must unum be a loner?) That test sequence now seems the most provocative part of the film, hovering between satire and anthem. It also suggests how far *The Parallax View* needs a level of random, documentary-like descant—the pandemonium of TV coverage, or persistence, the unholy flux of information and advertisement. That is the mix that really opens up the paranoid vision of America.

The test is conducted in a large room, a kind of church that reminds us of the chamber where the commission had passed judgment on its lone Seattle gunman—or of a grand cinema. (As we watch, we feel we are taking the test.)

Fig. 21. Frady sits for—and passes—the Parallax Test (*The Parallax View*, Alan Pakula, 1974, Paramount Pictures).

There is a large chair for the subject. He must sit there, with his fingertips touching the sensors that record his reactions. The room goes dark, the music swells, and this movie begins—a montage of still shots, the iconography of Americana, sex and violence, family and fruitfulness, with those interposing titles—LOVE, MOTHER, FATHER, ME. . . . What messages would your fingertips be sending if you had taken the test, in 1974? Did you LOVE ME and GOD? Or would you have been horrified at being asked? Do you find the test sinister or comic? Do you realize how many Trump voters would have passed the Parallax test?

The movie offers Joe (and us) the test reel as if to say, there, isn't that code awful? It may be, but that piety is insufficient when most of us much of the time are suckers for the stuff in the test reel and the verve that puts it across. Donald Trump's identity is not of a man with political beliefs, or critical thinking, but that of an image that inflates on self-promotion. Just think of a film—it might deserve the wild comedy of Preston Sturges—about a crusading spirit who approaches the big bad world of Parallax, *and falls for it*—and who has a chance of being a leader. Suppose he becomes its mouthpiece, a mixture of Lonesome Rhodes (from Kazan's *A Face in the Crowd*) and Donald Trump, as comic and menacing as anyone we've seen. And if comedy and menace don't mesh, can we resolve our difficulty in deciding he's ridiculous?

Preston Sturges doing *The Parallax View*? You may decide that I am out of my mind—but isn't dysfunction to the point of imbalance what Pakula hoped he was getting at? And isn't it possible that American self-awareness and its pessimism have tended too much toward noir introspection instead of surreal riot? After all, people not quite seeing straight—a condition of parallax—are as likely in farce as in tragedy. I understand that assassinating senators is not the normal material of farce—or I did, before I saw enough senators in action. Are we really at a point where the life of Congress can still be reformed by grave lectures on its moral purpose and the history of freedom—or does it need to be exploded through comic outrage? Is Capra-ism really more responsible than the Marx Brothers?

A sentimental respect has grown over noir. It wants to assume that an adolescent fatalism will not just vouchsafe seriousness, but guarantee that pessimism can save the day. Be suspicious enough and you won't be a sucker. But consider the possibility that the ethos of America is to make suckers of us all—like proposing life, liberty, and the pursuit of happiness when those three approaches may be cracker-barrel ads. So I'm suggesting that Joe Frady could become more like John McCabe, less vain and more foolish. But maybe that's a half measure. Suppose, instead, that Frady was played by Jim Carrey . . . or Jerry Lewis.

Don't let your fingertips crackle with static. I realize, Carrey was not ready yet in 1974 (though that Seahaven community from *The Truman Show* does seem like a Parallax project). I know that Jerry Lewis sounds outrageous. But Jerry was in his prime still not quite fifty, and still thoroughly committed to the Muscular Dystrophy Telethon, and that—I submit—was another show that an enterprising Parallax Corporation could have been mounting, with its demented contrast of energy and entropy in America. Think of Lewis playing Joe as a half-scary, half-endearing huckster who veers from believing in the worst to trying to sell the best. That might show us something about our psychotic desire for recognition.

I am not disrespecting muscular dystrophy, or being facetious about America. But noir (a glorious genre over the years) has a tendency to slip into dreamy but solemn humbug, as opposed to critical thinking. We do need to reexamine our story forms. Genres are the mountain ranges of American cinema, and persistent myths in our collective unconscious. So the western is still said to be a moral template, no matter that it can be ludicrous when compared with the actuality of American history in the West of the country. *Casablanca* may be a "great" brooding noir romance for people safe at home in 1943, but it is a travesty for anyone who lived and suffered under the Gestapo.

Genres need prodding and subverting if they are not to become frauds. Think of *The Big Sleep*. People still say that great Hawks film is a noir, a mystery story, a private eye film, and a study in the way terse dialogue, cigarette smoke, innuendo, kissing the beautiful dame, and staying suave can handle corruption. So be it: those elements *are* there in the picture. But *The Big Sleep* is also a screwball romance in which a man and a woman say who cares who killed whom, when they can cuddle a bit, have witty telephone calls, and generally be so insolent you know they're dreaming of having sex. And why not?

These speculations may be unsettling (like rumors of conspiracies), but I am trying to rethink what happened in American film in the sixties and seventies—that last golden age? If you think the question mark is merited at the end of that sentence, then you are living with some thought or hope that American movies should stand as a commentary on America itself—instead of just an unprincipled way of making money.

Where was American cinema going in the era of *The Parallax View*? And how important were the "statements" made by movies in the 1970s? Look at the key example: the first two *Godfather* films are endlessly rewarding, beautiful in the sultry ways of movie, and a landmark. But what do those films urge upon us except that in times of crisis and stress don't we long to be part of some steadfast family, in a pact of togetherness, even if the purpose of the pact is a life of organized crime? Although those films think they are saying Michael Corleone is a very bad man (so get him out of our sight), don't we cherish his dark example as much as we are drawn in by Pacino's meticulous shyness? Don't we want him as *our* godfather and yearn for the conviction that comes from being a Corleone? That is a dire ambition, but I think it's the fantasy that takes me back to the films year after year. And I tremble at myself for the addiction. But that's where a better or more challenging version of *The Parallax View* might begin to get at the appeal of the organization and its test reel.

To twist that knife home a little more, test the reliability of what *All the President's Men* had to offer. Bernstein and Woodward are with us still, and they do books from time to time. There's always a new *Fear*. They have an emeritus place in the ongoing coverage of contemporary politics. The *Washington Post* exists, owned by the master of Amazon, in a media society where newspapers are desperate over their survival. Did that film preserve the presidency or protect the Constitution—not just from Nixonian rascals, but from the deterioration of American institutions and their idealism? Like many other countries, America faces a horizon of problems so daunting as to threaten a feeling of futility in the political process—and the largest of these problems seem essentially beyond politics. Some sections of our political world even deny they exist. That is how Congress can seem like a nasty club to which very few are paying attention. That is how a monster of farcical incompetence became a candidate for ultimate leadership. Donald Trump may be counted on to destroy himself. But suppose the next Trump proves as cool as Obama, as charming as JFK, and as idealistic as Bernie Sanders. Such a leader could win and draw us closer to fascism. That's when the archetype of a Michael Corleone can become so important, and ominous. And Michael is an impeccable monster of efficiency: his most fascist streak is in saying bosses don't make fools of themselves, and of us.

The best movies of the seventies are sometimes archaic now because their narrative structures cling to realism, to cause and effect, to tidy cross-cutting and the suspenseful battle between good and evil, when our real lives (our experience) are crowded with futility and disorders that hardly weigh good and evil any longer. TV coverage (hundreds of simultaneous channels) is a profuseness that has undermined and mocked the tidiness of satisfying stories. And we do not know how to generate new movie narratives—or art and entertainment as a whole—that can contain this disorder, let alone say much useful about it. Instead, the leviathan sprawl of our media has become both our subject and our form. That is our chaos and our chaos theory.

These matters may be larger than most movies care to contain. Some of our best films stick with small stories or local situations—like *A Man Escaped*, *The Shop Around the Corner*, and even *The Big Sleep*. But *The Parallax View* offers an oblique commentary on nearly everything American, and on whether the cause of justice and the task of reporting and writing can keep that everything in order. The best comparison I can think of is with Ken Burns's and Lynn Novick's eighteen-hour *The Vietnam War*, which embraces the panorama of America in the age of that war—and ever since.

Joe Frady gets lost in that enormous, shadowy America, and Pakula ended this film in retreat and disarray: Joe is dead, Rintels is dead, Lee is dead, presidential candidates are dead, the mystery persists, but there will always be a panel of wise white men ready to explain away the loss as individual aberration or madness—in a fascist state, being mad can be one of the last freedoms that remain. So often, the leaders of those states are the template for insanity.

There's a strange coda to all this. On November 4, 1998, Alan Pakula was driving on the Long Island Expressway, near the town of Melville in Suffolk County. A vehicle in front of him struck a piece of metal piping on the road. It jumped up, came through Pakula's windshield, and killed him outright. This was a tragic mishap—just one of those things—but Joe Frady would have known how to read its meaning.

CHAPTER 7

CINEMATIC TONE IN POLANSKI'S *CHINATOWN*
Can "Life" Itself Be "False"?

Robert Pippin

> Wrong life cannot be lived rightly.
> (Es gibt kein richtiges Leben im falschen.)
> THEODOR ADORNO, *Minima Moralia*

Villainy, often extreme, horrific, satanic villainy, is as much a staple of American film noir as the entrance of the femme fatale, confusing double or triple plots, the weakness and fragility of the grip of moral norms, and ironic, "unhappy" endings. In Roman Polanski's *Chinatown* (1974), often cited as the finest example of the "neo-noir" genre, as well as in many of the best noirs, what appears to be the ordinary world of rational expectations, planning, moral courage, and attempts at mutual understanding is in reality, we learn, a world where none of this really matters or is even possible, that events are actually manipulated by unseen and malevolent self-interested forces that frequently cannot even be identified. But very often the malevolence has a source, an arch-villain. Kaspar Gutman (Sydney Greenstreet) and Joel Cairo (Peter Lorre) in *The Maltese Falcon* (1941), Johnny Prince (Dan Duryea) in *Scarlet Street* (1945), Ballin Mundson (George Macready) in *Gilda* (1946), Whit Sterling (Kirk Douglas) in *Out of the Past* (1947), Arthur Bannister (Everett Sloane) in *The Lady from Shanghai* (1947), Mike Lagana (Alexander Scourby) and his brutal henchman Vince Stone (Lee Marvin) in *The Big Heat* (1953), Hank Quinlen (Orson Welles) in *Touch of Evil* (1958), and such female villains as Barbara Stanwyck in *Double Indemnity* (1944) and Lana Turner in *The Postman Always Rings Twice* (1946) would only be the beginning of a long list.

Chinatown successfully re-creates many of these markers of the "noir world"—or at least as many as it can in a color, Panavision anamorphic format film, most of which occurs in daylight[1]—both by cinematic means (dialogue, the score, narrative pacing, and the characters' sense of futility and confusion) and by setting the film in the Los Angeles of 1937, near the beginning of the noir period, conventionally fixed at 1941 and *The Maltese Falcon*. (The aptness of such a setting and such a bleak moral atmosphere for indirectly representing the United States of the 1970s is also no doubt intentionally suggested.) This is the setting in which we meet Noah Cross (played with cunning and flair by John Huston), whose perfidy is mythic in scale, willing to build shoddy dams that burst and kill hundreds, willing to cheat farmers out of their water in a drought so that he could buy their land, to treat the public or common good as wholly his to profit from, to murder anyone in his way, and to impregnate his daughter and groom his granddaughter for the same fate. It is hard to imagine a noir villain remotely his equal.

Pointing to such similarities raises an obvious but very broad question, unmanageable in this limited context. Among the many characteristics of the role of genre in Hollywood production, one of the oddest is that some genres appear to have births and deaths; others, not so much. Romantic comedies, suspense thrillers, crime procedurals, bio-pics, historical epics, all extend back from the present into the heart of the "classic Hollywood" period, the thirties, forties, and much of the fifties. Musicals, westerns, melodramas, and noirs all became extremely popular for a period of time, and then seemed to fade away in importance and frequency. Noirs are a bit of an exception, since the bleakness, fatalism, and general style or atmosphere of noirs persist in crime pictures and in other genres too. There are noir westerns, and if we count some of the work of Dennis Potter, even noir musicals. But, as noted above, the convention is by now pretty fixed that film noir should be dated from 1941 and *The Maltese Falcon* (interestingly, for our purposes, a John Huston film) to either 1955 and Robert Aldrich's *Kiss Me Deadly*, or 1958 and Orson Welles's *Touch of Evil*. This flourishing period seems to have had something to do with postwar unease, paranoia, and anxiety, especially about the changing status of woman that war production required. The reemergence of a complexly plotted, bleak, clearly noirish Hollywood feature film in 1974, one that inspired passionate pro and con reactions[2]—much like the reception of noirs themselves—poses a social and historical question worthy of reflection in itself. As noted, the film even seems to have a classic noir villain, played by the man credited with making the first film noir, John Huston. But even more interestingly, that apparent similarity can be misleading.

For the film's theme is not individual moral evil itself, and does not appear to attribute the source of the evil we see simply to Cross as an individual character, although the temptation to do so is overwhelming. The theme is, rather, as the title announces, "Chinatown," a marker for something unfathomable, inexplicable, an evil "unattributable" to a villain (no one knows who is responsible for what in "Chinatown"), but characteristic of a world itself, and not just the world of Chinese immigrants in Los Angeles. For example, the film's famous, signature closing line, "Forget it Jake; it's Chinatown," makes no literal sense. Cross's murder of his former partner, his swindle, his rape of his daughter, all of which culminate in the police shooting the fleeing Evelyn Mulwray and Cross getting his clutches on his granddaughter, have nothing to do with Chinatown. That place is simply where the final scene occurs. At least, it makes no sense unless the speaker means to refer to what we have just seen, that Evelyn and Noah Cross exemplify "Chinatown." In fact, the reference seems meant to do duty for the whole social and historical world set out by the film, and the most prominent characteristic of that world appears to be its *unintelligibility*—already an invocation, among many others, of a crude stereotype, Asian "inscrutability"—an unintelligibility that has a number of particular inflections and implications in Polanski's treatment.

"Chinatown"

This idea or image of Chinatown is like a spectral presence throughout the film, both to suggest that no matter how confusing and dangerous Los Angeles can seem, at least it is not Chinatown, and, much more ominously, and more and more prominently, that the distinction between Chinatown and Los Angeles is an illusion, that we—the bourgeois world and its rule of law—are *in* such an unfathomable world, and can never escape. The references, that is, work to create a foreboding atmosphere of dread, anxiety, uncertainty, and confusion about our own situation that the characters displace or project onto this "other" place, until finally the last words spoken are truer than the speaker realizes. The world of Los Angeles itself is Chinatown, and the advice being offered Jake (forget it; do nothing because nothing can be done) is a chilling expression of a despairing cynicism in the face of this fact.

The screenwriter, Robert Towne, apparently originally conceived the title to refer to Jake's psychology. As the producer, Robert Evans, remembers an early conversation between them:

> " . . . what's it called?"
> "*Chinatown.*"
> "What's that got to do with it? You mean, it's set in Chinatown?"

"No. 'Chinatown' is a state of mind—Jake Gittes's fucked up state of mind."

"I see," I said, not seeing at all.[3]

But once Polanski made the script into a film, the reference is hardly so limited—the only thing "fucking up" Jake Gittes's mind is his memory of a particular and, we will find, typical failure in Chinatown—and the ironic identification of Chinatown, as moral anarchy and unintelligibility, with Los Angeles (for Polanski, the Los Angeles of the Tate-LaBianca murders as well) gradually becomes inescapable, as the vastness of the corruption and the extent of the evil everywhere become ever clearer to our representative in the film, Jake. (Except for one or two exceptions, the story is narrated from Jake's point of view, and that point of view is ours. We see and learn what he sees and learns as he does.)[4] None of this is explicit or is pointed out by anyone, except ironically in the last words, and is more intimated by Polanski's creation of a general tonality or atmosphere. Chinatown, and what it comes to mean, hovers over *everything* that happens; it cannot be confined to a distinct place. Nothing anywhere is what it seems; Jake's naïve confidence that he can figure everything out seems less and less credible; the musical score, dominated by a plaintive, melancholic solo trumpet, constantly suggests that this will all not turn out well, no matter what anyone does, or thinks he has discovered; and the references to Chinatown keep reappearing throughout.

The allusions begin with a racist joke told to Jake by his barber to distract Jake from his anger at another customer who had disparaged Jake's profession. (Jake believes he has discovered a "love nest" where Hollis Mulwray meets his

Fig. 22. Director Roman Polanski flashes a knife in *Chinatown* (Roman Polanski, 1974, Paramount Pictures).

mistress, and the newspapers blast this scandal all over the front page of the paper the customer is reading. In reality, Mulwray is helping his wife protect the young girl from Noah Cross, the father of both Evelyn and the young girl, Katherine.) The customer, it turns out, is a mortgage banker, and Jake points out to him that at least he, Jake, does not foreclose and throw people out of their homes. Already, the moral taint unavoidable just by inhabiting the contemporary world is suggested: one can either be a snoop, making what should be private more or less public, or a banker who throws people into the street, or a barber who cannot afford to make moral judgments. Everyone is a customer. Everyone has to make a living, and that means everyone has to participate in the ruthless profit machine. (As we are reminded later, even the police must "swim in the same water as the rest of us," a disturbing image since the big fish there in the water with us is Noah Cross.) Jake rushes back to the office to relay the joke to his operatives, and we see the ironic inverse of the femme fatale entrance. Evelyn is not the object of a male gaze, but stands behind Jake, unobserved, powerful and rich (her lawyer is with her, armed with a lawsuit) and hears him repeat his tawdry Chinaman screwing joke.[5] In an instant, Jake's seeming coolness, his unflappable air and so his apparent inheriting the sang-froid superiority of Sam Spade and Philip Marlowe, are forever destroyed. He is little more than a braying adolescent male. So much for Evelyn's "first impressions."[6] And this early diminution of Jake's status is reemphasized throughout the film, physically denoted by his cut nose, a somewhat odd feature of the character, judged by standard hard-boiled detectives in other films. He is easily set up by the fake Mrs. Mulwray, Ida Sessions; ultimately understands very little of what is going on (he does not finally even seem to understand what Evelyn tells him about the incest). And he is largely incidental to the action, which is generated by the attempt on Evelyn's part to keep her daughter/sister away from her father, Noah Cross, an attempt that is understandably hysterically ramped up when Evelyn loses her protector from Cross, her husband Hollis Mulwray. Jake even manages to set up, and then to lead everyone of relevance to the site of the final scene, the scene of Evelyn's death. But any judgment about Jake depends on the role of the references to Chinatown in the film, and, given that role, what it would be reasonable to expect anyone to know and to do.

At Mulwray's mansion, Jake finds an Asian butler, maid, chauffeur, and gardener, and again a stereotype is invoked. The gardener is trying to tell Jake what he is doing, that the salt water in the tide pool is very bad for the grass, but he says, and Jake repeats, that the water is "velly bad for the glass." If Jake had heard anything other than the mispronunciation, he would already have had the film's most important clue. The fact that the water is salt water is what reveals that Mulwray was murdered in the tide pool, and that will lead Jake, finally, to conclude that Noah Cross was the murderer. These stereotypes, and there are more to come, appear to function as defense mechanisms. Chinatown may be a dangerous and unfathomable place, but the crude stereotypes create the illusion that "we know" what "they" are like, and we are superior to them, can make them the butt of jokes. In "our" world, they are not dangerous but humorous, an obviously fatal piece of self-deceit.

When Jake discovers the place where Mulwray's body was discovered, he meets there an old police colleague from Jake's own Chinatown days, Lou Escobar. He asks Lou if he is still arresting Chinamen for spitting in the laundry, and Lou tells Jake that, in the first place, Jake is behind the times. They have steam irons now. Jake's knowledge of Chinatown and its mores is out of date, a sign perhaps that his imagination is not up to what "Chinatown-as-LA" is now capable of. And second, Escobar says that he has made lieutenant and made it out of Chinatown, creating the suggestion that Jake, whatever he may think, has not really made it out.

When Jake is summoned to meet Cross, he is warned by Cross that, while Jake may think he knows what he is dealing with, he most certainly does not. Jake replies that that was what they used to tell him when he worked in Chinatown. Ironically, Jake gives plenty of signs that he believes that this *is* true of Chinatown, that no one, at least no one from the outside, knows what is really going on there, who is running what show, what the rules are. If Jake could have carried that lesson with him in his new PI job, he might have been more hesitant to trust what he thinks he has figured out, that Evelyn committed the murder. Then again that lesson might be better expressed by what Jake says when asked what he did in Chinatown. "As little as possible." This is also one of the closing pieces of dialogue in the film, a somewhat neglected line, said

Fig. 23. Jake Gittes (Jack Nicholson) and Noah Cross (John Huston) in *Chinatown* (Roman Polanski, 1973, Paramount Pictures)

quietly by Jake (almost inaudibly) as he contemplates the mess that has been created: Evelyn dead, Cross with his daughter/granddaughter.

Jake and Evelyn finally sleep together in a scene marked both by tenderness and a notable lack of erotic charge. Neither of them seems much interested in sex,[7] and Polanski does not even hint that Jake is the kind of lady-killer associated with the private detective stereotype. Evelyn wants to know about Jake, in their postcoital, cigarette afterward scene. He tells her that he was a policeman in Chinatown, occasionally wearing a uniform (perhaps intimating that he occasionally did what a police officer should do, but only occasionally) and that the experience was very painful, that he does not want to talk about it. She presses him, and he says that he was trying to protect a woman, and in so trying, he ensured that she did end up "hurt."[8] This is exactly what he is about to do to/for Evelyn, reminding us again that the presumed difference between LA and Chinatown is an illusion, and that one of the most dangerous entanglements in such a world is love.[9] Chinatown (Los Angeles, the contemporary world) is a world where good intentions and commitment to others not only do not much matter, but they can even be dangerous. They assume what moral action always does—that one knows one's own motives, that one understands what is happening, and that one can predict safely what a course of action will bring about. Since none of these assumptions is true, doing "as little as possible" seems the safest choice. Assuming these conditions have been met is not only naïve, but very dangerous.[10]

Finally, the polysemous "Chinatown" is invoked in other, related ways. When Jake is being prodded by Evelyn to tell her more about Chinatown, he finally says, "You can't always tell what's going on . . ." but instead of saying "there," he turns more toward her and says ". . . with you." *She* is now his Chinatown, dangerously opaque to him, even as he begins to trust her.[11] Here the dialogue makes Towne's original point with Evans, that "Chinatown" is also state of mind, as in "you may think you know what you are dealing with, but, believe me, you don't," although in this case he at least knows what he doesn't know, that Evelyn, however attractive, is still hiding something and may be quite dangerous. For one thing, she, or her eye, is "flawed." There is a black mark in the green of her iris—a stain, it would seem; ultimately the ineradicable stain of incest, and the site also of her death, the mark of why "life" for her is impossible, as the policeman's bullet seems to pass through her and out that eye. The image is nicely echoed in Jake's pursuit of her after she receives the phone call that prompts her departure. He kicks out one of her taillights and follows the "one-eyed" vehicle and the "flawed" Evelyn to the house where he will learn the truth. This is the "flaw" that likely makes her so wary, closed off, mistrustful; and Jake's suspicions about what she is holding back, combined with that wariness, is what likely makes the "romance" between them so tentative and even somewhat formal. In fact, from her point of view, the stain is even harder to bear because she assumes some responsibility for it. When, after the famous (and much parodied) "she's my daughter, she's my sister" slapping scene, she begins to tell Jake what happened and starts, "My father and I . . ." Not "My father used to come into my room" or something similar to other incest revelations in films and television. And even more remarkably, when Jake offers, "He raped you," Evelyn, weeping, looks directly at Jake and shakes her head decisively.[12] Whatever it was, she is insisting, it was not rape. She participated. The unfathomability of "what's going on" with Evelyn, introduced in the scene in bed as another dimension of the unfathomability of Chinatown, has reached an even darker, more horrific region.

In sum, the film's repeated references to and warnings about "Chinatown" create an atmosphere or tonality so ominous and threatening that it raises the question of whether the unambiguous and profound evil present in the film might not be the product of one or a few bad individuals, but that a whole form of life can be said to have "gone wrong," become "false," not "truly" what a human life must be to count as such, so damaged (*beschädigt*) that no "right" life in such a world is conceivable. (The possibility that Evelyn's flaw or stain is not just hers, but the "*human* stain"—she calls it a sort of "birthmark"—or that the form of life we experience in the film is not a "damaged" form, but *the* form of human life, inherently and irremediably deeply corrupt, is a possibility we will consider later.)

A film, that is, can have a mood suffused through it, something not quite the same as a signature style, but an effect of a consistent, controlled style. John Ford's westerns, the great ones, create a mood of historical fundamentality, that matters of great political and social significance are at stake (the place of violence in a civilized life, for example); Alfred Hitchcock's films sustain a mood of brittle anxiety and eventually dread, given that we and the characters never know what they need to know; Douglas Sirk can create scenes of desperate emotional intensity, and can even string several such scenes together successively; David Lynch can create a sense of perversity in the way a character smiles or walks or eats. In this film at least, Polanski creates and sustains a constant, uneasy mood among all the unknowing characters, that *something is not at all right here*, and this is the reason people are so often reminded of Chinatown. They sense the situation is beyond them, either beyond their limited capacity to understand (ever), or, as in the case of Cross's relation with his daughter, beyond any being's capacity to understand; that there is nothing here that is understandable.

This is the clear implication of the epigram cited above from Adorno's *Minima Moralia*, subtitled "Reflections on a Damaged Life."[13] (The moral corollary of the claim: "Today . . . it is part of morality not to be at home in one's home." At the most metaphysical: "Life does not live.")[14] Adorno meant the life of late capitalism (a "profit economy"), mass consumer societies, manipulated by the "culture industry" to such an extent that "right life" is not *possible*; objectively available coherent courses of action, even possible ways of living, are all compromised or "damaged." But the bearing of this mode of assessment, shifting our attention from individual moral agents (while not denying their individual culpability) to a different notion of "wrongness," one borne by a form of life itself, as unjust, exploitative, dehumanizing in its very nature, should be clear. In any such world, one is morally complicit with such wrongness just by surviving, by existing at all. We might think this a radical and initially implausible notion. We immediately call to mind moral heroes under Nazism, or people of conscience in all sorts of horrific and objectively hopeless corrupt and depraved societies. But Adorno does not say that moments of right action are not possible, but rather that no *right life* is possible, and these moments of moral heroism are not instances of living rightly, but—if only at least once—acting rightly. Even so, given what was said above about noir villains in general, and the singular villainy of Noah Cross in particular, such a sweeping indictment does not seem plausible. There seems a clear center of responsibility for what is so wrong about Los Angeles: Cross and those who serve him. But what does Cross have to do with "Chinatown"? That is the question that can be illuminated by what I've referred to as "tonality" or a cinematic representation of a mood or common "attunement" in the narration. Something like these terms are needed because the issue does not concern false beliefs, even collectively held false beliefs, or a society subject to delusions that need to be, and can be, corrected. *Life itself* has become "false," and this is not a feature representable discursively (by a set of propositions listing what is commonly felt, believed, hoped for, etc.), but in the way a life is, can be, cannot be, lived. Cinema is well positioned to give us some sense of what that might mean or at least "look" and "feel" like, and that is especially true of this movie. We need to discuss first one more prominent feature of the film's narrative.

The Double Plot

As other commentators on the film have pointed out, the structure of the film forces us to ask what the two plots, the water swindle plot and the incest plot, have to do with one another, if anything. Their relationship is not a standard plot and subplot relation, for one thing, because it is not at all clear which is to be the major focus and which the minor. Psychoanalytically inclined critics obviously focus on the incest plot, and the sociohistorical critics on the water plot, but for many in each camp, the other plot is a digression, diversion, or distraction.[15] And it is certainly true that the film itself had an impact on water policy in California, that that plot, loosely based on the Owens Valley case, had a real-world effect.[16] The details of the real event and the film's treatment of it are in some dispute, but Shetley sets out what appears to be the most reasonable and widely accepted view:

> No one disputes the fact that a group of the city's wealthiest men, privy to inside information about the plans of the Department of Water and Power, bought up land cheaply in the San Fernando Valley and realized enormous profits on their purchases when the Owens Valley Aqueduct, completed in 1913, made water available to irrigate that land. Though the dates have been shifted from the early part of the century to the 1930s, the film presents with a fair degree of accuracy the fundamental structure of the San Fernando conspiracy, a conspiracy in which wealthy and powerful interests manipulated public agencies for private profit.[17]

Robert Towne, at least, had a clear idea that the water plot was the most important. He said, "A man violating his own child is not as serious as a man who is willing to violate everyone's children. . . . Maybe it's because America is a puritanical country. I felt the only way to drive home the outrage about water and power was to . . . cap it with incest."[18] On this account, the incest plot is a kind of intensifier; it is there to intensify our outrage at what Cross is willing to do. That may be so; the revelation after the slapping scene certainly intensifies our disgust with Cross, but that can hardly be the end of the relationship between the plots.

For one thing, it remains unclear in the film just what Cross did and was willing to do and why. This confusion is not helped by the fact that the film ends with so little of the plot elements resolved, so few that each plot, as a narrative, does not seem to have the clear end point in standard beginning, middle, and end narratives. Evelyn dies, but that "resolves" very little. We don't really find out just why Cross murdered his own business partner, and are left with the fact that their last, photographed fiery conversation could have been about either Hollis's discovery of the plot to force farmers out of the valley by denying them water and blowing up buildings, poisoning reservoirs, which is what Jake thinks, or about what appear to be Hollis's attempts to hide Katherine from him, which is what Cross himself suggests when he answers Jake's question about the argument by saying it was about "the girl."[19] Nothing about Cross's motives is all that clear either. He doesn't need the money he will gain by the success of the water swindle, as he admits to Jake, saying it is all about "the future," whatever that means. Towne's remarks are a bit hysterical here. Cross is not willing to "violate everyone's children." He wants the desert valley to become a garden, with plenty of children, just as long as he owns the land and profits from the great bounty that will result from the building of the dam. This is in itself already mysterious, or at least confusing. If he really doesn't care about the money, why not let the dam be built and the farmers already there on the land in the valley prosper? His tactics are illegal, and he certainly is willing to harm the families now on the land, but this is basically an insider trading sort of offense, and as far as I can see, it completely pales in comparison with the incest plot. It would be a different matter indeed if, for example, he knew the water were contaminated, and that he was consigning many future generations to cancer and other diseases.

Moreover, are we to believe that the police will write off Hollis's murder to Evelyn, which is why they are pursuing her and forcing Jake to help them, because they believe she did it in a jealous rage? Will they even pursue the case? Are we to think that they will just not believe Jake, or figure there is too much danger to themselves in believing him? Are there to be no legal services involved in the determination of what should happen to Katherine? Cross just gets to "take" her, fold her physically into himself in an ugly parody of intimacy when he takes her out of the car, shielding her eyes with his hand. How will anyone establish that he is her grandfather, as he claims, after briefly stumbling about what he should call his relation to his young daughter?

One thing we do know about the incomplete resolution of each plot is that no one attempting the "right thing," in the loosest sense—Jake's wanting the truth to come out, Evelyn's wanting to protect Katherine from Cross—succeeds, and this leads us closer to the question of "no possible right life" suggested above. For the plots do share a strong metaphorical link. The link is voiced in an utterance by Evelyn in the climactic scene, "He *owns* the police," and by Cross when he is trying to persuade Evelyn to back off, "She's *mine* too." The legitimacy of private property, which should begin in the right over my own body, the entitlement to noninterference by others, does not settle the question of rightful extent of ownership, or the question of what may be privately owned. The Romans may have treated children as property of the father, but no serious theorist of capitalist modernity has ever advanced such a claim. Katherine is not and cannot be "his," any more than Evelyn was. But it is also not enough to show that in both cases, the issue for Cross and men like him is simply power, the power especially never to be subject to the will of another, always to be able to subject others' will to one's own. Not that this is insignificant. As Shetley points out, both water and daughters represent the possibility of fertility and in that sense the power to control the future. As he compellingly puts it, "Each [water and daughter] is a means of projecting oneself into the future, either through bloodlines, or the creation of wealth, for what is capital but wealth that has outlived its creation, even its creator? Noah Cross's incestuous acts and his land swindles turn on his desire to monopolize for himself the possibilities of life and fertility that water and daughters represent; in both cases, what ought to be exchanged is instead hoarded, what should circulate is instead entrapped and held back."[20]

But this still leaves somewhat mysterious why Cross, mortal being like the rest of us, should expend such energy, take such risks in the service of such megalomaniacal control of a future he will not see. At one point he seems to suggest that he wants it simply because he can have it. In a crucial scene by the tide pool, he tells Jake that he doesn't blame himself for the incest, and he expresses what appears to be one of his founding principles, if not his lodestar, "You see, Mr. Gittes, most people never have to face the fact that at the right time in the right place, they're capable of *anything*." This is not the film's finest moment. Such nihilism is simplistic, and although we are three years from the sexual-assault-on-a-minor charge that eventually led to Polanski's exile, the assertion sounds creepily like the director's own all-purpose excuse for his behavior. Our natural or immediate reaction is to think of the line as Cross's self-deceived and pathetic excuse for himself, but the more we note that the center of "wrongness" in the film is "Chinatown" (or LA, or the US, or capitalism, or even modernity), the line begins to emerge as the film's point of view. This need not be meant as some comment on human nature, as it is characteristic of this distinctive form of life, the one so mysteriously and elusively evoked in the film by the mere mention of "Chinatown."

The tide pool scene also resonates unintentionally with our theme. Cross tells Jake that Hollis Mulwray loved tide pools, because they were where life mysteriously began; they were the source. This tide pool, though, was the site of Mulwray's death. That life itself should now be the site of death sounds like Adorno's quotation from Kürnbirger, that "life does not live." The source of life now—now in Los Angeles and the industrialized West with its social organization based on acquisition and consumption—is the place of death; more generally of "death in life."

But in this case, the exercise of power made possible by unimaginable wealth has a central dimension crucial to the effectiveness of the film, and that "locates" to some extent the Chinatown social pathology (or locates Evelyn's flaw, Cross's limp, Jake's scar). For the idea of capitalism as a legal system, as rightful, requires a distinction between public and private that is both acknowledged in the regime's basic law and attended to and actively sustained by enforcement and official expression. The idea that there can be a collective allegiance to a common good is also the idea that the state's monopoly on the use of legitimate coercive violence cannot be understood as at the service of whatever private interests are predominant at a time. In such a case there would be no state, no genuinely public sphere, no politics, just some (putative) collective means to ensure that the use of public power be consistent with some sort of like use for all, always subject to manipulation by anyone with wealth enough to manipulate without penalty. This returns us to the "false life" issue.

"False Life"?

Clearly, the somewhat vatic pronouncement that "life does not live," or that there is no "right" way to live in a false life, means to refer to a normative, not physical breakdown. Everyone who is alive obviously exists, is living, not dead. But life in some sociohistorical setting might not be lived "as life should," as a human life. Elephants performing their dreary routines in circuses are alive, but not living the life-cycle of elephants. And we do not mean that some aspect of their lives is not as it should be, but rather they are simply not at all living as they should. Their whole way of life could be said to be false to what is "truly being" the creatures they are; there is no "right" way to be an elephant in a circus. As we have been seeing, the references to Chinatown all suggest a moral chaos at *this* level of generality. *Everything* there is inscrutable; and this is because *no one* seems to know what the rules are; *no one* seems to know who is running the show; the best thing one can do there is "as little as possible." There is no reliable public agent; law is only a means. The one thing we do seem to know is that, whatever is "really" going on there, it is corrupt and dangerous; only someone very wise in its ways could survive for very long, and imagining such a person is very difficult for those of us, most of us, who are not such persons.

Once the characters and the audience have come to realize the disturbing truth that there is very little if any difference between LA and its Chinatown, we also seem to be prompted to come to the disturbing conclusion that Jake may have reached: that there is nothing to be done. We will never understand enough of what we need to know to manage to live as life is meant to be lived. The suspicion that *this* is our fate is, I have suggested, indirectly created by the film's tonality, its sustaining a mood throughout of confusion, justifiable paranoia, and outcomes that do not at all match what was intended, and this keeps building an *atmosphere* of confusion and impotence among the principals—not something one can be said to "come to believe." There could be no determinate content to such a belief. The main feature of LA-Chinatown is that no one can figure out *what* is appropriate to believe about their station.[21] It is heroic in a way, or antiheroic, that Jake refuses Evelyn's offer to "drop the whole thing" after she drops the lawsuit, but it is his pressing forward on the matter that dooms all the principals to the final Chinatown scene. Evelyn does not understand why Jake has been hired to snoop around Hollis, but, veteran Cross that she is, she is willing to back off, do nothing, "forget it." This makes it unclear why she filed suit in the first place. That is certainly not going to help with the publicity problem. It is also not clear why she later hires Jake when he tells her that it is likely that someone murdered Hollis. If someone murdered Hollis, she must have a pretty good idea who it was. Jake's conclusion that Evelyn murdered her husband leads him to take several steps that finally reveal to Cross and to the police where Evelyn and Katherine are. The many close-ups of pained, confused, suspicious, and befuddled faces (especially Faye Dunaway's brilliant, intense, brittle, barely in control performance) build this sense of futility and frustration among the participants and in the viewer. So it is appropriate that we too, the viewers of the film, are left so confused about such things as Cross's motives, the police's intentions, the fate of Katherine, or what it means to suggest that Jake should just "forget" about the fact that a vast water swindle is succeeding, and that a sexual predator has gotten his hands on a new young victim.

We have noted that the one thing one can say about Noah Cross and, we have to assume, the real world as he (and perhaps Polanski) sees it, the "dark world" meant in the same paranoid sense as "the dark state," is that the main feature prized in such a world is power, control, even over "the future." In general, this in itself is not surprising. Human beings cannot assure themselves and their kin of their own welfare if they are subject to the will of others who are primarily interested in *their* good. A degree of independence, or freedom from interference, is a feature of what makes a human life human. But so is the inescapable fact of our dependence on other persons. We are finite beings who depend on others for the achievement of our ends, and in a world of highly divided labor, this dependence is more and more unavoidable. The most significant arena in which this tension must play out is the political world, and

Fig. 24. "Forget it Jake, it's Chinatown." (*Chinatown*, Roman Polanski, 1973, Paramount Pictures)

that means especially the state's assumption of a monopoly on the legitimate use of coercive violence. If it becomes more and more likely that there is no such thing as "the state," that the police can be owned, that we cannot be assured that there is a genuinely public sphere in which a collective commitment to a common, rather than private good is possible, and instead that we can detect everywhere nothing but the play of private advantage, then it becomes more credible to think that the first condition in a genuine human life being led as distinctly human has not been met. (Stated in the terms of modern political thought: the state of nature must be exited. The "war of all against all" must cease.) So there is something almost pathetic in the final scene when Jake, of all people, encourages Evelyn, "Let the police handle this," a plaintive expression of hope that is immediately and, by this point, compellingly for most viewers, countered by Evelyn: "He *owns* the police."[22]

It would be comforting to think in more straightforward moral and legal terms. Cross is an evil man, and he is a criminal, guilty of tyrannical and unrestrained sexual predation and of corrupting to the point of unrecognizability the public world, making it "his." We might think: at least we could arrest and condemn him, all as a confident rejoinder to "Forget it, Jake. It's Chinatown." But by this point, the film has created that undercurrent of futility, confusion, and paranoia, such that the title of the film should remind us yet again that the problem is not Cross, but "Chinatown." No one who thinks they have found the truth can do anything with such a truth. (Another pathos at the end: Jake screaming all the details of what he has discovered, and no one is listening.) No one who thinks they have left Chinatown really has. Jake thought he had left it behind, but he finds himself staring at the same carnage he brought about there: "I was trying to keep someone from being hurt. I ended up making sure she was hurt."[23]

CHAPTER 8

"I DON'T KNOW WHAT TO DO WITH MY HANDS"

John Cassavetes's *The Killing of a Chinese Bookie*

George Kouvaros

At the end of *The Killing of a Chinese Bookie* (John Cassavetes, 1976/1978), Cosmo Vitelli (Ben Gazzara) stands outside the club whose proprietorship he has tenaciously defended. As part of his travails to retain control of the club, he manages to perform a seemingly impossible hit and also to turn the tables on the mobsters who tried to double-cross him. Cosmo's triumph is signaled in his penultimate scene when, for the first time in the film, he abandons his position in the wings as the unseen announcer and maestro and walks onstage to quell his audience's hostility at the show's delay. His onstage patter belies the toll exacted by these labors: "They say that everything is sex and sex is everything. Here at the Crazy Horse West, we give you a lot more than that." The only indications that something is amiss are the moments when his lowered gaze suggests a weary entanglement of internal ruminations. In order to buy his performers a little more time to get ready, he offers each of his patrons a free drink, acknowledges the hard work of his bar staff, and raises his glass in farewell to Rachel (Azizi Johari)—his girlfriend and club favorite. Once Mr. Sophistication (Meade Roberts) and his Delovelies arrive onstage, he takes his leave. He is last seen standing outside the club gazing at the blood that seeps through his coat pocket, seemingly more annoyed than actually concerned about the mortal threat the bullet wound poses.

"You think you're gonna live with the bullet in you?" These words, spoken by Betty (Virginia Carrington), the mother of Cosmo's girlfriend, encapsulate the strange sense of dissociation that dominates the film's final moments. The

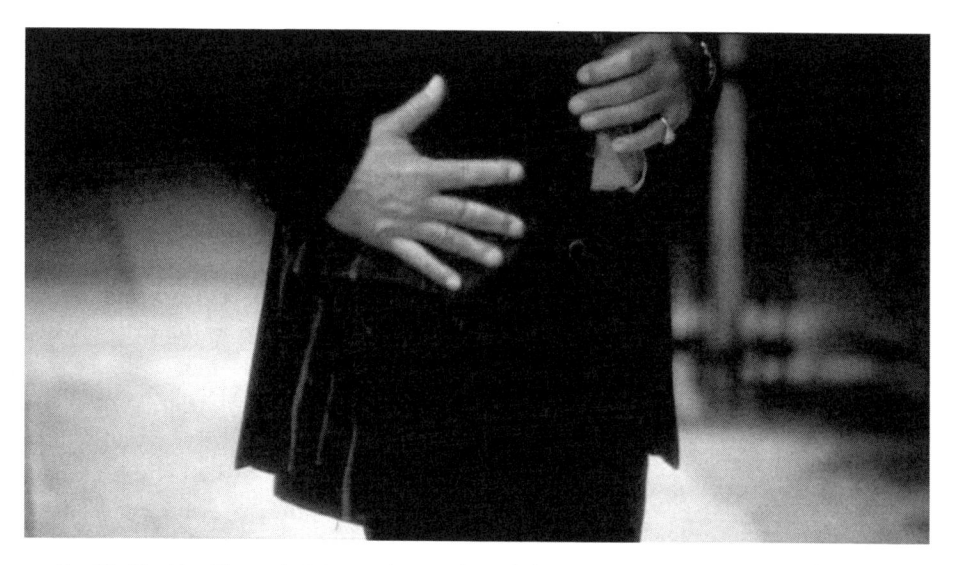

Fig. 25. The blood from a bullet wound seeps through the coat pocket of Cosmo Vitelli (Ben Gazzara) near the end of *The Killing of a Chinese Bookie* (John Cassavetes, 1976, Faces Distribution).

wound in Cosmo's side is a low priority bit of business that must wait for more important matters such as the show. Given Cosmo's apparent indifference, it is appropriate that the camera does not dwell on his discomfort and instead returns one final time to the stage of the Crazy Horse West and Mr. Sophistication, who is struggling through a rendition of "I Can't Give You Anything but Love, Baby." In his top hat, pancake makeup, and deadpan expression, Mr. Sophistication is both master of ceremonies and fall guy to the Delovelies who taunt and disrupt his performance—much in the same way that the gangsters had taunted Cosmo when they first visited his club in pursuit of the debt. When Mr. Sophistication departs and the closing credits start to roll, we are presented with a series of still images of the performers. On the soundtrack we hear a quick reprise of Mr. Sophistication's theme song, clapping, cheering, and catcalling. And, almost last of all, Cosmo's voice can be heard back announcing the act. Eventually this gives way to a cacophony of sound and audience applause that fades out with the voice of one of the Delovelies: "He thinks we don't love him, but we really do."

In making sense of the tangle of events that constitute the film's denouement, much depends on how we read the film's engagement with the gangster film. Recounting his discussions with the director during the filming, Ben Gazzara argues that Cosmo's struggle to retain control of the club must be read biographically: "The gangsters were a metaphor, and Cosmo was John, certainly. The club was where Vitelli created beauty, with its girls, the music, the jokes, the spectacle—that was the best part of Cosmo. The gambling, the drink, that was the dark side of the artist, and the gangsters were the system, which was so hard on John."[1] Al Ruban, Cassavetes's frequent producer, occasional cinematographer, and sometime actor, echoes this reading of the film's significance: "The club was the world that he created and valued more than anything, much like the films that John made and was so protective of, and the gangsters were the men in the suits, the pressures that came to bear not only to sign you up but to change you to their will."[2] For the most part, critics and writers have stuck closely to this reading of the film, utilizing the director's biography as a key to unlocking its significance—a tendency that dominates the writing on Cassavetes's work, more generally. "The gangsters are producers," claims Ray Carney, "and Cosmo is every filmmaker who agrees to adhere to someone else's script and 'shoot' something he doesn't really believe in in order to clear a debt."[3] Likewise, Gilberto Perez positions Cosmo as an onscreen stand-in for the director. In danger of being forced to assume the role of a puppet in a much larger scheme, Cosmo manages "to become his own director, which enables him finally to wear with real feeling the mask of grace under pressure."[4]

The most interesting version of this reading of the film is provided by Ivone Margulies. Like Carney and Perez, she understands Cosmo's devotion to the Crazy Horse West as an allegory of the director's own dogged pursuit of artistic independence in the corporatized environment of Hollywood filmmaking. But rather than stopping here, she considers how the interruptions, false starts, and errors that distinguish the events occurring onstage encapsulate a distinctive set of filmmaking principles: "As a director and screenwriter, Cassavetes multiplies the occasions for small pathetic spectacles—on and off stage.... He feeds off the breakdown of polished showmanship and polite behavior, and his characters' ultimate dignity is measured precisely in challenging received ideas of what is proper."[5] Marguiles's summation opens the door for a more nuanced understanding of the film's significance, one in which the tropes and conventions of the gangster film—personal overreach, extortion, murder, and betrayal—enable, rather than contain, an exploration of the disparate energies and material circumstances that determine the film's staging. Much more than an affirmation "of the amateur as the bearer of artistic independence"—as Margulies has it—the erratic onstage spectacles encapsulate a principle of representation at its limits that animates and estranges the world created in the film.

Interestingly, the idea of approaching the film as an exercise in world creation is something that Cassavetes himself proposes: "I was wondering ... what kind of person would own a place where groups of people would sit silently and look at flesh, and what kind of people would perform, and why do they perform?" *The Killing of a Chinese Bookie* is not a gangster film, he insists, but the precise rendition of a world: "The fun and challenge of the film was to imagine a self-contained world different from the one I live in: to move into it and live in it."[6]

By looking closely at the way in which he sets the terms of this inhabitation we can clarify the significance of this film in his body of work as well as some of the complexities that define his place in the New Hollywood. Nearly three decades after his death, Cassavetes has emerged as one of the most widely acknowledged influences on a number of different generations of filmmakers, for example, Elaine May, Martin Scorsese, Peter Bogdanovich, John Sayles, Jim Jarmusch, Sean Penn, Nicolas Winding Refn, Pedro Almodóvar, and Olivier Assayas.[7] This acknowledgment is matched by an ever-growing body of critical writing devoted to elucidating the nature and impact of his work.[8] Where once the task for scholars and critics was to rectify a perceived neglect of Cassavetes's films or to debunk erroneous assumptions about their production circumstances, it is now something more challenging—to better understand the contexts that inform their emergence. The context that I will consider concerns certain formal and thematic shifts that cut across the distinction between independent and studio-funded filmmaking during the 1960s and 1970s. In Cassavetes's case, the outcome of these shifts was the creation of particular types of filmic worlds grounded in the affective volatility of the filmmaking process itself.

White Events

In an influential survey published at the midpoint of the seventies, Thomas Elsaesser observes that, while the protagonists in films such as *Two-Lane Blacktop* (Monte Hellman, 1971), *Five Easy Pieces* (Bob Rafelson, 1970), *The Last Detail* (Hal Ashby, 1973), and *California Split* (Robert Altman, 1974) share attributes with their classical counterparts, their behavior is disconnected from a motivating context. This abjuring of motivation, he argues, gives rise to a dramaturgy quite distinct from that found in classical Hollywood narrative: "Classical narrative was essentially based on a dramaturgy of intrigue and strongly accentuated plot. The image or scene not only pointed forward and backward to what had been and what was to come, but also helped to develop a motivational logic that functioned as an implicit causality, enveloping the hero and connecting him to his world."[9] The motivation connecting the hero to his world provides the narrative with direction and purpose: "Contradictions were resolved and obstacles overcome by having them played out in dramatic-dynamic terms or by personal initiative: whatever the problem, one could do something about it, and even eventually solve it" (281). In films such as those cited above, contradictions and obstacles are no longer amenable to the application of personal initiative. Taking as his exemplar *Two-Lane Blacktop*, Elsaesser identifies a deliberate downplaying of intrigue or interpersonal conflict in the film's rendition of the journey: "There is only the merest shadow of an intrigue, the action provocatively avoids the interpersonal conflicts potentially inherent both in the triangular relationship and in the challenge personified by the Warren Oates character" (281).

The larger question shadowing Elsaesser's comments has direct relevance for how we understand this era of American filmmaking: How far is it possible to consider the New Hollywood as experimental? For Elsaesser, the answer comes down to whether or not the skepticism about motives gives rise to narratives free of "parasitic and synthetic causality" (283). After surveying the work of different American directors, he sees some cause for optimism. He notes that while European directors such as Jean-Marie Straub, Jacques Rivette, and Luis Buñuel "can work at purely situational narratives . . . in the comforting knowledge of an appreciative intellectual audience," the pressures on such experimentation in Hollywood cinema mean that American directors pursue a more familiar course: "Consequently, the innovatory line in the American cinema can be seen to progress not via conceptual abstraction but by shifting and modifying traditional genres and themes, while never quite shedding their support, be it to facilitate recognition or for structuring the narrative" (287).

Elsaesser's survey provides a handy starting point for understanding Cassavetes's approach in *The Killing of a Chinese Bookie*. Here too we encounter a constant reworking rather than abandonment of generic tropes and conventions. Both Carney and Richard Combs comment on the way in which the director deftly translates the harsh tonal juxtapositions of classic fifties film noir into the medium of color film stock.[10] During the course of the film, we move between the glare of spotlights and the afternoon sun to darkened corridors and corners that seem to both draw us in and hide their contents. Most of the action takes place at night or under the garish artificial lighting of the club. In this nocturnal environment the faces and expressions of the characters are isolated against backgrounds that are often either out of focus or shrouded in darkness. In Alexandre Astruc's famous account of F. W. Murnau's films, he describes a tension between composition and annihilation at work in the very construction of the image, a tension that we might cautiously connect to *The Killing of a Chinese Bookie* as a way to describe its formal energies.[11] At times, Cassavetes's filming seems to eat away at the characters, showering them in too much light or losing them in a deliberate underexposure. When Cosmo is bundled into a car by the mobsters and given his instructions on how to perform the hit on the Chinese bookie that serves as the film's narrative centerpiece, the scene is filmed in almost total darkness. It is impossible to tell where the voices are coming from and who is speaking. Like the central character, we remain suspended in a world whose contours and borders are always at the point of receding into darkness.

This perceptual transformation of the world is connected to a broader disturbance of tempo and causal linkages. When Cosmo, Rachel, and two of the other performers, Sherry (Alice Friedland) and Margo Donna (Donna Marie Gordon), take a trip to Chinatown to contact the Chinese bookie, the scene begins in bright sunshine. As the group walk toward the camera, the backgrounds shimmer in the heat and glare of the sun. Even the bright oranges and yellows of the women's dresses are rendered diffuse by the intensity of the diurnal light. The scene cuts to a high-angle shot of the group sitting in a restaurant, but only long enough for Cosmo to suggest going to a movie. We then cut again to a shot of the group rising from their seats in a still-darkened cinema. The exaggerated punches and groans emanating from the martial arts film play on regardless of the group's departure. When we next see them outside the cinema, all hell breaks loose. Cosmo suddenly realizes it's night: "Jesus Christ . . . What time is it?" From then on, it becomes a mad rush to get back to the club in time for the evening's show. The journey to Chinatown takes just over a minute of screen time. But in that period, Cassavetes's montage of over-illuminated bodies, incidental actions, arrivals and departures creates an acute sense of something happening too fast, of time getting way. This sense of temporal disturbance is crucial to the film's downplaying of causal linkages. No sooner does Cosmo pay off the debt than he once again plunges back into debt. Between these two events there is no cataclysmic turning point or moment of fatal error, but rather a series of low-key incidents—often just to the side of where we imagine the central action to be occurring—each with its own mystery and drama: a solitary drink in a bar; the preparations for a night out; the boredom and discomfort of Cosmo's female entourage waiting for him to finish the game; and the final humiliation of waiting to be called in by the mobsters to render an account, trapped in a florescent hell of white walls, nautical themes, and deck chairs.

These events follow each other in a consecutive pattern; yet what has been curtailed is the motivating connection that could adequately explain how we have come to be where we are, how we get from one point to the next. The various events that push the narrative forward lack a gravitational force and tend to deviate our attention away from the central drama. Even when Cosmo is refused further credit at the gaming table, the camera's attention is not on the central character arguing with the casino employee, but on Rachel looking onto a scene in which—depending how you look at it—she either plays no part or is the central part.

"Linkages, connections, or liaisons are deliberately weak," Gilles Deleuze writes in his own account of this period of American filmmaking. "Sometimes the event delays and is lost in idle periods, sometimes it is there too quickly, but it does not belong to the one to whom it happens (even death . . .)."[12] He refers to these disconnected events as "white events": "events which never truly concern the person who provokes or is subject to them, even when they strike him in his flesh." Detached from causal linkages, white events find their natural extension in the directionless ground-level movements of an urban wanderer: "How could there be a nerve fibre or a sensory-motor structure between the driver of *Taxi Driver* [Martin Scorsese, 1976] and what he sees on the pavement in his driving mirror? And, in Sidney Lumet, everything happens in continual trips and in return journeys, at ground level, in aimless movements where characters behave like windscreen wipers (*Dog Day Afternoon* [1975], *Serpico* [1973])" (208).

Deleuze's description helps us to summarize the complex dramatic movements and tempos in *The Killing of a Chinese Bookie*. If in *Faces* (1968), *Husbands* (1970), and *Opening Night* (1978) Cassavetes constructs an experience of time predicated on repetition, habit, fatigue, and the elongation of actions to the point where meaning is lost or overturned, in *The Killing of a Chinese Bookie* he provides us with an experience of time that is more elusive yet also more abrupt. There is a gnawing sense of distraction, a sense of always being too soon or too late. It is as if the turning point that could reveal the significance of an event is just about to happen or has already happened prior to our arrival. Instead of giving us a series of defining actions, *The Killing of a Chinese Bookie* seems to focus on the interval between actions: the moment when an action is either not yet or no longer present—or else has happened too fast to be properly registered. Cosmo's elusive grins and mysterious gestures—shaking the condensation from a glass of scotch off his fingers, dancing a brief jig in front of the bar, muttering to himself in the limousine on the way to pick up the girls: "I'm amazing"—seem to be the aftereffects of events never witnessed directly, but still capable of registering a complicity with the camera.

The elusive tempo of an event is strikingly reflected in Cosmo's performance of the hit on the Chinese bookie. After he receives the extraordinarily complex set of directions, his journey to the bookie's house is suddenly interrupted by a blowout on the freeway. Forced to abandon the car, he phones for a cab to take him the rest of the way and also makes a quick call back to the club to check on the act. But when neither Vince (Vince Barbi) nor Sonny (Salvatore Aprile) is able to tell him which number is being performed, he is forced to sing into the receiver a few bars of Mr. Sophistication's signature tune, "I Can't Give You Anything but Love, Baby." The neon light of the phone booth seems to operate as his own personal spotlight, demanding that he come up with an

Fig. 26. Cosmo improvising "I Can't Give You Anything but Love, Baby" (John Cassavetes, 1976, Faces Distribution)

appropriate performance to an event that is constantly changing its terms and conditions.

Even the side trip to pick up the hamburgers required to distract the bookie's dogs is hijacked by a well-meaning waitress (Arlene Allison), who has trouble understanding Cosmo's request to not have the burgers individually wrapped. "You can't put twelve hamburgers in a brown paper bag," she insists. "You're gonna ruin it." In *The Killing of a Chinese Bookie* these encounters refuse to remain in the background. Like the young man riding in the back of the pickup who screams something out to Cosmo in the film's opening moments and is never seen again, the concerns and anxieties of the well-meaning waitress impose themselves on the film. They belong to a class of phenomena whose purpose is not simply to extend the scene out into the world, but also to change its direction. They do so by bringing it into engagement with incidents that may or may not have a role to play in the story. These incidents imbue the film with a remarkable sense of contingency; at the same time, they index a world whose dimensions extend beyond the necessarily limited purview of the central character.

The trials and interruptions that waylay Cosmo confirm that the tempo of an event—even the most generic—is not something inherent to that event but something that has to be performed and staged step by step and thus is subject to a range of possible rearrangements. In his book on the pre-cinematic motion studies of Étienne-Jules Marcy, François Dagognet provides an apt description of the implications that arise once our view of an action or gesture is rendered discontinuous: "The universe knows only surges and drops, fragments that we reassemble and that we thereby diminish. We ourselves fabricate a smoothed-out, rounded spectacle."[13] It is this sense of a "smoothed-out, rounded spectacle" that Cassavetes takes apart in *The Killing of a Chinese Bookie*. At stake in this disruption is the opening up of new possibilities of narrative as well as the rendering of different forms of temporal sensation and affect.

When Cosmo arrives at the bookie's house, the camera travels through a series of exits, corridors, and doorways following Cosmo, but also at times seeming to lose him in the maze. Eventually the camera stumbles upon an old man (Soto Joe Hugh) contentedly splashing around in a large bath with a young female companion. For a time, the film seems to forget about Cosmo, intent rather to observe the playful behavior of the old man. His emaciated body seems far too vulnerable and earthbound for the role in which he has been cast. When the old man moves to an adjoining room, the camera patiently observes his slow movements as he takes off his glasses and wades into the waist-deep water of an indoor swimming pool. He glances a number of times in the general direction of where we assume Cosmo is standing, without registering his presence. When he finally acknowledges Cosmo's presence, the old man blinks hard as if trying to assure himself that what he is seeing is not a ghost. The only verbal contact between the two occurs just before the old man is shot, when he mumbles in a barely audible tone, "I'm real bad. I'm so sorry."

In the melee of actions, gunshots, and sounds that follow the assassination, it is unclear whether Cosmo has been wounded by one of the bookie's men. It is only when he steps out of the cab and collapses at Rachel's house that the seriousness of the wound becomes apparent. But in *The Killing of a Chinese Bookie* not even death is allowed to run its proper course. Instead of using Cosmo's injury as a way of determining his hero's fate and bringing the narrative to a conclusion, Cassavetes slows things down even further, wrapping the remaining forty-seven minutes in a hypnotic web of botched actions and personal crises. When Cosmo goes back to the club, he is picked up by one of the gangsters, Flo (Timothy Carey) and taken to a warehouse, presumably for execution. As he waits for his colleagues to arrive, Flo seems to mentally unravel. "You're an amateur," Cosmo tells him. "Take a walk." He then manages to outplay the other two gangsters who are sent to kill him: the first is caught unaware by Cosmo's ability to appear out of nowhere, while the second and most tenacious of the gangsters blindly wanders through the warehouse—calling out to Cosmo to show himself—while Cosmo patiently waits in a dark corner until he is able to calmly escape.

In Cosmo's final performance, he returns to the club, manages to soothe Mr. Sophistication's wounded ego, and gets the show back on the road. His

Fig. 27. Cosmo explaining to his clientele the importance of being "comfortable" (John Cassavetes, 1976, Faces Distribution)

triumph is signaled when he goes onstage to address his audience and introduce the act. In a film dominated by truncated framings, oblique angles, and disjointed representations of space, Cassavetes's framing of Cosmo's onstage appearance in a classic medium close-up shot is one of the few moments in which the central character is located within a stable representation of space. This moment suggests that, despite everything, Cosmo has finally achieved that state of grace he describes simply as "being comfortable." But the intensity of the light that shines on his face as he addresses his audience carries with it a sense of menace. The disconcerting nature of this illumination suggests that it is not just a matter of light, but also the generation of heat burning a hole in the image and placing the figure it illuminates under an intense pressure.

This intense illumination affirms that the act of inhabiting a world described by the director involves something much larger and more immersive than the rendering of a fictional story. It involves the employment of cinematic materials—spaces, durations, and rhythms—so as to convey how this world is lived and experienced at its most particular: its rises and falls, waves and lulls. It necessitates the creation of moments of recognition that bridge the world onscreen to previous film worlds, as well as the creation of moments of estrangement that suspend this connection, moments in which we are inducted into a world whose terms and conditions we must negotiate step by step. Nicole Brenez argues that the tawdry spectacle occurring onstage at the Crazy Horse West affirms "the possibility that one can still create something beautiful in a world of money."[14] Mr. Sophistication and his Delovelies function as "a little machine of love, freedom and fantasy—unmanageable, uncontrollable, unmemorisable... a pure expenditure of energy, desire and narcissistic claims lacking any guarantee that they will ever function properly." Brenez is right to emphasize the film's unswerving commitment to the creative possibilities of the show. But it is not a valorization of beauty or love—at least not in their conventional sense—that emerges as a result. Rather, it is something more volatile—as in the Latin root of this word: *volare*, given to flight—that, in the end, does not lift us above the demands of the mobsters, but, at best, enables fleeting moments of pleasure and connection between all those who have been granted entry to the world of the film.

"Lower-Case Observations"

The question that we need to return to is how does this shape our understanding of Cassavetes's relationship to the New Hollywood? Elsaesser argues that the de-dramatizing of narrative coincides with the rise of other strategies that define this period of American filmmaking, for example, the use of parody and pastiche in *The Long Goodbye* (Robert Altman, 1973) and *Thieves Like Us* (Altman, 1974) and the penchant for pathos in *Easy Rider* (Dennis Hopper, 1969) and *Butch Cassidy and the Sundance Kid* (George Roy Hill, 1969). He detects a "realism of sentiment" that is the outcrop of a negative view of recent American history: "By foregoing the dramaturgy of interpersonal conflict, suspense and intrigue or the self-alienated aggressiveness of emotional frustrations, the films are somehow led to stylising despair or helplessness into the pathos of failure" (286–87). Right at the end of the article, he gleans one other feature of this period of filmmaking that is left undiscussed. In *Two-Lane Blacktop* the de-dramatizing of narrative coincides with a strengthening of the "inner dynamism" of the scene: "The momentum of action gives way to the moment of gesture and the body. A new form of mise-en-scène seems in the making that could mean a revaluation of physical reality on the far side of either fetishistic fixation on the image or conceptual abstraction of the form" (292).

Two years after Elsaesser, Patricia Patterson and Manny Farber elaborate some of the characteristics of this new form of mise-en-scène. In an overview of post–New Wave filmmaking, they identify two recurring structures. The first is a "shallow stage" filming that utilizes a "low-population image squared to the edges of the frame. Facing a fairly close camera, the formal-abstract intellectualized content evolves at right angles to the camera, and usually signifies a filmmaker who has intellectually surrounded the material."[15] They cite as examples Hollis Frampton's *Nostalgia* (1969), Nagisa Oshima's *In the Realm of the Senses* (1976), and Rainer Werner Fassbinder's *Katzelmacher* (1969). The second structure is closer to the model of mise-en-scène identified by Elsaesser: "dispersal" space filming. By this they mean films committed to "the idea of non-solidity, that everything is a mass of energy particles, and the aim, structurally, is a flux-like space to go with the atomized content and the idea of keeping the freshness and energy of a real world within the frame." This style of filmmaking is exemplified by films such as Michael Snow's *Rameau's Nephew* (1974), Jacques Rivette's *Celine and Julie Go Boating* (1974), and Fassbinder's *Beware of the Holy Whore* (1971). Also included in this list are two key films of the New Hollywood: Altman's *McCabe & Mrs. Miller* (1971) and Scorsese's *Mean Streets* (1973). Both films embody what the authors describe as "a profoundly rhythmic filmmaking with a lot of lower-case observations, a brusque, ragged movement in *Mean Streets* and a ballad-like rhythm in Altman's *McCabe*." Instead of definitive positions and claims about the motivations of their protagonists, both films concentrate on minor movements and gestures: "What is picked up about the trudging, muttering McCabe character, with his derby and long overcoat, is a half sentence ('got poetry in me—ain't gonna put it down'), a suspicious and balky glance."[16]

Cassavetes's films do not appear in the story sketched by Patterson and Farber. Nonetheless, they anticipate some of the central tendencies identified in their remarks, specifically, the skepticism regarding big statements and the opening of character to a type of scrutiny that is intensely focused on the minute, the particular, yet fundamentally cautious in its claims to truth. In *Faces* we witness an almost obsessive investigation of the inconsistencies and foibles associated with each of the characters. Yet this investigation does not uncover a hard-won knowledge. "When I'm working on a film, I forbid myself to have any opinions," the director explained in an interview published in 1969. "I just want to record what people said, film what they did, intervening as little as possible, or, in any case, trying never to film inside them, so to speak."[17] These remarks illustrate the simultaneous effect of proximity and distance that characterizes *Faces*. While the director's insistence on keeping the camera close to the characters allows the fiction to be guided by the pulsations and false starts of the performances, he refuses to define these actions according to an inner logic—to "film inside" the characters, as he puts it. Like many of the other revelations in the film, when Richard (John Marley) confesses to Jeannie (Gena Rowlands) that he has buried eight relatives in the past six years, it seems to come from nowhere and quickly dissolves into laughter. The significance that this remark may have in terms of the events portrayed is left open and undefined. In *Faces*, laughter, tears, and anger seem to exist on a slippery continuum that has lost its proper sequence. In a similar manner, Cassavetes's insistent use of the close-up does not facilitate identification or emphasize a dramatic point. Rather, it draws attention to details and expressions that fray the edges of the narrative—it affirms the limits of what we can say or know about the film.

In *Faces* the array of facial close-ups seems to be letting us in on a level of dramatic action occurring simultaneous to the main story. In a film where the flow of verbal and physical expression has overwhelmed the possibility of communication, the faces of the characters become a kind of privileged space where the mystery of human emotion peeks out and registers a special affinity with the camera. The point to emphasize is that it is not the subjectivity of these emotions—their wellspring or secret meaning—that is central in Cassavetes's approach, but the traces they leave on the faces of the actors, traces that can only be revealed through the camera's special scrutiny. The end result is an interior dimension glimpsed at through a haze of dispersed actions and lowercase observations that the camera both reveals and struggles to decipher.

A Realism of the Body

This refusal to explain the motivations guiding the characters' outbursts and actions coincides with a heightened attention to the actor's body—its capacity to serve as a meeting point for a series of transferences and dramatic forces that shape the space of the film. In *Husbands, A Woman under the Influence* (1975), *Opening Night*, and *Love Streams* (1984), the bodies of the characters bear the weight of time figured as either a dilemma of aging—time running out, the fear of being left behind, no longer knowing how to act—or as something that constantly slips through our fingers and disturbs our sense of the present. This anxiety is conveyed through the attitudes and postures adopted by the actors: overwhelmed, agitated, collapsed. In *Love Streams* the two central characters Robert (John Cassavetes) and Sarah (Gena Rowlands) are both continually overwhelmed by space. Their bodies seem to be at war with the world around them, cut, bloodied, and, at various times, submerged by an accumulation of alcohol, luggage, and animals. This process of bodily dissolution leads Yann Lardeau to describe the drama in *Love Streams* as a series of "electric shocks of variable intensity which twist, swell, pound, project, dislocate and disjoint grimacing beings in the same way as the burlesque puppets of yesteryear."[18] Lardeau's comments draw attention to the body's openness to the world. This openness is manifested in moments of contact or collision that define the relationships explored in the films, for example, in *Faces* when Chet (Seymour Cassel) attempts to resuscitate Maria (Lynn Carlin) by forcing her to vomit the sleeping pills she has swallowed. During Mabel's nervous breakdown in *A Woman under the Influence*, Nick (Peter Falk) tries to break through her fears (and allay his own anxieties) by pressing himself against her and demanding "Come back to me!" A less violent process of bodily resuscitation occurs near the end of the film when Mabel's children swarm around her prone body, refusing to be dragged away by their father.

In *Opening Night* it is this type of physical contact and support that Myrtle (Gena Rowlands) seems to demand as she staggers to her dressing room on the night of the New York premiere. As Thierry Jousse observes in relation to this scene: "What appears to us as a moment of coquetry is undoubtedly only the pathos of a woman trying by all means to reattach herself to the world and therefore to a human body."[19] The body's openness is also evident in the way in which Myrtle's fans grab at the actress as she enters and exits the theater. The young female fan Nancy (Laura Johnson) who pushes her way through the crowd and is later knocked down and killed by a car seems to threaten Myrtle with the ferocity of her adoration. This threat will become explicit when she returns as an apparition accompanying Myrtle in her crisis. At first it seems as if Nancy has been conjured into being by Myrtle as a device for the performance—an attempt to "stay in touch" with a set of emotions that are fast receding and a way of transforming the scenario of aging and passivity built into the role that she is playing. What quickly becomes apparent is the danger of such conjurings. This danger is registered in the dead fan's brutal actions and Myrtle's equally violent final response.

As Myrtle is pummeled by Nancy, the threat of madness that hovers over her struggle with the role is steered away from a question of psychological crisis to one of physical disintegration. Nancy is neither simply a figment of Myrtle's imagination—her presence is too carnal and the final exorcism too brutal—nor a separate paranormal presence seeking vengeance for an act of neglect outside the theater. She is, over and above these other possibilities, a physical force or energy of disruption that overwhelms not just Myrtle, but also the time and space of the film—a violent tearing of performative space by something singular, exorbitant, and unaccountable that transforms the terms of engagement between the spectator and the film and between the character and the scene.

On another level, the insistence on bodily contact relates to a broader imperative—its capacity to become the source of a sudden revelation. In their constant reaching out to—and pushing away—of others, Cassavetes's performers engage in an endless re-creation of the body. This is not a matter of improvisation. Rather, it is based on an attentiveness—on the part of the actors as much as the filmmaker—to moments when the body enters into arrangements with other bodies. These arrangements go to what the narrative cannot speak of directly: experiences and emotions that lie at the cusp of comprehension or naming.

The closest point of association is Elaine May's *Mikey and Nicky* (1976). Begun in 1973 yet not released until three years later, this film models the type of reworking of the gangster film that Cassavetes follows in *The Killing of a Chinese Bookie*. In both films, moments of errancy and resistance are central to the rendition of a social world that imposes itself on the central characters, not the other way round: for example, the growing frustration of Mikey (Peter Falk) with the uncooperative café proprietor (Peter R. Scoppa) who will not sell him milk without coffee; the discovery of the hit man (Ned Beatty) that instead of heading south as instructed, he is heading north; the violent argument with the bus driver (M. Emmet Walsh) who insists that, as per company policy, Nicky (John Cassavetes) must exit via the back door of the bus. Looming over these encounters is what Jonathan Rosenbaum describes as the central theme in all of May's films: "the secret betrayal of one member of a couple by the other."[20] Two images crystallize the film's treatment of this theme. The first appears near the start. Summoned to the hotel where Nicky has taken refuge from the mobsters who have placed a contract on his life, Mikey is refused entry. As Nicky cowers on the other side of the door—desperate for his friend's support yet too terrified to let him in—Mikey improvises a lullaby: "Open the door, Nicky. Open the door and let me in." When this fails he starts to pound and kick against the door. The second moment occurs right at the end; it involves a mirror reversal of the first moment. This time it is Nicky who is standing on one side of a locked door while Mikey is on the other side, instructing his wife

Fig. 28. Nicky (John Cassavetes) pounding on Mikey's door demanding to be let in at the end of *Mikey and Nicky* (Elaine May, 1976, Paramount Pictures)

(Rose Arrick) to refuse his friend's pleas to be let in. As the hit man closes in, Nicky throws himself against the door, screaming in horror: "I don't feel well. Get me a doctor, Mikey. Get me a doctor. I'm sick."

Appearing near the start and right at the end, these two scenes actualize what is perhaps the film's underlying theme: an all-pervading fear of death—its capacity to render all affiliations, relationships, and histories null and void. "Everyone we knew when we were kids is dead," Nicky tries to tell his friend during the detour to visit his mother's grave. He then provides a roll call of the departed: "I wish my mother was alive. I wish your mother was alive. . . . I wish your father was alive. I wish my father was alive. I wish your brother Izzy was alive." More than a narrative device driving their flight across the city, death is the secret bond that links the two friends, a bond that is made visible through the repetition of gesture.

Mikey and Nicky thus stands as a key influence on Cassavetes's reassembling of the gangster genre in *The Killing of a Chinese Bookie*; at the same time, it connects with the issues explored in his earlier film *Husbands*.[21] Here, too, death is the starting point for a series of bodily exertions that place language in check. Indeed, from the moment near the start of the film when the quiet of the funeral is brutally interrupted by a harsh cut to a cacophony of car engines and screeching tires as the mourners flee the cemetery, the impact of the death of Stuart (David Rowlands) is registered in and through the intensities of experience it generates. The singing on the footpath; the basketball game and swim in the pool; the long singing contest where Harry (Ben Gazzara), Gus (John Cassavetes), and Archie (Peter Falk) consume beer after beer; the vomiting; the flight to London: each of these episodes is part of the catalog of experience and sensation that follows in the wake of Stuart's death. So too are those interludes when nothing in particular happens, moments when the three friends catch their breath or simply exchange a nervous look as if they are seeking reassurance for what they have done or are about to do. The uncertainty generated by Stuart's death culminates when, at the end of an extended drinking session, Archie and Gus retreat to the privacy of a small toilet cubicle. In this highly compressed space, Archie insists that Gus listen to him in silence. He insists that he has something important to say: "I want to tell you how I really feel. I mean I want to tell you what's really bothering me. I'm going to tell you, now, what it is . . . what it must be, 'cause it's not the sickness. I can live with that. No. Here's what it is. . . . It's . . . it's ah . . . it's a tremendous need . . . an anxiety. It's a ah . . . you see, that's what happens. I forget what it is."

In Cassavetes's films the only experiences and emotions worth talking about, it seems, are those where language and words come up short and a different form of articulation must step in. During these moments, the body of the actor has a dual purpose: it is in the service of the fiction and able to figure elusive currents of feeling and affect. This duality is maintained through a superimposition of two kinds of labor: that of the character struggling to make sense of an experience whose contingency places language in check and that of the actor working under the weight of a role whose borders and limits remain deliberately undefined—a role whose essential lack of definition serves as a fault line for the performance.

In their commitment to maintaining the visibility of both forms of labor, Cassavetes's films exemplify what Elsaesser—as well as Patterson and Farber—glean in their reflections on the New Hollywood: a realism grounded in the productivity of the body: its capacity to show us not just the character, but also the actor—her struggles, capacities, and potential. This dual emphasis is evident in the work of directors such as May, Hellman, Altman, and Scorsese. But it is in Cassavetes's films that it achieves its most sustained realization. The concern with forms of corporeal experience that press against the limits of what can be said or known also reveals how decisively the realism found in his films shades into its rival, a modernism overtly concerned with the limits of representational processes. Grounded in the volatile materiality of filmic space, the worlds created in these films are both intently engaged with the entanglements of interpersonal relationships and highly conscious of their own operations as cinema.

This, too, is how the New Hollywood stakes its claim for innovation: not simply by modifying and adapting traditional genres or suspending causality and motivation, but also by unsettling the distinctions and terms that dominate the classification and history of twentieth-century art.

What I Live Through

After Cosmo escapes from the warehouse where he has been taken for execution, he returns to Rachel's house holding a single red rose. He sits down to talk things through with Betty. The conversation between Betty and Cosmo is not really a conversation as such. It is more a type of performance at the very limit of comprehension. "Ahh . . . I'm not feeling well . . . to tell you the truth," Cosmo tells Betty as they sit opposite each other at a table. "My stomach's upset. . . . I need some ah . . . some ah . . . I don't know what I need." He then launches into an anecdote about his mother: "My mother was very funny. Had a great sense of humor. . . . She was so funny she ran off with a big fat butcher." But he is not really interested in this story, and, sensing that neither is Betty, his words trail off. As if to relieve the pressure of these words going nowhere, Cosmo runs his fingers across his eyelids and cheeks. When Betty finally breaks her silence, she announces that she doesn't give a shit about Cosmo's mother or his father, and they become embroiled in a brief yet spectacular confrontation across the table.

After sitting back down, Cosmo notices the cup of coffee in the foreground of the shot, takes a sip, and immediately spits it out. Unable to comprehend why on earth he attempted to drink cold coffee, he declares: "I don't know what to do with my hands." Todd Berliner claims that a distinguishing feature of the dialogue in Cassavetes's films lies in the way in which "speech mimics the rambling quality of thought."[22] While this claim has merit in distancing these films from dominant conventions of movie dialogue, it does not explain the disquiet generated by Cosmo's words and the unpredictability of his actions. Rather than mimicking the rambling quality of thought, the conversation with Betty seems to be about the struggle to express feelings and sensations that disturb thought. This disturbance strips words of their utilitarian purpose; but it also enables them to express a range of subterranean impressions and disturbances that are central to the drama. "I don't know what to do with my hands" is the most direct statement of this crisis *and* a reminder of the theatrical stakes surrounding the scene, its commitment to a form of experimentation grounded in the actor's labor. In Cosmo's excruciating movement toward death, the body of the performer—slowly emptying itself of blood and words—becomes the stage for a series of outbursts and actions that place representation in check.

That hands figure so prominently in the film's rendition of this labor is clearly no accident. Earlier, when Cosmo retreats to a bar to celebrate his final payment to Marty (Al Ruban), the sounds of conversations just off-screen, glasses clinking, and music slowly rising from the jukebox are part of the scene's rendition of a dynamic auditory field. After he orders a scotch and water from the bar, the handheld camera moves closer to Cosmo as if something important is about to be revealed. Cosmo picks up the glass and in a single drink consumes the entire contents. Turning away from the bar, he looks down at his wet fingers and starts to shake his hand as if to remove some unwanted substance. He waves at someone off-screen and claps his hands together. A voice calls out, and Cosmo starts to dance. Despite the obvious sense of triumph in Cosmo's little jig, it is not his victory over pecuniary forces that rings out. It is rather the strange insistence of the world: an insistence of objects and sounds that, like the glass of scotch, leave their mark on Cosmo.

This insistence is reaffirmed near the end of the film when Cosmo once again looks down at his hand. This time the substance that he is trying to comprehend is the blood from the bullet wound. The strangeness of this moment is heightened by the way in which the camera zooms into a close-up of his cupped hand, almost as if it has a life independent of the body to which it is attached. When the camera pans up to his face, it is not, as first suggested, an expression of indifference that we encounter, but something more complicated and harder to read: the registration of experiences and sensations that are not ours to own—experiences and sensations that disturb thought and must be negotiated step by step. In Cassavetes's films this negotiation coincides with an emphasis on the openness and productivity of the actor's body. "The world is not what I think but what I live through," writes Maurice Merleau-Ponty. "I am open to the world, I have no doubt that I am in communication with it, but I do not possess it."[23] Perhaps this is the best way to define the innovation of *The Killing of a Chinese Bookie*, its connection to the history of the New Hollywood as well as its own distinctive place: it reveals us in communication with the world—not above it, nor at a safe distance, but in constant tactile engagement with its inexhaustibility and its mystery.

CHAPTER 9

THE SPIRIT OF '76
Travis, Rocky, and Jimmy Carter

J. Hoberman

America was baptized anew in the bicentennial year 1976—or in a phrase made suddenly current, the nation was born again.[1]

On one hand, there was the nostalgia-infused Disneyfication of the past, particularly airbrushing the decade recast as the "fabulous fifties." On the other hand, there was a desire for a ritual cleansing. "All the animals come out at night—whores, skunk pussies, buggers, queens, fairies, dopers, junkies, sick, venal," the antihero of Martin Scorsese's *Taxi Driver*, released in early 1976, would muse as he cruised for fares in Times Square. "Someday a real rain will come and wash all this scum off the streets."

After going through a long litany of social ills, Howard Beale, the populist TV demagogue in *Network*, which would open three weeks after the 1976 presidential election, gave viewers their marching orders: "I want all of you to get up out of your chairs. I want you to get up right now and go to the window. Open it, and stick your head out, and yell, *'I'm mad as hell, and I'm not going to take this anymore!'*"

The fugitive Patty Hearst had been arrested in September 1975, but active terrorist cells remained. The bicentennial year was punctuated by bombs, some planted by the Bay Area's New World Liberation Front, others—mainly in New York and Chicago—by the Puerto Rican nationalists of the Fuerzas Armadas de Liberación Nacional (FALN). The menace had not yet been exorcized. *The Omen*, the big movie during the summer of '76, wound up with the president of the United States unwittingly adopting a five-year-old Antichrist.

All politicians were suspect. The crusading post-Watergate Congress served to pry open the crypt. Hearings held by the United States Senate Select

Committee to Study Governmental Operations with Respect to Intelligence Activities opened in September 1975 and, chaired by presidential hopeful Frank Church of Idaho, revealed information on a host of unsavory practices, dirty tricks, and abuses of power.

As if on cue, the self-conscious post-Watergate thriller *Three Days of the Condor* had its premiere eight days into the Church hearings. Robert Redford played a shaggy CIA operative—not a spy but a creator of alternative scenarios—who discovers a secret CIA within the CIA and, as Vincent Canby noted in his *New York Times* review, "comes close to wreaking more havoc on the CIA in three days than any number of House and Senate investigating committees have done in years."

As the political thriller built upon current events, the western approached obsolescence. Marlon Brando played a lunatic bounty hunter in Arthur Penn's *The Missouri Breaks*. John Wayne made what was to be his swan song in *The Shootist*, essentially playing himself as an aging gunslinger dying of cancer. *The Last Hard Men* would end with the retired sheriff Charlton Heston dead in the dust.

Yet, the bicentennial year was also notable for Hollywood's interest in American folk heroes, old and new. The investigative reporters Woodward and Bernstein would became household names; Robert Altman cast Paul Newman as Buffalo Bill; the white Indian hero of *A Man Called Horse* was called back to America to re-right Kiowa wrongs; Elia Kazan gave Robert De Niro the lead as a crypto Irving Thalberg in *The Last Tycoon*.[2]

The Old Left remembered itself; history was revised. *The Front* revisited the blacklist; *The Bingo Long Traveling All-Stars & Motor Kings* celebrated the Negro baseball leagues. Gordon Parks made a film about the folk singer Leadbelly, and Hal Ashby adapted Woody Guthrie's memoir *Bound for Glory* with David Carradine as Guthrie. (The role was dangled before Bob Dylan, who turned it down while offering to direct.)

Television prepared to assume its world-historical role as chronicler of the American past and mirror of the American present. Starting in October 1975, NBC's *Saturday Night Live* subjected President Ford to near continuous ridicule. ABC prepared the miniseries *Roots*, which, telecast in January 1977, would be the most watched TV program in history, while the bicentennial year began with the syndication of Norman Lear's most experimental show, the meta-soap opera *Mary Hartman, Mary Hartman*.

The counterculture dwindled, but movie stars with a measure of countercultural credibility remained ascendant: Redford topped the 1975 Quigley exhibitors poll of box office stars as he had in 1974, when he supplanted Clint Eastwood, and would again in 1976. Jack Nicholson, ranked no. 8 in 1974, would rise to no. 2 in 1976, with Dustin Hoffman at no. 3. (After a four-year hiatus, Hoffman returned to the top ten, although 1976 marked the end of Paul Newman's decade-long run.) It was during 1976 that *The Rocky Horror Picture Show*, a flop when it opened commercially, would become an ecstatic cult film—the ritually repeated viewings, costumed participation, and celebration of pansexuality suggested the continuation of the counterculture by other means.

Still, as far as Hollywood was concerned, 1975 was the sixties' last hurrah. *Nashville* received multiple Oscar nominations, and Miloš Forman's adaptation of Ken Kesey's *One Flew over the Cuckoo's Nest*, a novel with an antiestablishment polemic exceeded only by *Catch-22*'s, won five Oscars (Best Picture, Actor, Actress, Director, and Adapted Screenplay), befitting a movie that, save for *Jaws*, had been the year's biggest hit.[3]

Not just westerns but the cycles of the early seventies—blaxploitation and upscale porn, cop and vigilante films, disaster epics and road movies—were fading. Soon new tendencies would take their place. In 1977 and 1978, remakes, redneck and slapstick comedies, working-class inspirationals, space operas, and slasher flicks would come to the fore. But first, there was the New Hollywood epitome and cosmic bummer that was *Taxi Driver*.

A powerfully summarizing work, directed by thirty-three-year-old Martin Scorsese from a screenplay by twenty-nine-year-old former film critic Paul Schrader, *Taxi Driver* was an eruption out of the national id. Embodied by Robert De Niro, the antihero Travis Bickle—a would-be assassin of a would-be president—almost instantly became a character in the American narrative alongside Huck Finn and Holden Caulfield.

Steeped in libidinal politics, celebrity worship, sexual exploitation, the fetishization of guns, and racial stereotyping, *Taxi Driver* synthesized film noir, neorealist, and nouvelle vague stylistics. The Bickle story—an unstable ex-marine driven mad by New York City's sleaze pits—assimilated Hollywood's vigilante and Viet-vet cycles, as well as gritty, downbeat Fun City *policiers* like *The French Connection*, while drafting blaxploitation in the service of a presumed tell-it-like-it-is naturalism that, predicated on a frank, unrelenting representation of racism, violence, and misogyny, was even more racist, violent, and misogynist than the movie itself allowed.[4]

In production during New York's festering summer of *Jaws*, during a heat wave and a garbage strike, *Taxi Driver* crystallized one of the worst moments in the city's history. Mass transit faltered, roads cracked, crime rose, jobs hemorrhaged, businesses fled, and buildings were abandoned. The city trembled on the brink of fiscal catastrophe—America's pariah, a crime-ridden, fiscally profligate, graffiti-festooned moral cesspool.

A native New Yorker, Scorsese upped the ante by returning endlessly to his boyhood movie realm, Forty-Second Street, now a lurid land of triple X-rated

Fig. 29. Robert De Niro as Travis Bickle in *Taxi Driver* (Martin Scorsese, 1976, Columbia Pictures)

movies, skeevy massage parlors, cruising pimpmobiles, sidewalks crammed with hot-pants hookers and the customers who on any given weekday evening, according to NYPD stats, were patronizing porn shops at the rate of eight thousand per hour.

Recalling his youth, Baudelaire wrote of simultaneously experiencing the horror and the ecstasy of existence. So it was with *Taxi Driver*. The pagan debauchery that the boy Scorsese witnessed in Pax Americana spectacles like *Quo Vadis* is played out in the Manhattan of AD 1975. The movie's coproducer Julia Phillips would recall (or imagine) that it was a project fueled by cocaine. "Big pressure, short schedule, and short money, New York in the summer. Night shooting. I have only visited the set once and they are all doing blow. I don't see it. I just know it."

In early September, the *Wall Street Journal* called on New York to declare bankruptcy; Ronald Reagan repeatedly used his radio show to denounce the city's union leaders, news media, and elected officials, as well as its "wild spending, dirty streets, pornography," and "general decline in civility," warning that New York was "an example of what can happen to this entire country if we don't re-chart our course," and praying that the federal government would not bail out the city. It was while *Taxi Driver* was in postproduction that President Ford threatened to veto any federal financial assistance to New York, and the *Daily News* ran the headline, "FORD TO CITY: DROP DEAD."

Brilliant and yet repellent, at times even hateful, *Taxi Driver* inspired an understandable ambivalence both toward the movie and the antihero who called himself God's Lonely Man. For the first time, a Hollywood movie provided a pathology and a human face for the Secret Agent of History, the mysterious Lone Gunman seemingly conjured into existence by the great extinguished star-pol, John F. Kennedy.[5]

Prophesied by *The Manchurian Candidate* (1962), this figure was given material form by Lee Harvey Oswald and subsequent political assassins. Post-Watergate fascination with corporate or governmental conspiracies suggested that the Secret Agent of History might be an avatar of the System (as in *The Parallax View*), but *Taxi Driver* was partially inspired by the diaries of George Wallace's failed assassin, Arthur Bremer, and hence interested in the Secret Agent as a social symptom. In her memoir *You'll Never Eat Lunch in This Town Again*, Phillips recalls Scorsese expressing concern that the would-be Ford assassin Sara Jane Moore might "hurt the picture."

Scorsese and Schrader may have regarded Travis as a menace, but as Stuart Byron observed, many of the movie's patrons saw *Taxi Driver* as "a more sophisticated, kinkier *Death Wish*, the story of a man driven mad by the realities of urban life, and who therefore reacts in an understandably violent way."[6] Citizen of a sodden Sodom where the steamy streets are always wet with tears, among other bodily fluids, Travis is a skid row Captain Ahab embarking each evening on a glistening sea of sleaze in search of some monstrous leviathan.

Seen through Travis's rain-smeared windshield, Manhattan is a movie—call it "Malignopolis." The cab driver lives by night in a world of myth, populated by a host of supporting archetypes: the astonishing Jodie Foster as Iris, a runaway twelve-year-old hooker living the life in the rat's-ass end of the sixties yet dreaming of a commune in Vermont, and Harvey Keitel as her affably nauseating pimp. Peter Boyle's witless working-class sage speaks for the salt of the earth, while Cybill Shepherd's bratty golden girl plays a suitably petit bourgeois Daisy Buchanan to Travis's lumpen Gatsby.

Hysterical yet sublime, the twelfth-top-grossing movie of 1976, *Taxi Driver* was not just a hit but, like *Psycho* in 1960 or *Bonnie and Clyde* in 1967, an event in American popular culture—perhaps even an intervention. Inspired in part by one failed assassination, it would inadvertently trigger another.[7]

The 1976 campaign was well under way when *Taxi Driver*, which included a presidential campaign, opened on February 8, 1976.[8] Ronald Reagan, the former two-term governor of California, was challenging the sitting Republican president, Gerald Ford. After perennial heir apparent Ted Kennedy made clear his disinclination to seek the office, and in the absence of the old warhorse Hubert Humphrey, Senator Henry "Scoop" Jackson of Washington was the designated frontrunner in a crowded Democratic field.

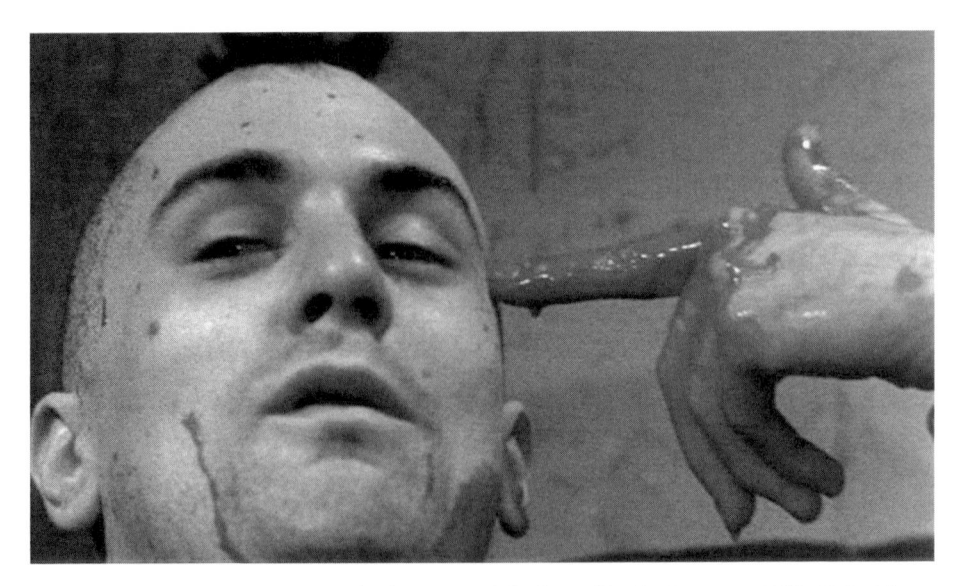

Fig. 30. *Taxi Driver*—the bloody (and controversial) climax (Martin Scorsese, 1976, Columbia Pictures)

Conventional wisdom was upended on January 19 when former Georgia governor James Earl "Jimmy" Carter handily won the Iowa caucuses over Indiana senator Birch Bayh and Arizona congressman Morris Udall, albeit losing to Uncommitted.

On the eve of the bicentennial year, the *New York Times Magazine* had introduced a fascinating new folk hero in a cover story titled "A Peanut Farmer for President." The fifty-one-year-old Carter's journey had taken him from "farm boy to naval officer/nuclear scientist to peanut farmer/politician."

Patrick Anderson's article described Carter as "a soft-spoken thoughtful, likeable man" who was a "stubborn" antisegregationist with a "conservative background" tempered by his "liberal instincts." He also seemed to be something of an opportunist. "Carter and his advisors think that next year's election may be decided more on personality—on character—than on issues," Anderson wrote. "They hope that his aura of honesty and sincerity will make the difference in post-Watergate America."

Most intriguingly, Carter positioned himself as a beneficiary of the counterculture, characterized by Anderson (who would become Carter's chief speechwriter) as "an introspective man who enjoys the songs of Bob Dylan." Let no one say that this one-term Georgia governor was a man who, like Dylan's Mr. Jones, did not know something was happening. Two weeks into *Taxi Driver*'s run, Carter beat Udall in New Hampshire in what *New York*

Times columnist William Safire called "a triumph of evangelical pseudo-conservatism."

Another campaign began, less than a week later, when Francis Ford Coppola and his family departed for the Philippines. There Coppola would begin shooting if not the Great American Movie he intended, then certainly Hollywood's greatest periodization of the sixties, and supreme disaster film: *Apocalypse Now*.

Inspired by Joseph Conrad's novella *Heart of Darkness*, the movie had its origin in a 16 mm project that John Milius and George Lucas had originally hoped to film in Vietnam while war was still being waged. Ambivalence was part of the package. The pro-war Milius saw the movie as a celebration of "surfing and bombs," while the antiwar Lucas thought it might be a new *Dr. Strangelove*.

A few years later, still envisioning a 16 mm film shot with real soldiers, Lucas imagined *Apocalypse Now* as his follow-up to *American Graffiti*. But Coppola, who produced *American Graffiti* and inherited the rights to *Apocalypse Now*, offered Lucas a deal so penurious that Lucas turned it down. Then, in 1974, with Lucas already involved with *Star Wars*, Coppola became suddenly enthusiastic, deeming the project a perfect bicentennial film. Lucas asked Coppola to wait for him to finish *Star Wars*. Coppola declined and, after failing to recruit Milius to make the film, decided to direct it himself.[9]

Having made with *The Godfather* the greatest popular movie of the era, Coppola sought to remake the Vietnam War, or so it came to seem. The idea that a madly extravagant movie and an out-of-control imperial war might be kindred forms of endeavor was scarcely lost on him. The filmmaker would assert that *Apocalypse Now* was not about Vietnam, it was Vietnam—up to its confused, anticlimactic ending, not to mention the destructive effect on his subsequent career.

Coppola put himself and his consciousness at the center of the narrative. *Apocalypse Now* was something new—the manifestation of a personal struggle to make a movie, an auteur psychodrama. Few movies have ever identified so closely with their own grueling production stories. Not since D. W. Griffith had a director so blatantly attempted the grandiose simulation of a historical event. Now envisioned as a suitably megalomaniacal postscript to the most convulsive episode in American history since the Civil War, *Apocalypse Now* went into production less than a year after the fall of Saigon.

Like the New Frontiersmen who initiated U.S. involvement in Vietnam, Coppola undertook *Apocalypse Now* for what he believed to be a noble cause, namely the creation of his Zoetrope studio. And, as the American government had, he found himself confounded by nature, beholden to unsavory dictators— leasing planes and other equipment from the Philippine strongman Ferdinand

Marcos—and bogged down in an epic quagmire. Like LBJ, Coppola was tough on his subordinates. He would fire his first leading man, Harvey Keitel, and drive Keitel's successor, Martin Sheen, to a heart attack. And like Nixon, Coppola had no idea how to end his extravaganza. In a sodden paroxysm of irrationality, he would hire Marlon Brando to be his white whale and prayed that once the actor arrived on location, something resembling a climax would occur.

March 6, Scoop Jackson won the Massachusetts primary. Carter came in fourth, but Jackson had peaked. The rest of March belonged to Carter, then widely compared—even by *TV Guide*—to Hal Phillip Walker, the mysterious presidential candidate in Robert Altman's *Nashville*. Carter scored victories over and thus neutralized his southern rival, George Wallace, in Florida, Illinois, and North Carolina, where, for the first time, he began speaking of his evangelical faith. North Carolina also gave Ronald Reagan, who had campaigned extensively with James Stewart, his first win. The victory was attributed to a last-minute, recycled TV address in which Reagan called for the "re-establishment of American superiority."

On April 6, Carter squeaked past Udall in Wisconsin—the next day, Francis Coppola threw himself a birthday bash in the jungle. An enormous cake (forty-eight square feet) and gourmet goodies were flown in from California—an extravagance anticipating the *Apocalypse Now* barbecue scene. The memory of the war was merging with the reality of the movie. "There's a rumor that rebels are in the hills about ten miles away," Eleanor Coppola noted in her diary, adding that "several hundred South Vietnamese people were recruited from a refugee camp near Manila to play North Vietnamese in the film."

Opening on April 9, three days after Carter's win in Wisconsin, *All the President's Men* celebrated the downfall of Richard Nixon, crediting his ouster to a pair of dogged, long-haired reporters, Bob Woodward and Carl Bernstein, played by Robert Redford and Dustin Hoffman. Although in many ways a conventional thriller—Vincent Canby called it "the thinking man's *Jaws*"—the movie was also a counterculture victory: the Sundance Kid and the Graduate take down Nixon.[10] The film was visualized as the Watergate scandal unfolded; its release melded with the publication of *The Final Days*, Woodward and Bernstein's sensational follow-up to their Watergate reporting, which, largely unsourced although clearly drawing on material furnished by Henry Kissinger or secondhand by his aides, depicts a drunken, distraught, possibly suicidal Nixon.[11]

Deep in the jungle another putsch was under way. Coppola secretly left the *Apocalypse Now* set on April 16 and flew to Los Angeles to fire his principal actor Harvey Keitel. His reality testing was such that, while there he telegraphed Secretary of Defense Donald Rumsfeld inquiring as to the possibility of renting US military equipment as had been, for example, made available to *The Green Berets*. He also interviewed Martin Sheen, Keitel's replacement, in a lounge at the LA airport.

With *All the President's Men* in theaters, outsider-ness was ascendant: On May 1, Carter won Texas, Georgia, and Indiana. So did Reagan. On May 4, Carter won Georgia, Indiana, and Washington, DC. *Time* and *Newsweek* put him on their covers as the presumptive nominee. Reagan beat Ford in Georgia, Alabama, and, with a dramatic final surge, Indiana. May 18, Carter narrowly defeated Udall in Michigan, but the same day in Maryland, his juggernaut was unexpectedly derailed by an even more outside outsider, Reagan's successor, California's thirty-eight-year-old governor Jerry Brown. Brown did not have to quote Bob Dylan; he dated the beautiful folk-rock singer Linda Ronstadt, cast himself as a Zen Catholic, and was the first national politician with personal experience of the counterculture.

For the rest of the month, Carter and Reagan absorbed a series of split decisions. May 25, Carter won Arkansas and Kentucky while losing Nevada to Brown and Oregon to Senator Frank Church; Reagan took Arkansas, Idaho, and Nevada but lost to Ford in Kentucky, Tennessee, and Oregon. Three days later, *Taxi Driver* won the Palme d'Or at Cannes. (The announcement was greeted with boos.)

On June 8, Reagan won Montana, South Dakota, and California. Brown won his home state as well but ended his chances by failing to contest New Jersey and Ohio. Both went to Carter, who reached out to another constituency, the future fans of Steven Spielberg's *Close Encounters of the Third Kind* (currently shooting on a closed set in Gillette, Wyoming), when the June 8 issue of the *National Enquirer* reported his belief in UFOs and a pledge: "If I become president, I'll make every piece of information this country has about UFO sightings available to the public and the scientists."

Opening in mid-July, around the time George Lucas wrapped *Star Wars*, the Democratic convention turned out to be a love-in that, as if to exorcize Travis Bickle, was held in New York City. Carter accepted the nomination and the wisdom of the counterculture, telling delegates, "We have an America that, in Bob Dylan's phrase, is busy being born—not busy dying."

America's reigning male star had his own statement. During the Democratic convention, *The Outlaw Josey Wales* opened in Los Angeles: by virtue of his charisma, Clint Eastwood's unreconciled, largely unsmiling Confederate soldier unites Native Americans and white settlers, a hippie chick among them, in a sort of ad hoc commune dedicated to doing one's own thing and resisting the corrupt federal government. *Josey Wales* was not only Eastwood's bicentennial election year movie, an ambitious synthesis of the classic Fordian western with the "dirty" last sixties and even the counterculture westerns, but his post-Watergate, post-Vietnam statement as well. "All of us died a little in that damn war!" Josey tells the cavalryman who has been pursuing him over the course of Hollywood's first (and only) Carter western.[12]

A month later, the Republicans gathered in Kansas City for the party's first open convention since 1940, Ford and Reagan locked in a virtual tie. The convention's penultimate night featured a televised battle of the wives. Betty Ford upstaged Nancy Reagan by gamely dancing the bump with leering pop star Tony Orlando. In the end, her husband prevailed—winning the nomination on the first ballot by seventeen votes. Meanwhile in New York, *All the President's Men* went back into wide release.

September 23, some weeks after Marlon Brando (and Dennis Hopper) arrived in the Philippine jungle, Carter and Ford met for the first of three presidential debates, notable mainly for the twenty-seven-minute loss of sound that left the men frozen behind their podiums. During the second debate, Ford made a remarkable gaffe. As if scripted by *Saturday Night Live*, he declared that Poland was not a Soviet satellite and never would be under his presidency. The third debate was inconsequential. On November 2, Carter was narrowly elected, with 50 percent of the popular vote to Ford's 48 percent and an electoral margin of fifty-seven votes.

Nineteen days after Jimmy Carter's victory, another redeemer arrived, although his coming had been heralded for several months: stoical, sweet-natured Rocky Balboa, a character invented and played by Sylvester Stallone.

Stallone had hoped to open *Rocky* on July 4, 1976. Even so, his timing was nothing short of miraculous. No less than the born-again Christianity that Carter helped popularize or the bicentennial rebirth hoopla, the passion of Stallone's burnt-out pugilist was predicated on the grace of a second chance.

Rocky was another auteurist psychodrama. As with *Apocalypse Now*, the movie's story was indistinguishable from its backstory. The advertising tagline "His life was a million-to-one shot" described both the movie's protagonist and its creator. Scripting his own vehicle, Stallone made the movie he wanted to live—and did. A good-natured palooka fought the world heavyweight champion to a standstill; an obscure thirty-year-old actor knocked out Hollywood.

Opening with the image of Jesus Christ presiding over a boxing ring, *Rocky* resurrected the sports inspirational (a mode that served Ronald Reagan twice, first as a juvenile in the 1940 *Knute Rockne All American* and twelve years later as star of *The Winning Team*). At the same time, *Rocky* affirmed traditional American values—evoking and endorsing the importance of honesty, perseverance, and hard work, not to mention love, trust, make-believe, happy endings, and Hollywood hype. Bickle's New York was hell; Rocky's Philadelphia was purgatory.[13]

Fig. 31. Sylvester Stallone in *Rocky* (John Avildsen, 1976, United Artists)

By resurrecting the Horatio Alger myth on the mean streets of South Philadelphia and sprinkling pixie dust on Scorsese's urban grit, Stallone confirmed blue-collar white ethnics as heirs to the American dream. Putting a positive spin on the fatalistic *Godfather* movies, he implicitly celebrated the rise of Italian American directors and actors—Francis Coppola, Martin Scorsese, Al Pacino, and Robert De Niro, none of whom would ever make or star in a western.

Archie Bunker notwithstanding, the luckless club fighter and tenderhearted debt collector Rocky Balboa was the first working-class icon to capture the public imagination in the half-dozen years since the eponymous hardhat in *Joe* opened fire on the hippie spawn of the degenerate middle class—the movie that had been the maiden effort of *Rocky*'s director, John Avildsen. While *Joe*, released a few months after the Kent State massacre and widely shown throughout the 1970 electoral season, was one of the most divisive of American movies, Rocky proved to be all but universal.

According to the legend, published numerous times in late 1976, Stallone felt that his acting career had stalled. His wife was pregnant. The rent was overdue. Then his mother, an amateur astrologist, advised him to seek success as a writer. Three and a half days later, Stallone had the first draft of a screenplay, inspired by the 1975 Muhammad Ali–Chuck Wepner title bout. The studios saw *Rocky* as a possible vehicle for Burt Reynolds, James Caan, Ryan O'Neal, or even Robert Redford, but Stallone, whose major credit was a supporting role in *The Lords of Flatbush* (1974), a post–*American Graffiti* youth film that also featured *Happy Days*'s future Fonzie, Henry Winkler, held out for the starring role.

Rocky was positioned as the ultimate sleeper, even though weeks before the movie opened in New York on November 21, Stallone's media presence was so ubiquitous that the *New York Post* would joke that he had "granted more interviews than any American short of [the president-elect's mother] Lillian Carter." Advertised sans title only as an Oscar contender, the movie had a sneak preview at the Baronet, a first-run Manhattan theater on the Upper East Side, on August 8, a week before Republicans began to gather in Kansas City. *New York Times* reporter Guy Flatley saw the ad and paid his way in. "The audience went wild, and so I—on my own—contacted Stallone in Hollywood for the interview," he recalled.

Flatley's piece appeared in the same edition that reported the "generally genteel" first Ford-Carter debate. Around the time Ford blundered in early October, *Village Voice* writer Pete Hamill, then out in Los Angeles, got wind of *Rocky* and had the movie's coproducer set up a special screening. Almost immediately after, Hamill found himself scooped by *New York Magazine* and its sister publication *New West*, both of which ran a lengthy profile entitled "*Rocky*: It Could Be a Contender" in their October 18 issues. Upping the ante, Hamill channeled Hemingway in a cover story, "Rocky KOs Movie Biz," which appeared in the *Voice*, the morning after Carter's victory: "The word is everywhere: Stallone is a star. A new star. As big as Brando, maybe. And a writer, too. Maybe even a director. The picture will be huge."

Leading the premiere by nearly two weeks, *Time* joined the parade, waxing sociological: "Boggled by grim, paranoid plots like *Marathon Man* and savage heroes like the Taxi Driver, audiences may be ready to buy into [Stallone's] gentler, uncomplicated machismo." Rocky was inherently chivalrous and kind, despite his day job as an underworld enforcer.

Although he was clearly of an age to have served in Vietnam, Rocky's relation to the war is vague, as was Stallone's. Nevertheless, Rocky provided a paradigm for post-Vietnam masculinity. Stallone himself felt that it was the manliness of Rocky's character that made the film a hit: "I don't think that even women's lib wants all men to become limp-wristed librarians. There doesn't seem to be enough real men to go around." A column Beth Gillin Pombeiro wrote for the *Philadelphia Inquirer*, published on the day of *Rocky*'s New York opening, made the essential point: "*Rocky* is a film for our times—with a real hero."

Rocky redeemed boxing, show biz, America, and post-Vietnam masculinity as well as the movies.

The very day *Rocky* opened in New York, Vincent Canby published a Sunday think piece, "Cynical Cinema Is Chic," citing *Network*, *Three Days of the*

Condor, and *The Parallax View* among other movies demonstrating "the extent to which the political events in this country in the sixties, for which Watergate was the grand finale, have shaped hopelessness as a perfectly acceptable, popular attitude."

Although not unanimously favorable, the early reviews were near universal in their analysis. Canby described *Rocky* as "purest Hollywood make-believe of the 1930s." Frank Rich concurred: "It has an innocence we associate with the uplifting Hollywood films of the Great Depression." Kathleen Carroll was even more specific in comparing it to "the movies of Frank Capra." While Pauline Kael called *Rocky* "a threadbare patchwork of old movie bits," *Newsweek* clinched the connection: "Just as Jimmy Carter prevailed by harking back to the old values of love and trust, *Rocky* resembles nothing so much as a throwback—to the 1950s Cinderella hit *Marty* and to the 1930s brand of optimism known as 'Capra-corn.'"

Rocky also recalled Elia Kazan's *On the Waterfront* (1954), back from the Dream Life. Some twenty-three years before, Marlon Brando had played another over-the-hill palooka, mixed up with gangsters, and looking for self-respect. "What separates Stallone from Brando is that everything Stallone does has one purpose: to make you like him," Pauline Kael wrote.[14]

"I knew Carter was going to win two-and-a-half years ago," Stallone told the *Philadelphia Inquirer*, reveling in his new role as prophet. "I saw him on a television show in Los Angeles with a circulation of about 15 people, the Mort Sahl show. Sahl introduced him and people said, 'Who is he?' They thought he was there to sell aluminum siding, or maybe he was waiting for a bus. He said, 'I'm gonna be President,' and I said, 'He's gonna make it.'"[15]

Reporting from Manhattan's Cinema II, Frank Rich noted in the *New York Post* on December 4, 1976, that "the crowds pouring out of a new American film called *Rocky* are behaving in a most unruly manner":

> These moviegoers just can't contain themselves: They leave the theater beaming and boisterous, as if they'd won a door prize rather than parted with the price of a first-run ticket, and they volunteer ecstatic opinions of the film to the people waiting on line for the next show. It's a Hollywood mogul's wet dream come to life.... Amazingly enough, this film offers incontestable proof that American audiences have a latent will to believe in the Protestant ethic, the magic of love, and the Easter Bunny.

Rocky was a thing, or at least a full-fledged symptom. "The Hollywood Movie Hero Has Returned," Ernest Schier of the *Philadelphia Bulletin* explained on January 9, 1977; "Audiences grew restless and silent watching Paul Newman or Robert Redford go down to defeat. It was closer to life.

It was depressing. Societies need heroes to carry their hopes." Such was Rocky's burden.[16]

In the Dream Life, the restoration of the underdog White Champ and the elevation of a long-shot conciliatory southern Democrat to the White House coincided with the phenomenon that was *Roots*. Telecast by ABC over the course of a week, starting three days after Jimmy Carter's inaugural, the miniseries attracted one hundred million viewers—a record that, appropriately, eclipsed that of NBC's November 1976 telecast of *Gone with the Wind*—and stimulated a national conversation on slavery even as it suggested that enslaved Africans were sustained as a people thanks to their belief in the family unit.

As the candidate of faith and family, Carter made a strong appeal to African Americans; *Rocky*, however, profited from a white backlash. "Race is the force of the original film and of the sequels," Joe Flaherty would write on the occasion of *Rocky III* (1982). From the moment that the hero's locker is taken by a black fighter through his patronizing treatment by a black TV newswoman to his titanic clash with the black champion Apollo Creed, *Rocky* is a tale of displacement and revenge.[17]

Creed, who taunts the American public by capering about dressed as Uncle Sam, was transparently modeled on Muhammad Ali, on whom, Flaherty declared, "our great lust for revenge was denied until Stallone rewrote history." If Ali were simply the world champion, he would not be so potent a demon. He was also an embodiment of the sixties, whose sins included a conversion to Islam, a refusal to be inducted into the army, and identification with the Third World. Rocky, by contrast, is named for and identifies with Rocky Marciano, the last white American heavyweight champion, who won the crown in 1952 and retired undefeated four years later.

Rocky would hardly work if Creed had been a white champion or Rocky an underdog black challenger. It is necessary that Rocky lives in a reverse Bantustan where blacks have all the power and prestige or, at the very least, seem to have appropriated the wheels and levers of American life. At the same time, the movie's overt racist comments are mainly made by blacks. Creed, who cooked up the idea of fighting an unknown Italian fighter on the bicentennial and thus for whom Rocky is less a man than a money-making gimmick, refers derisively to his opponent as the "Eye-talian Stallion" and makes other disparaging remarks, while color-blind Rocky is incredulous and offended when a bartender calls Creed a "jig clown."[18]

For Creed, the American people are a bunch of media-blitzed rubes. (This, of course, is Stallone's most brilliant sleight of hand.) Creed is arrogant, street-smart, and rich, while Rocky is humble, innocent, and poor. Structurally, *Rocky* resembles the second half of *The Birth of a Nation*, with blacks having displaced whites, and whites—or at least a white—redeemed when Rocky goes the distance. Creed wins a split decision and refuses a rematch (only to demand one in *Rocky II*). Thus, as Flaherty wrote, *Rocky* borders on a "colonial restoration" in which a creature of the 1950s miraculously returns to defeat a demon of the 1960s. (In Hollywood terms, Stallone dethroned Robert Redford as the number one box office attraction.)

And thus, the bicentennial year that began in a city of dreadful night haunted by the insane would-be savior Travis Bickle ended with the beatification of the sweet-natured long-shot Rocky Balboa, hailed by *New York Magazine* critic John Simon as "the most likable and unaggressive of punks."[19] Unlike Travis, Rocky was a deservedly successful megalomaniac.

Five myth-making movies were nominated for the bicentennial's Best Picture: *All the President's Men*, *Bound for Glory*, *Network*, *Rocky*, and *Taxi Driver*. *All the President's Men* was the first movie that Jimmy Carter would screen in the White House, on January 22, two days after his inauguration. But inevitably, on Oscar night 1977, it was the endearing folk tale *Rocky*, a movie whose grosses were one hundred times its budget, that the Academy canonized.[20]

Aggressively innocent and proudly upbeat, Stallone's underdog psychodrama demonstrated that movies were about making audiences feel good about themselves (and America). The fantasy of realizing an impossible dream against all odds was resurrected as a Hollywood staple, even as the *Rocky* theme would become the default musical introduction for American politicians. "*Rocky* is shameless, and that's why—on a certain level—it works," Pauline Kael noted.

If *Taxi Driver* was Hollywood's last great feel-bad movie, *Rocky* created the template for the feel-good movies that would endure for the rest of the twentieth century and beyond. In 1990, Mark Crispin Miller analyzed a new happy ending, founded on the inscription of cheering spectators, among other forms of on-screen audience euphoria, observing that *"feeling warmly watched by everyone* now seems a sweeter fantasy than the fictitious heroisms of past cinema."[21]

Rocky was the exemplar of this fantasy and a harbinger of Hollywood's subsequent found illusions. The bicentennial year saw a dip in box-office figures, but the setback was only momentary: grosses took off over the next few years as a new zeitgeist came to roost. Powered by the astounding, unforeseen success of *Star Wars* in 1977, the period between November 1976 and November 1978 proved to be a watershed for the themes and trends of the next half-dozen years. *Apocalypse Now*, which from early 1976 through mid-1979 had been Hollywood's most notorious work in progress, did not open until July 1979, having woefully missed its moment.

CODA

WHAT "GOLDEN AGE"?
A Dissenting Opinion

Phillip Lopate

I am not a lover of the New Hollywood. Taking into consideration the enormous reverence that quite intelligent people have for these movies, let us start from the assumption that I am wrong. But perhaps not entirely: as with any perversely contrarian stance, a grain of truth may be uncovered.

Before going into the reasons for my resisting, or at least not being wowed by, the films of the New Hollywood when they first appeared, I should clarify where I was coming from. As a film buff in college, 1960 to 1964, I had fallen in love with art movies. Attracted first to the iconoclastic energy of Godard and the French New Wave, the austerities of Antonioni, and the perverse subversions of Buñuel, I came shortly afterward to honor most of all the sad wisdom and classical restraint exemplified by movies such as Max Ophüls's *The Earrings of Madame De*, Kenji Mizoguchi's *Ugetsu*, Satyajit Ray's *Apu Trilogy*, Yasujirō Ozu's *Late Spring*, Robert Bresson's *Diary of a Country Priest*, and Carl Theodor Dreyer's *Day of Wrath*. These contemplative, burnished masterpieces constituted my gold standard. Even with comedies and musicals, I was drawn to the poised acceptance of heartache found in Vincente Minnelli's *Meet Me in St. Louis*, say, or the bittersweet worldliness in Ernst Lubitsch's *Trouble in Paradise* and *The Shop around the Corner*. If my first love was foreign films, I came to appreciate more and more the Hollywood movies of the forties and fifties that represented, to my mind, a perfection in the handling of space and an emotional maturity. For it was maturity that I was after: the urge to be rescued from my unfinished, awkward, and unpolished young man's state.

Revering the work of directors such as John Ford, William Wyler, Alfred Hitchcock, Otto Preminger, Vincente Minnelli, Nicholas Ray, George Cukor, Anthony Mann, and Douglas Sirk, I had been tutored in this taste by the critical perspectives of André Bazin and Andrew Sarris. I was much more a Sarrisite than a Paulette, preferring Sarris's formalist, mise-en-scène analysis and his prematurely middle-aged humanist values to Kael's giddy, roller-coaster idea of the fun to be had at the movies. Sarris was unapologetically historically minded, would go back again and again to re-view old movies, changing his mind and saying so in print, whereas Kael boasted that she saw a movie only once, trusting to her remarkable memory, which could bring back each jolt or sigh of boredom. She was not one to dwell on the felicities of Frank Borzage or Raoul Walsh, but gave herself rapturously to the promise of newcomers, like her favorites Francis Ford Coppola, Martin Scorsese, Sam Peckinpah, Philip Kaufman, and Brian De Palma, whom collectively she once compared to the nineteenth-century American Renaissance of Hawthorne, Melville, Emerson, and Thoreau (to my mind, a stretch).

Given the fact that I thought Hollywood had already achieved a golden age, with films such as Ford's *She Wore a Yellow Ribbon* and *The Searchers*, Ray's *The Lusty Men* and *Bigger Than Life*, Preminger's *Laura* and *Bunny Lake Is Missing*, Sirk's *Written on the Wind* and *Imitation of Life*, Hitchcock's *Notorious* and *Vertigo*, Cukor's *A Star Is Born* and *The Marrying Kind*, it was hard for me to be swayed by the hype that accompanied the new generation's crop of films. In some cases, my objection came down to finding the seventies' directors technique inconsistently eclectic and inelegant; in other cases, to what I saw as the too self-approving, heavy-handed, trendy didacticism of their content.

Of course, it makes no sense to denigrate more than a decade's worth of American cinema, and I do recognize that the New Hollywood brought a fresh excitement to audiences. Still, I am left with remembering my lack of instinctive enthusiasm for this movement. Take *The Graduate*, that ur–New Hollywood work. I have never been able to warm to Mike Nichols's visual style—or lack of style. *Catch-22*, *Carnal Knowledge*, *Regarding Henry*—at best it is serviceable, at worst, hit-or-miss arty (see *The Graduate*'s underwater pool shot). As a director, Nichols is most celebrated for his skillful handling of actors. And yet the protagonist, Benjamin, makes no sense to me as portrayed by Dustin Hoffman. He is supposed to have been a college athlete, yet he walks duck-footed and graceless, like a Jewish schlemiel out of Jerry Lewis's playbook, and he talks so slowly and registers points so belatedly that he seems to be on the autism spectrum, halfway to his performance in *Rain Man*. Hoffman's Benjamin is intensely watchable and indeed unforgettable, even if he doesn't quite jibe with the character in Buck Henry's screenplay. (Years hence, we may come to regard the New Hollywood as a triumphant playground for actors, a performers' rather than a directors' cinema—but that's for another essay.)[1] *The Graduate*, now considered a classic (i.e., enough people like it for it to stick around and be taught in film appreciation courses), was very popular at its release; it certainly tapped into the zeitgeist, which made me mistrust it automatically. What exactly was its message that so suited the zeitgeist? That young people were lovable dreamers who had the right idea, and all adults were idiots, corrupt fools trapped in the corporate rat race, or sexual predators like Mrs. Robinson, who wanted what beautiful youth had? Pauline Kael, offended by the ugly portrayal of an older woman pouncing on a naïve young man, nailed the triteness and one-sidedness of this material.

On the other hand, Kael fell utterly for Arthur Penn's *Bonnie and Clyde*, which she defended on the very same grounds she had denounced *The Graduate*: because it captured the spirit of the moment.[2] She would probably have said *The Graduate* pandered to its audience through its anodyne portrait of sensitive youth, while *Bonnie and Clyde* was daringly edgy, by virtue of its pessimism and satire of the American go-getter mentality. But I resented the way that movie kept winking at the audience with its ironic happy-music soundtrack, or its too-careful placing of Depression period details, and asked us to feel superior to these cretinous yokels who stumbled from one holdup to another. Clyde and his clumsy, clueless gang made the outlaw couples in *They Live by Night* or *Gun Crazy* seem positively thoughtful by comparison. It isn't so much that I was put off by its celebration of criminality, as resistant to the movie's cynical attitude that there was no moral middle ground in America: outlaws were essentially no different from robber-bankers. As a critique of capitalism, it felt to me lacking in nuance, too broad-brushed.

I once heard *Bonnie and Clyde* cited as a paradigm shift in American movies. That it was, but not all paradigm shifts are for the good. Penn's mix-and-match cinematic technique, which went from Fritz Lang–like overhead shots to bouncy satiric montages to slow-motion *Liebestod*, made me uneasy.

On a technical level, what was being compromised, I felt, in many New Hollywood movies was the integrity of the image. By that I mean the classical balance between foreground and background that linked characters to their environment; mise-en-scène that encouraged fluid traversing of space through camera movement; preference for long-duration medium or long shots over close-ups and quick cutting. This style had been brought to a high polish with the wide-screen Cinemascope of the fifties and early sixties. If you look again at a movie like Preminger's *Anatomy of a Murder*, you see apt camera placement and framing in every shot, which allowed for the subtle complexity of interactions between characters, such as the understated erotic current between

James Stewart and Lee Remick. The same is true for Robert Rossen's *The Hustler*, or a restrained melodrama like *Strangers When We Meet*. But from the late sixties on, a jittery, destabilized approach to the shot began to take over: more close-ups (adapting to television's shallower depth of field), quicker cutting, greater use of the zoom over the tracking shot (which made for a fuzzier image and less crisp compositions), and darker, duller interiors. Increased film stock speeds made it possible to shoot with minimal lighting setups or none at all, a convenience but also a loss in the art of lighting's expressive potential. We suddenly got all those muddy brown-orange interiors, from *Godfather II* onward.

The New Hollywood directors, many of whom had gone to film school—the first such generation to have done so—were certainly cognizant of the craft employed by the older masters, but their very borrowing often suffered from an anything-goes appropriation—mixing montage, tracking, and extreme close-ups. What had been audacious solutions in the past became a bag of tricks: Brian De Palma's *Obsession*, for instance, features a 360-degree tracking shot that is obviously an homage to *Vertigo*, but has none of the emotional power of the original, because the characters involved are relative ciphers. Peter Bogdanovich's nostalgic *The Last Picture Show*, while consistently Fordian in its approach to the shot, comes off as painfully academic, like a graduate student copying his professor. Such were my formalist objections.

Thematically, I was bothered by the New Hollywood's continuous flattery of youth culture and its pseudo-anti-Establishment stance (pseudo because many of these pictures were obviously financed by corporate conglomerates). A string of movies, some good, some bad, featured right-wing conspiracies, fashionable paranoia, and self-satisfied denunciations of the American Way of genocide and corruption (*Mickey One*, *Little Big Man*, *The Parallax View*, *Zabriskie Point* . . .). The smirk directed against the military can be traced back to Kubrick's *Dr. Strangelove*, embraced prematurely by the *bien-pensant* as a comic masterpiece. Somehow I couldn't join in the laughter at cowboy soldiers riding atomic bombs. I hasten to add that I myself was draft age, vehemently against the Vietnam War, and situated on the left; but perhaps for that very reason, I disliked the glib *MacBird*-type satires and the privileging of youth as the new moral standard-bearer. *Easy Rider* seemed practically a cartoon representation of longhairs' self-pity: why can't the Man just leave us alone to smoke our dope and party in peace?

Radical shifts in politics are often sparked by youth movements, and those of the 1960s and '70s deserve every credit for helping to end an atrocious war. The problem is that we may have spearheaded the antiwar movement, but that did not mean we had a solid purchase on wisdom. The young tend to see things in morally simplistic, black-and-white terms. If America was the bad guy in Vietnam, or a hotbed of racism, then the Communists were the good guys everywhere. Stalin and Mao were reevaluated as heroes. The year after graduating from college I had lived in Franco's Spain, where I got a close-up view of how a truly Fascist government operated, so I was far less willing to go along with those who insisted on portraying America as "Amerikkka."

The movies of the New Hollywood focused obsessively and sentimentally on the young. Suddenly the worldly, mature type of character that Jimmy Stewart played in *Anatomy of a Murder*—the experienced guy who had carried so many of the dramas of the forties and sixties—disappeared, was no longer to be found onscreen. Humphrey Bogart, Robert Mitchum, John Wayne, James Stewart, Gary Cooper, Gregory Peck, and Cary Grant were either dead or put out to pasture, replaced by charmers like Dustin Hoffman, Elliot Gould, Al Pacino, Robert De Niro, who played either crazily out-of-control types or horny, sexually inexperienced boy-men. Part of the reason for this shift had to do with the political mood: middle-aged men were no longer seen as positive role models but as potential war criminals, responsible for the mess in Vietnam. The very name "John Wayne" (a fine actor whatever his politics) suddenly become shorthand for all that was ludicrous and abhorrent in the warrior ideal. Mature masculinity suddenly seemed suspect, potency itself a dubious construct. Just as the hip audience had been quick to sneer at the general in *Dr. Strangelove* (played by Sterling Hayden) for holding in his semen because it would dilute his strength, so it chuckled knowingly at the Freudian joke that Warren Beatty's killer Clyde had an impotence problem.

The young flailed rather than ascending the old ladder of growing up. A film like Martin Scorsese's *Mean Streets*, though thrilling to watch and listen to, failed to engage me more than viscerally: there were limits to how much could I invest in the Robert De Niro character's blind careening and self-destructive acting-out. By contrast, the protagonists in Jean-Pierre Melville's gangster movies, like *Le samouraï* or *Le doulos*, might be just as violent, but they were acting according to a code, and taking responsibility at every turn for their misdeeds. However amoral Melville's criminals might be, the moral vision of the director's was rock solid. Could we say the same for Scorsese's *Taxi Driver*, where the takeaway was a bemused shrug of confusion at a shootout blurring De Niro's good guy avenger and bad guy psycho?

That quintessential New Hollywood picture, *Five Easy Pieces*, intriguing up to a point as a study of the regressive American male refusing to grow up, before its script petered out in the last third, could not hold a candle to Jean Eustache's trenchant 1973 study of male immaturity, *The Mother and the Whore*. That Eustache movie, I have come to see, was both the fulfillment and outgrowing of the *nouvelle vague*. Here a paradox is in order: the New Hollywood directors were besotted with the French New Wave, and longed to make movies of similar freedom. But those French breakthrough films were also rife with young men's suicidal self-pity and misogyny. Not until Françoise Lebrun's great climactic speech in *The Mother and the Whore* excoriated these young people for aimlessly smoking endless cigarettes in cafés and cheating on each other was the order of narcissistic youth challenged. Sex, the Lebrun character said, was trifling, unless it led to something bigger (in her case, she wanted a child). The hero's rootless rutting was this time being called to account. It was time to grow up.

Éric Rohmer's protagonist in *My Night at Maud's*, eager to settle down with a good Catholic girl, abstains from sleeping with the very desirable Maud for reasons both principled and cowardly. (Rohmer followed up this film with other tales of sexual restraint, such as *Claire's Knee* and *Chloe in the Afternoon*.) Was there a single New Hollywood movie in which the male star turned down an offer to bed a pretty woman to whom he was attracted? Maybe *Klute*, but otherwise I can't think of any. Benjamin in *The Graduate* both sleeps with Mrs. Robinson and acts victimized about it.

Mark Greif, who writes about the nefarious aftereffects of America's enthroning youth as the pinnacle of sexual desirability in his book *Against Everything* (and who may be even more of a contrarian than I am), puts it well: "the de-emphasis of sex and the denigration of youth will have to start with an act of willful evaluation. It will require preferring the values of adulthood: intellect over enthusiasm, autonomy over adventure, elegance over vitality, sophistication over innocence—and, perhaps, a pursuit of the confirmation or repetition of experience rather than the experience of novelty."[3] It is not a question of returning to puritanical attitudes about sexuality but acknowledging a more worldly perspective regarding desire and its consequences. What I would have given, in any New Hollywood film, for the sophistication of the three principals in *The Earrings of Madame De*, the General, his wife, and her diplomat suitor, adults who knew the score even as they took fatalistic paths.

A major reason I did not swoon over the products of the New Hollywood was that I was deriving too much satisfaction from foreign cinema during the seventies and eighties. I was following the work of Chantal Akerman, Jean Eustache, Maurice Pialat, Éric Rohmer, Roberto Rossellini, Andrei Tarkovsky, Rainer Werner Fassbinder, Hou hsiao-hsien, Edward Yang, Alexi German, Larisa Shepitko, Abbas Kiarostami, Otar Iosseliani, Theo Angelopoulos, Sergio Leone, Nanni Moretti, Lino Brocka, Shohei Imamura. . . . Where was the New Hollywood equivalent of Ingmar Bergman's *Scenes from a Marriage*? Certainly not *Bob & Carol & Ted & Alice*, fun though that was. The only American picture I can think of that came close to capturing the complexity of marriage during this period was Alan Parker's *Shoot the Moon*, with Diane Keaton languidly smoking a joint in the bathtub and singing to herself. The Godard

Fig. 32. Erland Josephson and Liv Ullmann in *Scenes from a Marriage* (Ingmar Bergman, 1973, Cinematograph AB)

film I most admired, in the end, was not *Breathless* or *Band Apart*, with their doomed young people's hijinks, but *Contempt*, the story of a marriage going off the rails (as mine was at the time). I needed guidance in the realities of male-female relationships, more than outlaw larks that turned violent.

And I needed therapy. How did the New Hollywood films' sensationalized treatment of cracking up compare to the clarity of *Jeanne Dielman, 23, quai du Commerce, 1080 Bruxelles*? Though the mystery of Akerman's heroine's breakdown is never explicitly accounted for, the very composure with which it is shown on-screen, without any false attempt to replicate cinematically the hurly-burly of going mad, allows us to accept it as simply factual.

The New Hollywood's embrace of *confusion* as a vanguard position was, in its way, truly innovative, even if it prevented evocative films such as John Cassavetes's *A Woman under the Influence*, Jerry Schatzberg's *Puzzle of a Downfall Child*, Robert Altman's *3 Women*, or Scorsese's *Taxi Driver* from being fully comprehensible or artistically resolved. Cassavetes plunged us into an atmosphere of turmoil and mental disorder in *A Woman under the Influence*, *Faces*, and *Husbands*, though it was not entirely clear whether these swirling interactions were meant to be accurate portraits of people falling apart or documentaries of seemingly improvised Method acting exercises (even if, it turned out, they were entirely scripted). It wasn't until *The Killing of a Chinese Bookie* that I began to admire Cassavetes's aesthetic, relishing that film's calmer, more Apollonian balance between nightclub milieu and threatened, courtly hero; and then I went back to appreciate his earlier films for whatever frissons they could deliver. I still felt uneasy about the glamorizing of mental disorder, a remnant of the sixties' / R. D. Laing's irresponsible idealization of schizophrenia as a valid adaptation to society's madness. On a formal level, I simply had to give up the expectation that every moment advanced the narrative, and watch patiently for behavioral grace notes.

Over the years, I have come to appreciate more the New Hollywood's muzziness (in both visual and emotional senses), at least as applies to some of its directors whom I now esteem. I am thinking especially of Sidney Lumet and Robert Altman. Lumet, who came out of live television drama, brought that on-the-fly, opportunistic approach to the film set, with visual results that were somewhat muddled and not as sharp as the great Hollywood studio stylists of the forties and fifties. Indeed, Lumet never developed a consistent mise-en-scène or a compositional sense of elegant inevitability. But he made up for it by the depth of his characters and the sturdy, gritty realism of his settings (especially those shot in New York, like *Prince of the City*, *Serpico*, *Dog Day Afternoon*, *Just Tell Me What You Want*). The acting performances he elicited were often amazing, not just from Al Pacino but from the whole cast of *Long Day's Journey into Night*, which demonstrated a rootedness in classical American theater that nourished his filmmaking, more so than most of his New Hollywood comperes.

As for Altman, I was a skeptic until I happened upon *The Long Goodbye*, whose lovingly downbeat atmospherics and nuanced character touches trumped any genre expectations it might have pretended to fulfill. After that, I found myself liking almost every Altman movie—up to a point, realizing that there would always be transcendent moments if not fully rounded aesthetic experiences. Altman evolved a sophisticated visual style, which he carried from film to film, though I still found it mystifying that he could be so wildly uneven, one year making a beauty like *California Split*, the next a woeful mess like *A Wedding* or *HealtH*.

Then there is *Nashville*, still Altman's most important film, and a distillation of all that is brilliantly energetic and disturbingly caricaturing in his approach. Almost every character in the twenty-four-member cast is shown to be craven, vain, self-serving, or lost to addictive substances, with a few rare exceptions. The vividly staged humiliations of the Gwen Welles and Ronee

Blakely characters and especially the BBC reporter by Geraldine Chaplin are done with a bit too much gusto, suggesting Altman's cruel enjoyment of these takedowns. The director also seemed to be sneering a good deal at the foolish citizens in the background, caught in a celebrity-worshipping culture. These mindless mass-media-shaped zombies are perhaps the true subject of *Nashville*, reminiscent of Nathaniel West's Hollywood premiere–gaping mob in *The Day of the Locust*, though minus an authorial narrative intelligence to guide us toward the possible existence of a more humane perspective. The movie opens with a smugly patriotic song, "We must be doing something right / to last two hundred years," and ends with the number "It Don't Worry Me," the supposed response to a pointless assassination, bookending a too-facile dig at American unconsciousness, complacency, and indifference. No one is accorded the dignity of self-reflection, much less critical self-awareness.

The message seems to be: This is us, America, and we are fucked.

Despite the media clamor at the time to declare it a masterpiece, I was not alone in my reservations about *Nashville*. Reviewing the film, the fine critic William S. Pechter wrote,

> Clearly [the subject] isn't Nashville but nothing less than America itself: America as it really is, stripped of myth and idealization, on this eve of its bicentennial celebration. . . . What, in fact, Nashville amounts to specifically, with its horde of hayseed characters seen in all their malice, venality, and scrambling opportunism, is the movies' biggest bout of hick-baiting since A Face in the Crowd. . . . But when one populates a work of art with numerous characters toward whom one's salient attitude is a contemptuous condescension, one is involved, I think, in trashing of a different and more deeply offensive sort. . . . And when you thus trash not only your subject but your own characters and their emotions, you lay yourself open to criticism that goes beyond questions of artistic virtuosity and artistic finesse. In fact, what's revealed in such a moment is a coarseness of sensibility, an ugliness, of a kind one glimpses at moments in a number of Altman's films.[4]

I want to make clear that I am not faulting Robert Altman or by extension the New Hollywood for being critical of American society. The film noir classics of the postwar era and the fifties were steadfast in showing the dingy downside of the American dream. But there was more of a sense of balance: they posited the darker elements against a foreground of desired and desirable normalcy. A film noir like Max Ophüls's forever haunting *The Reckless Moment* critically exposes the Joan Bennett character's entrapment in a bourgeois housewife suburban box, but it also allows for a tenderness to develop between her and James Mason's complexly intelligent crook, such as would be out of keeping in a New Hollywood picture, and it leaves us with a feeling that, for all its complacency, there is a good deal positive to say about the protective safety of the American family unit. Nicholas Ray's *On Dangerous Ground*, which begins with a horrific portrait of the urban jungle where thugs and a brutal, disenchanted cop (played memorably by Robert Ryan) battle it out, evolves into a rather surprising pastorale, as Ryan is sent to the countryside to work on a case and encounters the sympathetically adult Ida Lupino. America was not hopelessly lost; there are still pockets of sanity to stumble upon.

If the New Hollywood overreached itself in its grand epic statements, it showed more prowess working small. Some of the films I cherish most from this alleged "golden age" were lean, modest, genre pieces or slices of life, where the obligatory New Hollywood sourness was less self-congratulatory and more organically embedded in the narrative. I'm thinking particularly of films like Ivan Passer's *Cutter's Way*, Ulu Grosbard's *Straight Time*, Roman Polanski's *Chinatown* (curious how many of the émigré directors got it right), William Friedkin's *Sorcerer* and *To Live and Die in L.A.*, Barbara Loden's *Wanda*, Alan Pakula's *Klute*, Peter Yates's *The Friends of Eddie Coyle*, Sydney Pollack's *Three Days of the Condor*, Michael Mann's *Thief*, and Elaine May's *Mikey and Nicky*. In these movies, disillusionment with the American dream was not made such a big deal of, but treated with a grown-up sense of stoic resignation: we were not put on earth to be happy. (Again, in this regard they came closer to Jean-Pierre Melville's icy *policiers*). It was not the conspiracy plot in *Three*

Fig. 33. Faye Dunaway and Robert Redford in *Three Days of the Condor* (Sydney Pollack, 1975, Paramount Pictures)

Days of the Condor that impressed me, but the slowing-down of that headlong narrative with Robert Redford admiring Faye Dunaway's photographs, or trying to, at least, thanks to a beautiful script by the veteran screenwriter Lorenzo Semple Jr. The wandering-around dialogues in *Mikey and Nicky* between Peter Falk and John Cassavetes resulted in what I like to think of as one of Cassavetes's best films (even if Elaine May directed it).

I know I am distinctly a minority in finding what most people would consider the pinnacle of New Hollywood achievement, Francis Coppola's *The Godfather*, overrated; the first part especially feels turgidly stately and self-important to me. It so wants to be an Epic About America that it keeps nudging us in the ribs to make its points. *Godfather, Part II* is a little more relaxed, and therefore less grating, but still too earnestly monumental. By contrast, Coppola's *The Conversation* strikes me as highly disciplined, rigorous, engrossing, and never hyperventilating—the equivalent of a good European art film.

Here I ought to draw a distinction between art cinema and popular cinema, which may clarify my (possibly wrongheaded) judgment of the New Hollywood. Please remember that my earliest film appreciation training was in art cinema, and so I tend to judge all movies by that rubric. *The Graduate* is undoubtedly a successful piece of popular filmmaking, but it does not pass the higher standards of art cinema—nor did it necessarily set out to do so. *The Godfather* is a more complicated case, partly because Coppola is more of a gifted, self-conscious film artist than Mike Nichols, and partly because of the trilogy's soaring ambitions. In my opinion, we might tentatively say that *The Godfather* is both triumphant popular cinema and a flawed art film. In the case of Coppola's *One from the Heart*, it might be better to say that it is not a botched work of popular filmmaking but an intriguing example of megalomaniac experimental hunch-playing, of the sort that Stuart Klawans analyzed in his excellent book, *Film Follies*.[5]

Undoubtedly, some of the heroes of the New Hollywood, like Coppola, Michael Cimino, and Scorsese, were enormously gifted cineastes, but their wanting to make movies with the freedom of the French New Wave resulted often in self-indulgent, bloated (if endearing) follies like *One from the Heart*, *Apocalypse Now*, *New York, New York*, or *Heaven's Gate*. Without necessarily referencing Peter Biskind's book,[6] one wonders how much coke and other drugs influenced these ragged, overblown, underwritten, and finally incoherent statements. No, this is unfair: I must stop thinking of the decentering effects of the New Hollywood as somehow inadvertent. Its obstinately unclassical efforts were clearly intentional, the fruit of a rebellion against the aesthetic status quo, which mirrored the political protests of the time against the Establishment. In my case, I may have shared their antiwar politics, but I remained too steeped in the love of an older cinematic tradition (Ozu, Renoir, Dreyer,

Ford, Ophüls) to rejoice in their overturning the apple cart. And it went further than cinematic tradition: I looked to the past for instructions on how to live.

I married young, the first time. I so wanted to be thought mature that I could never be a good hippie: I would listen obediently to the new Jimi Hendrix LP, then gladly put on Mozart's *Requiem*. I sought answers not in the playful New Age goofiness of Richard Brautigan but in the ironic writings of Stendhal, Machado de Assis, and Italo Svevo. All taste is finally personal and autobiographical. Others with their eye on liberation from society's shackles would undoubtedly find more satisfaction in New Hollywood's fireworks. I needed a different balm. Without going into the details of my childhood and background, I will simply say that sexual repression was not our family's problem. If anything, the opposite: I had to find a more stoical, stable alternative to self-indulgence in the name of liberation. Given my circumstances, I could develop a moderate taste for the New Hollywood without buying into all the hoopla surrounding it, or assenting to the notion that its promise was ever fulfilled.

In conclusion, I would like to say a kind word for the New Hollywood filmmakers. The lads did the best they could. They were like the Decembrists plotting against the tsar, except instead of being shot they were feted, covered with medals and glory. Well, why not? During the seventies they were the best game in town, in this country, anyway. Old and wise as I am now, I applaud the vitality of their best work. My problem in assessing it is, I cannot forget that when these pictures first came out, I was not enthused, I wanted something different, a ripened, refined, Mizoguchi-like acceptance of suffering and mortality, or Lubitsch's wryly Old World perspective that I could aspire to. These Young Turks irritated me. They reminded me too much of my own callowness. If I seem cranky regarding the New Hollywood, you may chalk it up to being irritated at my own long-wished-for, too-long-delayed maturity.

APPENDIX

TIME LINE: THE NEW HOLLYWOOD YEARS

1966 **January 17**: Simon & Garfunkel release *Sounds of Silence*
May 16: Jack Valenti becomes head of Motion Picture Association of America (MPAA)
May 16: Bob Dylan releases *Blonde on Blonde*
May 16: The Beach Boys release *Pet Sounds*
June 21: *Who's Afraid of Virginia Woolf?* (Mike Nichols)
June 30: National Organization for Women (NOW) founded in Washington, DC
July 20: *The Wild Angels* (Roger Corman)
August 3: Comedian Lenny Bruce dies at age forty
August 5: The Beatles release *Revolver*
October 5: *Seconds* (John Frankenheimer)
October 6: LSD is banned in the US
October 16: Huey Newton and Bobby Seale found the Black Panther Party in Oakland, CA
October 23: Monte Hellman / Jack Nicholson collaborations in *Ride in the Whirlwind* (Hellman), *The Shooting* (Hellman)
November 8: Former actor Ronald Reagan elected governor of California
December 9: *You're a Big Boy Now* (Francis Ford Coppola)
December 18: New York premiere of *Blow-Up* (Michelangelo Antonioni)

1967 **February 5**: *Smothers Brothers Comedy Hour* premieres on CBS
April 4: Martin Luther King Jr. "Beyond Vietnam" speech at Riverside Church, Harlem
April 15: National Mobilization Committee to End the War in Vietnam march on the United Nations in New York City
April 28: Heavyweight boxing champion Muhammad Ali refuses induction into the army, is stripped of his title
May 17: *Don't Look Back* (D. A. Pennebaker)
June 1: The Beatles release *Sgt. Pepper*
June 10: Spencer Tracy dies
June 12: *Loving v. Virginia*: Supreme Court rules prohibition of interracial marriage unconstitutional
June 15: *The Dirty Dozen* (Robert Aldrich)
June 16-18: Monterey Pop Festival
July 12-17: Newark riots
July 26: *Hells Angels on Wheels* (Richard Rush)
August 2: *In the Heat of the Night* (Norman Jewison)
August 13: *Bonnie and Clyde* (Arthur Penn)
August 23: *The Trip* (Roger Corman)
August 30: *Point Blank* (John Boorman)
September 29: The American Film Institute (AFI) founded
October 9: Che Guevara executed in Bolivia
October 13: President Johnson signs executive order including sex discrimination on the list of prohibited forms of employment discrimination
October 21: Antiwar protesters march on the Pentagon, memorialized in Norman Mailer's Pulitzer Prize–winning book *Armies of the Night* (1968)
November 1: *Cool Hand Luke* (Richard Rosenberg)
November 9: Debut issue of *Rolling Stone* magazine
November 15: *Who's That Knocking at My Door?* (Martin Scorsese)
November 22: *The Producers* (Mel Brooks)
December 8: *Time Magazine* cover "The New Cinema: Violence . . . Sex . . . Art . . ."
December 14: *In Cold Blood* (Richard Brooks)
December 21: *The Graduate* (Mike Nichols)

1968 **January 22**: Series premiere of *Rowan & Martin's Laugh-In*
January 30: Beginning of the Tet Offensive
February 8: Orangeburg Massacre: three are killed protesting segregation at a bowling alley in South Carolina

February 12: Publication of *Soul on Ice* (Eldridge Cleaver)
March 6: *Psych-Out* (Richard Rush)
March 16: My Lai Massacre
March 21–April 30: Columbia University student strike, building occupations, protests, and police crackdown
March 31: President Johnson announces he will not run for a second term
April 2: *2001: A Space Odyssey* (Stanley Kubrick)
April 4: Martin Luther King Jr. assassinated in Memphis, TN
April 10: Academy Awards: Mike Nichols wins Best Director for *The Graduate*; Estelle Parsons wins Best Supporting Actress for *Bonnie and Clyde* (the awards ceremony was delayed by two days following the King assassination)
April 11: The Civil Rights Act of 1968 signed, prohibiting housing discrimination
May 1: *Countdown* (Robert Altman)
May 10: Beginning of the Paris peace negotiations (Vietnam War)
May 12: The Poor People's Campaign begins "Resurrection City" occupation in Washington, DC
May 13: General strike in Paris
May 18: Louis Malle, François Truffaut, and Jean-Luc Godard interrupt Cannes Film Festival screenings to express solidarity with student protests and general strike
June 3: Valerie Solanas shoots and gravely wounds Andy Warhol
June 5: Robert Kennedy assassinated
June 10: *Petulia* (Richard Lester)
June 12: *Rosemary's Baby* (Roman Polanksi)
June 13: Jonny Cash performs at Folsom State Prison
August 13: *Targets* (Peter Bogdanovich)
August 20: Soviet Union / Warsaw Pact invasion of Czechoslovakia
August 26–29: Democratic National Convention (DNC) in Chicago
August 28: Police riot in Chicago at the DNC
September 7: Feminists protest Miss America pageant, filling "freedom trash can" with symbols of normative femininity and disrupting ceremony on live television
September 22: *Faces* (John Cassavetes)
October 17: *Bullitt* (Peter Yates)
October 18: Tommie Smith and John Carlos black power salute at Mexico City Olympics
October 23: *Pretty Poison* (Noel Black)
October 25: *In the Year of the Pig* (Emile de Antonio)

November 1: MPAA film rating system goes into effect
November 5: Richard Nixon elected president
November 6: *Head* (Bob Rafelson)
November 22: Beatles release "the White Album"

1969   **January 28**: New York Film Critics Circle Awards: Mike Nichols wins Best Director for *The Graduate*
February 11: *Model Shop* (Jacques Demy)
March 20: John Lennon marries Yoko Ono
April 19: Black students take over Willard Straight Hall at Cornell University, demand black studies program; demonstrations follow at Colgate (April 25–28), City College of New York (May 8)
April 22: *Sympathy for the Devil* (Jean-Luc Godard)
April 30: Secret bombing of Cambodia begins
May 15: Bloody Thursday: Local sheriffs and National Guard forcibly eject people from "People's Park" in Berkeley, killing one and wounding several others
May 25: *Midnight Cowboy* (John Schlesinger)
June 8: *That Cold Day in the Park* (Robert Altman)
June 18: *The Wild Bunch* (Sam Peckinpah)
June 27: Police raid at Stonewall Inn
July 3: Founding member of the Rolling Stones Brian Jones dies at age twenty-seven
July 14: *Easy Rider* (Dennis Hopper)
July 20: Apollo 11 moon landing
August 8: Manson family murders of Sharon Tate, four others
August 15–18: Woodstock music festival
August 20: *Alice's Restaurant* (Arthur Penn)
August 27: *Medium Cool* (Haskell Wexler)
August 27: *The Rain People* (Francis Ford Coppola)
September: First female undergraduate students admitted to Yale
September 2: Ho Chi Minh dies
September 17: *Bob & Carol & Ted & Alice* (Paul Mazursky)
October 21: Jack Kerouac dies at age forty-seven
October 22: *The Sterile Cuckoo* (Alan Pakula)
October 23: *Butch Cassidy and the Sundance Kid* (George Roy Hill)
October 28: *Downhill Racer* (Michael Ritchie)
October 29: Bobby Seale gagged and chained to a chair while on trial with the "Chicago Seven"
November 15: Moratorium to End the War in Vietnam march on Washington in the largest antiwar demonstration in US history

November 28: Rolling Stones release *Let It Bleed*
December 6: Altamont free concert
December 10: *They Shoot Horses, Don't They?* (Sydney Pollack)

1970
January 1: California becomes the first state to adopt "no fault" divorce
January 25: New York Film Critics Circle Awards: John Voight wins Best Actor for *Midnight Cowboy*, Paul Mazursky and Larry Tucker win Best Screenplay for *Bob & Carol & Ted & Alice*
January 25: *MASH* (Robert Altman)
February 9: *Zabriskie Point* (Michelangelo Antonioni)
March 4: *Loving* (Irvin Kershner)
March 16: Forty-six women file suit against *Newsweek* management for sex discrimination
March 17: *The Boys in the Band* (William Friedkin)
March 22: US release of *My Night at Maud's* (Éric Rohmer)
March 26: *Woodstock* (Michael Wadleigh)
April 7: *Midnight Cowboy* wins three Oscars, including Best Picture and Best Director (John Schlesinger) despite X rating
April 27: *Hi, Mom!* (Brian De Palma)
April 28: US invasion of Cambodia
May 4: Kent State killings
May 8: Hard Hat Riot in New York City
May 9: Nixon mingles with protesters gathering overnight at Lincoln Memorial
May 13: *Let It Be* (Michael Lindsay-Hogg)
May 14: Jackson State killings
May 16: *MASH* wins Cannes Palme d'Or
May 20: *The Landlord* (Hal Ashby)
May 27: *Watermelon Man* (Melvin Van Peebles)
June 24: *Catch-22* (Mike Nichols)
July 15: *Joe* (John Avildsen)
August 10: *Diary of a Mad Housewife* (Frank Perry)
August 19: *WUSA* (Stuart Rosenberg)
August 26: Women's Strike for Equality
September 11: *Five Easy Pieces* (Bob Rafelson)
September 18: Jimi Hendrix dies at age twenty-seven
October 4: Janis Joplin dies at age twenty-seven
October 12: *I Walk the Line* (John Frankenheimer)
December 1: *Husbands* (John Cassavetes)
December 5: *Brewster McCloud* (Robert Altman)

December 6: *Gimme Shelter* (Albert Maysles, David Maysles, Charlotte Zwerin)
December 14: *Little Big Man* (Arthur Penn)
December 16: *Puzzle of a Downfall Child* (Jerry Schatzberg)
December 17: *Alex in Wonderland* (Paul Mazursky)
December 31: The Beatles break up

1971 **January 12**: Series premiere of *All in the Family*
January 18: New York Film Critics Circle Awards: *Five Easy Pieces* wins for Best Director (Bob Rafelson), Best Supporting Actress (Karen Black), and Best Film
January 25: Charles Manson and followers convicted of twenty-seven counts of first-degree murder
February 9: *Little Murders* (Alan Arkin)
February 23: *The Selling of the Pentagon* (Peter Davis)
February 28: *Wanda* (Barbara Loden)
March 11: *A New Leaf* (Elaine May)
March 11: *THX 1138* (George Lucas)
March 28: *Taking Off* (Miloš Forman)
April 20: *Swann v. Charlotte-Mecklenburg* upholds busing as a legitimate means to enforce racial integration in schools
April 23: Vietnam veterans protest the war at the US Capitol, throwing medals on the steps
April 23: *Sweet Sweetback's Baadasssss Song* (Melvin Van Peebles)
April 28: *Bananas* (Woody Allen)
May 21: *Drive, He Said* (Jack Nicholson)
May 21: Marvin Gaye releases *What's Going On*
June 13: Pentagon Papers begin to be published
June 23: *Klute* (Alan Pakula)
June 24: *McCabe & Mrs. Miller* (Robert Altman)
June 25: *Shaft* (Gordon Parks)
June 30: *Carnal Knowledge* (Mike Nichols)
July 3: Jim Morrison dies at age twenty-seven
July 7: *Two-Lane Blacktop* (Monte Hellman)
July 13: *The Panic in Needle Park* (Jerry Schatzberg)
July 16: *The Hired Hand* (Peter Fonda)
September 3: White House "plumbers" burglarize Daniel Ellsberg's psychiatrist's office
September 8: *Sunday Bloody Sunday* (John Schlesinger)
September 9: Attica Prison uprising

October 2: *The Last Picture Show* (Peter Bogdanovich)
October 7: *The French Connection* (William Friedkin)
October 15: *A Safe Place* (Henry Jaglom)
November 3: *Play Misty for Me* (Clint Eastwood)
December 19: *A Clockwork Orange* (Stanley Kubrick)
December 20: *Harold and Maude* (Hal Ashby)

1972   *The Joy of Sex* published
January 23: New York Film Critics Circle Awards: *Klute* wins for Best Actress (Jane Fonda), *The Last Picture Show* ties for Best Screenplay (Peter Bogdanovich and Larry McMurtry) with *Sunday Bloody Sunday*, and wins Best Supporting Actor (Ben Johnson)
February 21: Nixon goes to China
March 9: *What's Up, Doc?* (Peter Bogdanovich)
March 14: *The Godfather* (Francis Ford Coppola)
March 22: The Equal Rights Amendment is passed by Congress, but will not clear the state ratification process
March 22: *Eisenstadt v. Baird* : Supreme Court rules that right to privacy includes unmarried persons' right to use contraceptives
April 7: Academy Awards: Jane Fonda wins Best Actress for *Klute*; Cloris Leachman wins Best Supporting Actress and Ben Johnson wins Best Supporting Actor for *The Last Picture Show*; *The French Connection* (William Friedkin) wins Best Picture
May 2: Death of FBI director-for-life J. Edgar Hoover
May 15: Alabama governor and segregationist George Wallace shot and paralyzed while campaigning for Democratic nomination for president
June 4: Angela Davis found not guilty of murder, kidnapping, and criminal conspiracy
June 12: *Deep Throat* (Gerard Damiano)
June 17: Watergate break-in and arrest of "plumbers"
June 28: *Prime Cut* (Michael Ritchie)
June 29: *The Candidate* (Michael Ritchie)
July 21: George Carlin arrested in Milwaukee for violating obscenity laws after performing his "Seven Words You Can Never Say on Television" routine
July 30: *Deliverance* (John Boorman)
August 22: Jane Fonda delivers radio broadcast from Hanoi

October 4: *Hickey & Boggs* (Robert Culp)
October 8: *Images* (Robert Altman)
October 10: The *Washington Post* reports that FBI establishes a connection between Watergate break-in and Nixon's reelection effort
October 12: *The King of Marvin Gardens* (Bob Rafelson)
October 14: *Last Tango in Paris* (Bernardo Bertolucci)
October 19: *Play It as It Lays* (Frank Perry)
November 7: Nixon re-elected in landslide
November 8: Launch of HBO, the first pay-TV network
November 12: *Ulzana's Raid* (Robert Aldrich)
December 2: *Jeremiah Johnson* (Sydney Pollack)
December 17: *The Heartbreak Kid* (Elaine May)
December 21: *Up the Sandbox* (Irvin Kershner)

1973 **January 22**: *Roe v. Wade*: Supreme Court holds that the Fourteenth Amendment's protection of privacy rights extends to a woman's decision to have an abortion
January 27: Paris Peace Accord signed
January 30: G. Gordon Liddy and James W. McCord Jr. convicted of conspiracy, burglary, and wiretapping in the Watergate scandal
February 27–May 8: Wounded Knee: American Indian Movement occupies Pine Ridge Reservation in protest of tribal leadership and federal policy
March: End of draft announced
March 7: *The Long Goodbye* (Robert Altman)
March 27: *Sisters* (Brian De Palma)
April 8: Pablo Picasso dies
April 9: *Paper Moon* (Peter Bogdanovich)
April 11: *Scarecrow* (Jerry Schatzberg)
April 30: H. R. Haldeman, John Ehrlichman, and Attorney General Richard Kleindienst resign amid Watergate scandal
May 17: Beginning of televised Watergate hearings
May 23: *Pat Garrett and Billy the Kid* (Sam Peckinpah)
June 17: *Blume in Love* (Paul Mazursky)
June 26: *The Friends of Eddie Coyle* (Peter Yates)
July 13: Alexander Butterfield reveals the existence of Nixon tapes in testimony to Congress
August 29: Actor Mark Frechette from *Zabriskie Point* arrested for attempted bank robbery in Boston
August 31: Director John Ford dies

October 2: *Mean Streets* (Martin Scorsese)
October 5: US release of *The Mother and the Whore* (Jean Eustache)
October 10: Vice President Spiro Agnew resigns
October 12: US premiere of *The Bitter Tears of Petra von Kant* (Rainer Werner Fassbinder)
October 13: *Badlands* (Terrence Malick)
October 19: OPEC declares oil embargo in response to US involvement in Arab-Israeli War
October 20: The Saturday Night Massacre: Nixon fires special prosecutor Archibald Cox; Attorney General Elliot Richardson and Deputy Attorney General William Ruckelshaus resign
December 3: CBGB concert venue opens in Manhattan
December 5: *Serpico* (Sidney Lumet)
December 12: *The Last Detail* (Hal Ashby)
December 26: *The Exorcist* (William Friedkin)

1974 **February 5**: Patty Hearst kidnapped by the Symbionese Liberation Army
February 11: *Thieves Like Us* (Robert Altman)
March 24: *The Sugarland Express* (Steven Spielberg)
April: *Attica* (Cinda Firestone)
April 7: *The Conversation* (Francis Ford Coppola)
April 30: The White House releases edited transcripts of Nixon tapes to the House Judiciary Committee
May 1: *The Lords of Flatbush* (Martin Davidson, Stephen Verona)
May 9–24: Cannes Film Festival, premiere of *Hearts and Minds* (Peter Davis); *The Conversation* (Coppola) wins the Palme d'Or
May 22: *Daisy Miller* (Peter Bogdanovich)
May 22: *Thunderbolt and Lightfoot* (Michael Cimino)
June 15: Bob Woodward and Carl Bernstein's *All the President's Men* published
June 17: US release of *A Free Woman* (Volker Schlöndorff)
June 19: *The Parallax View* (Alan Pakula)
June 20: *Chinatown* (Roman Polanski)
June 24: *Jenkins v. Georgia*: Supreme Court overturns Georgia ruling that the film *Carnal Knowledge* (Nichols) was legally obscene
June 26: *Three the Hard Way* (Gordon Parks Jr.)
July 24: *United States v. Nixon*: Supreme Court requires Nixon to give tapes to investigators
July 27: The House Judiciary Committee passes the first of three articles of impeachment against Nixon
July 30: *Cockfighter* (Monte Hellman)

August 7: *California Split* (Robert Altman)
August 7: *Bring Me the Head of Alfredo Garcia* (Sam Peckinpah)
August 8: Nixon resigns
August 12: *Harry and Tonto* (Paul Mazursky)
October 2: *The Taking of Pelham One Two Three* (Joseph Sargent)
October 7: US release of *Celine and Julie Go Boating* (Jacques Rivette)
October 12: *A Woman under the Influence* (John Cassavetes)
December 9: *Alice Doesn't Live Here Anymore* (Martin Scorsese)
December 12: *The Godfather, Part II* (Francis Ford Coppola)

1975   **January 1**: Watergate conspirators including John Mitchell found guilty and sentenced to prison
January 20: Bob Dylan releases *Blood on the Tracks*
January 28: New York Film Critics Circle Awards: Jack Nicholson wins Best Actor for *Chinatown* (Polanski)
March 3: Pauline Kael publishes "preview" of *Nashville* (Robert Altman) in the *New Yorker*
March 13: *Shampoo* (Hal Ashby)
April 8: Academy Awards: *Hearts and Minds* (Peter Davis) wins Best Documentary
April 9: US release of *The Passenger* (Michelangelo Antonioni)
April 30: Fall of Saigon
May 25: *The French Connection II* (John Frankenheimer)
June 6: The Rockefeller Commission submits its report on CIA activities within the United States
June 10: *Love and Death* (Woody Allen)
June 11: *Nashville* (Altman)
June 11: *Night Moves* (Arthur Penn)
June 20: *Jaws* (Steven Spielberg)
July 8: *Fear of Fear* (Rainer Werner Fassbinder)
July 9: *Smile* (Michael Ritchie)
September 18: Patty Hearst arrested
September 21: *Dog Day Afternoon* (Sidney Lumet)
September 24: *Three Days of the Condor* (Syndey Pollack)
September 26: *The Rocky Horror Picture Show* (Jim Sherman)
October 3: *The Lost Honor of Katharina Blum* (Volker Schlöndorff, Margarethe von Trotta)
October 8: *Hard Times* (Walter Hill)
October 11: Premiere of TV show *Saturday Night Live*

October 19: *Hester Street* (Joan Micklin Silver)
October 30: *New York Daily News* "Ford to City: Drop Dead" headline
November 19: *One Flew over the Cuckoo's Nest* (Miloš Forman)
December 13: Patti Smith releases *Horses*
December 25: *Hustle* (Robert Aldrich)

1976   **January 25**: New York Film Critics Circle Awards: *Nashville* wins Best Director (Robert Altman), Best Supporting Actress (Lily Tomlin), and Best Film; Jack Nicholson wins Best Actor for *One Flew over the Cuckoo's Nest*
February 4: *Next Stop, Greenwich Village* (Paul Mazursky)
February 7: *Taxi Driver* (Martin Scorsese)
February 15: *The Killing of a Chinese Bookie* (John Cassavetes)
April 4: *All the President's Men* (Alan Pakula)
April 5: Producer/director Howard Hughes dies
April 25: *Stay Hungry* (Bob Rafelson)
May 13–28: Cannes Film Festival: *Taxi Driver* wins Palme d'Or
May 19: *The Missouri Breaks* (Arthur Penn)
May 28: *The Man Who Fell to Earth* (Nicholas Roeg)
June 1: *The Last Hard Men* (Andrew McLaglen)
June 24: *Buffalo Bill and the Indians, or Sitting Bull's History Lesson* (Robert Altman)
July 6: Robert Altman wins Golden Bear at Berlin Film Festival for *Buffalo Bill and the Indians, or Sitting Bull's History Lesson*
July 16: *The Bingo Long Traveling All-Stars & Motor Kings* (John Badham)
July 29: First "Son of Sam" murder in New York City
August 1: *Obsession* (Brian De Palma)
August 20: *The Shootist* (Don Siegel)
August 23: Tom Wolfe publishes "The 'Me' Decade and the Third Great Awakening" in *New York Magazine*
September 30: *The Front* (Martin Ritt)
October 8: *Marathon Man* (John Schlesinger)
October 26: FALN bombing in New York
November 2: Jimmy Carter elected president
November 11: US release of *Beware of a Holy Whore* (Rainer Werner Fassbinder)
November 14: *Network* (Sidney Lumet)
November 19: *The Last Tycoon* (Elia Kazan)

November 25: Martin Scorsese films the Band's last concert
December 3: *Rocky* (John Avildsen)
December 12: *Mikey and Nicky* (Elaine May)

1977 January 15: Peter Finch dies
January 23–30: *Roots* screened on television
January 30: New York Film Critics Circle Awards: *All the President's Men* wins Best Director (Alan Pakula), Best Supporting Actor (Jason Robards Jr.), and Best Film; Robert De Niro wins Best Actor for *Taxi Driver*, Paddy Chayefsky wins Best Screenplay for *Network*
March 29: Academy Awards: *Network* nominated in each major category, wins Best Actor (Peter Finch), Best Actress (Faye Dunaway), Best Supporting Actress (Beatrice Straight)
April 1: *In the Realm of the Senses* (Magisa Ôshima)
April 3: *3 Women* (Robert Altman)
April 20: *Annie Hall* (Woody Allen)
May 25: *Star Wars* (George Lucas)
June 3: US release of *Katzelmacher* (Rainer Werner Fassbinder)
June 24: *Sorcerer* (William Friedkin)
July 13: Electricity blackout in New York City
August 16: Elvis Presley dies
December 25: Charlie Chaplin dies
December 26: Howard Hawks dies

Thanks to Ed Quish for his invaluable work on the time line and research assistance in general.

NOTES ON CONTRIBUTORS

Molly Haskell is a film critic and author; a third edition of her landmark *From Reverence to Rape: The Treatment of Women in the Movies* was published in 2016. She has taught at Barnard, Columbia, and Sarah Lawrence College. Her most recent book is *Steven Spielberg: A Life in Films*.

Heather Hendershot is a professor of film and media at MIT and a former editor of *Cinema Journal*. Her most recent books are *What's Fair on the Air? Cold War Right-Wing Broadcasting and the Public Interest* and *Open to Debate: How William F. Buckley Put Liberal America on the Firing Line*.

J. Hoberman is a film critic and Gelb Professor of Humanities at Cooper Union. His recent books include *An Army of Phantoms: Hollywood and the Making of the Cold War* and *The Dream Life: Movies, Media, and the Mythology of the Sixties*. "The Spirit of '76: Travis, Rocky, and Jimmy Carter" is adapted from the third volume of his Cold War trilogy, still in progress, *Found Illusions or Remake My Day: The Reaganization of America*.

Jonathan Kirshner is professor of political science at Boston College. His numerous publications on international politics include *American Power after the Financial Crisis*. Kirshner is the author of *Hollywood's Last Golden Age: Politics, Society, and the Seventies Film in America*, and of the novel *Urban Flight*.

George Kouvaros is professor of film studies at the University of New South Wales, Sydney. He is the author of four books on leading figures and aspects of North American filmmaking. His monograph *Where Does It Happen? John Cassavetes and Cinema at the Breaking Point* is published by the University of Minnesota Press.

Jon Lewis is the Distinguished Professor of Film Studies at Oregon State University. He has published twelve books, including *Whom God Wishes to Destroy . . . Francis Coppola and the New Hollywood*; *Hollywood v. Hard Core: How the Struggle over Censorship Saved the Modern Film Industry*; and *Hard-Boiled Hollywood: Crime and Punishment in Postwar Los Angeles*.

Phillip Lopate is an author whose books range from fiction (*The Rug Merchant*, *Two Marriages*), to personal essays (*Against Joie de Vivre*, *Portrait inside My Head*), to poetry (*At the End of the Day*). His nonfiction works include *Waterfront* and *Notes on Sontag*. His writings on cinema have been collected in the volume *Totally Tenderly Tragically*.

Robert Pippin is the Evelyn Stefansson Nef Distinguished Professor in the Department of Philosophy at the University of Chicago. He is the author of several books on modern German philosophy, as well as *Hollywood Westerns and American Myth*, and *Fatalism in American Film Noir*.

David Sterritt is editor-in-chief of *Quarterly Review of Film and Video*, film professor at the Maryland Institute College of Art, and editor of *Robert Altman: Interviews* (2000). His writing on Altman has appeared in edited collections as well as *QRFV*, *Current*, and the *Christian Science Monitor*.

David Thomson is a film critic and author of the *New Biographical Dictionary of Film*, and, most recently, *Warner Bros: The Making of an American Movie Studio*. He is still writing about movies at the age of seventy-eight, despite current rumors that they no longer quite exist. He is still frightened by the films of Alan Pakula and believes there are Joe Fradys everywhere.

NOTES

Introduction

1. *Bonnie and Clyde* received ten Oscar nominations: Best Picture, Best Director, Best Actor in a Leading Role (Warren Beatty), Best Actress in a Leading Role (Faye Dunaway), Best Writing, Story, and Screenplay—Writing Directly for the Screen (Robert Benton and David Newman), Best Costume Design (Theadora Van Runkle), two for Best Actor in a Supporting Role (Gene Hackman and Michael J. Pollard), and won for Best Cinematography (Burnett Guffey) and Best Actress in a Supporting Role (Estelle Parsons).

2. See Louis Menand, "Paris Texas: How Hollywood Brought the Cinema Back from France," *New Yorker*, February 17 and 24, 2003, 169–77. See also Lester Friedman, *Bonnie and Clyde* (London: BFI, 2000).

3. David Newman and Robert Benton, "Lightning in a Bottle," in *The Bonnie and Clyde Book*, ed. Sandra Wake and Nicola Hayden (New York: Simon & Schuster, 1972), 13, 15, 23; Richard Brody, *Everything Is Cinema: The Working Life of Jean-Luc Godard* (New York: Metropolitan Books, 2008), 220–21, 222 (quote).

4. "Cinema: Low-Down Hoedown," *Time*, August 25, 1967.

5. Bosley Crowther, "Shoot-Em-Up Film Opens World Fete; 'Bonnie and Clyde' Cheered by Montreal First-Nighters," *New York Times*, August 7, 1967; Joseph Morgenstern, "Two for a Tommy Gun," *Newsweek*, August 21, 1967.

6. Joseph Morgenstern, "The Thin Red Line," *Newsweek*, August 28, 1967.

7. Roger Ebert, "Bonnie and Clyde," *Chicago Sun Times*, September 25, 1967; Pauline Kael, "Bonnie and Clyde," *New Yorker*, October 21, 1967, 147–71.

8. See Jon Lewis, *The Godfather* (London: BFI, 2010), 50.

9. On 1967 as a turning point see Mark Harris, *Pictures at a Revolution: Five Movies and the Birth of the New Hollywood* (New York: Penguin, 2008).

10. Michel Ciment, *John Boorman* (London: Faber and Faber, 1986), 78.

11. An irony is that although the film was indeed understood as almost a generational litmus test in 1967, over the years, especially for viewers seeing the film at different stages of their own lives, the film comes across, as Nichols intended, as suggesting similarities across the generations. See for example Ebert's contrasting reviews from 1967 and 1997.

12. In September 1978, Coppola screened a rough cut of *Apocalypse Now* for a roomful of United Artists (UA) executives. Coppola had gone into the screening with a plan to ask for more time and more money. But when the lights came up, the mood in the screening room had turned sour. One UA executive was so disappointed he leaked word to the press that the picture might never come out and then dubbed the film "Apocalypse Never." When the UA executives met again to discuss what to do about *Apocalypse*

Now, they decided to cut their investment in the film. Their reasoning was simple: so long as they could not control the project, so long as they could not control Coppola, they would let the auteur shoulder the risk. The decision proved to be one of the biggest blunders in modern Hollywood history. In exchange for a $7.5 million investment, UA retained domestic distribution rights to *Apocalypse Now*. The remaining $25 million in the production budget was technically loaned to Coppola, with his home and his future earnings from *The Godfather* put up as collateral (though even in combination they were not worth nearly $25 million). In limiting its cash investment, UA surrendered the copyright to Coppola, along with all future rights to pay and network TV, domestic and foreign home rentals and sales, foreign theatrical distribution, and the eventual director's cut reissue, *Apocalypse Now Redux* (released through the Disney subsidiary Miramax in 2001).

13. Friedkin followed *Boys in the Band* with two exemplary New Hollywood features, the Oscar-winning *The French Connection* (1971) and the blockbuster horror film *The Exorcist* (1973).

14. Barbara Koenig Quart, *Women Directors: The Emergence of a New Cinema* (New York: Praeger, 1988), 90.

15. Nathalie Léger, *Suite for Barbara Loden* (Dorothy, 2016).

16. The vast majority of these often ragtag entertainments had more in common with Roger Corman's seat-of-the-pants low-budget productions than with the arty ambitions of the New Hollywood.

17. Stanley Kauffmann, *A World on Film: Criticism and Comment* (New York: Harper & Row, 1966).

18. This book's necessarily selective engagement with many of the great films of the era, by scholars and critics reassessing their own (often seminal) assessments of the era, inevitably downplays the contributions of films and filmmakers that could have easily filled chapters, doubling or tripling the size of this volume. For example, we do not dwell on numerous notable period genres; in addition to blaxploitation (as noted), there were clusters of disaster films, horror, porn-chic, as well as, crucially, revisionist westerns, including the Vietnam War allegory *Ulzana's Raid* (1972, directed by Robert Aldrich and written by Alan Sharp, who also wrote *Night Moves*), Penn's *Little Big Man* (1970) and *The Missouri Breaks* (1976), and the many contributions of Sam Peckinpah, which included *The Wild Bunch* (1969) and *Pat Garrett and Billy the Kid* (1973). In addition to genres, additional directors whose important New Hollywood contributions could have been considered more closely include, among others, Hal Ashby (*Harold and Maude*, *The Last Detail*, *Shampoo*), Francis Ford Coppola (*The Rain People*, *The Godfather*, *The Conversation*), Monte Hellman (*The Shooting*, *Two-Lane Blacktop*, *Cockfighter*), Brian De Palma (*Hi, Mom!*, *Carrie*, *Sisters*, *Obsession*), Sydney Pollack (*They Shoot Horses, Don't They?*, *Jeremiah Johnson*, *Three Days of the Condor*), Paul Mazursky (*Bob & Carol & Ted & Alice*, *Alex in Wonderland*, *Blume in Love*), and Michael Ritchie (*Downhill Racer*, *Prime Cut*, *The Candidate*, *Smile*).

19. For more on the broad array of films from this period see Peter Biskind, *Easy Riders, Raging Bulls: How the Sex-Drugs-and-Rock 'n' Roll Generation Saved Hollywood* (New York: Simon & Schuster, 1999); David Cook, *Lost Illusions: American Cinema in the Shadow of Vietnam, 1970–1979* (Berkeley: University of California Press, 2000); Mark Harris, *Pictures at a Revolution: Five Movies and the Birth of a New Hollywood* (New York: Penguin, 1999), J. Hoberman, "Ten Years That Shook the World," *American Film* 10, no. 8 (1985); Diane Jacobs, *Hollywood Renaissance* (Cranbury, NJ: Barnes, 1977); Geoff King *New Hollywood Cinema* (New York: Columbia University Press, 2002); Jonathan Kirshner, *Hollywood's Last Golden Age: Politics, Society, and the Seventies Film in America* (Ithaca, NY: Cornell University Press, 2012); Robert Kolker, *A Cinema of Loneliness: Penn, Kubrick, Coppola, Scorsese, Altman* (Oxford: Oxford University Press, 1980); Peter Kramer, *The New Hollywood: From "Bonnie and Clyde" to "Star Wars"* (New York: Wallflower, 2006); James Monaco, *American Film Now* (Oxford: Oxford University Press, 1979); Michael Pye and Linda Myles, *The Movie Brats: How the Film Generation Took Over Hollywood* (New York: Holt, Rinehart and Winston, 1979); David Thomson, *Overexposures: The Crisis in American Filmmaking* (New York: Morrow, 1981); Robin Wood, *Hollywood from Vietnam to Reagan* (New York: Columbia University Press, 1985). See also the following anthologies: *Contemporary Hollywood Cinema*, ed. Steve Neale and Murray Smith (London: Routledge, 1998); *The Last Great American Picture Show: New Hollywood Cinema in the 1970s*, ed. Thomas Elsaesser, Alexander Horwath, and Noel King (Amsterdam: Amsterdam University Press 2004); *The New American Cinema*, ed. Jon Lewis (Durham, NC: Duke University Press, 1998).

20. Pauline Kael, *Reeling* (Boston: Little, Brown, 1976), xiii–xiv.

21. Pauline Kael titled her first book of collected essays and reviews, published in 1965, *I Lost It at the Movies* (New York: Bantam, 1966). The pun in the title, a reference to lost innocence of another kind, seems apt here.

1. The Mad Housewives of the Neo-Woman's Film

1. Molly Haskell, *From Reverence to Rape: The Treatment of Women in Movies*, 3rd ed. (Chicago: University of Chicago Press, 2016).
2. Betty Friedan, *The Feminine Mystique* (New York: Dell, 1964); Simone de Beauvoir, *The Second Sex* (Gallimard: Paris, 1949).
3. Molly Haskell, "The 2000-Year-Old Misunderstanding: Rape Fantasy," *Ms. Magazine*, November 1976.

2. Antonioni's America

1. *L'avventura* opened in the United States in March 1961, one month before Fellini's *La dolce vita*. Jean-Luc Godard's *Breathless* reached American screens in February. It was a very good year.
2. Andrew Sarris, "Andrew Sarris Demands You See This," *Village Voice*, March 23, 1961, www.villagevoice.com/news/andrew-sarris-demands-you-see-this-6723489.
3. Stanley Kaufmann, "Arrival of an Artist," *New Republic*, April 10, 1961, https://newrepublic.com/article/62856/arrival-artist-0.
4. See Stephen Holden, "Antonioni's Nothingness and Beauty," *New York Times*, June 4, 2006, www.nytimes.com/2006/06/04/movies/04hold.html.
5. "The Sight and Sound Top Ten Poll," *BFI Film Forever*, http://old.bfi.org.uk/sightandsound/polls/topten/1962/html.
6. I make this argument at length elsewhere. See Jon Lewis, *Hollywood v. Hard Core: How the Struggle over Censorship Saved the Modern Film Industry* (New York: NYU Press, 2000). A simple rule of thumb applies here: in the movie business, when they say it's not about the money, it's about the money. And (especially) when they say it's about morality, it's about the money.
7. "'Blow Up' B.O. Comforts Metro," *Variety*, March 22, 1967, 6.
8. "Advisory, Better Than Rigid, 'Classing,'" *Variety*, March 22, 1967, 6. This brief article was laid out directly above "'Blow Up' B.O. Comforts Metro."
9. Robert B. Frederick, "Valenti at Society of Mag Writers: Snobs Deify Foreign Film Directors Whose Name End with 'O' or 'I,'" *Variety*, September 18, 1968, 3, 17.
10. Frederick, "Valenti at Society of Mag Writers," 17.
11. Ronald Gold, "Valenti Won't 'Blow-Up' Prod. Code for Status Films; No Church Push," *Variety*, January 11, 1967, 1, 78.
12. The complex contract called for a total of three English-language films: *Blow-Up* (a negative pickup produced in the UK), *Zabriskie Point* (produced in the US by and for MGM, which also distributed the film), and *The Passenger*, an Italian, French, Spanish, and US (MGM) coproduction contracted for US distribution by Metro. Much as *Zabriskie Point* was a critical and box office disaster, *The Passenger* was for the director and the studio an unqualified success.
13. Gold, "Valenti Won't 'Blow-Up' Prod. Code for Status Films," 78.
14. Stefan Kanfer, "Advance Obit.," in *Film 69/70: An Anthology by the National Association of Film Critics*, ed. Joseph Morgenstern and Stefan Kanfer (New York: Simon & Schuster, 1970), 100.
15. Kael refers to the "super-blockbuster musicals" like *Paint Your Wagon* as Edsels, Ford's "car of the future" that failed to deliver for the company at the end of the fifties, posting a net loss of $250 million. See Pauline Kael, "*Paint Your Wagon*: Somebody Else's Success," in Morgenstern and Kanfer, *Film 69/70*, 111.
16. Kael, "*Paint Your Wagon*," 112.
17. The Grand Prix du Festival was the top prize (best-picture award) at Cannes from 1964 to 1974. It was renamed the Palme d'Or in 1975.
18. For a recounting of the complete production of *Zabriskie Point* see Beverly Walker, "Michelangelo and the Leviathan," *Film Comment*, September/October 1992, 36–49.
19. Roger Ebert, "An Interview with Michelangelo Antonioni," *Chicago Sun-Times*, June 19, 1969, www.rogerebert.com/interviews/interview-with-michelangelo-antonioni.
20. Ebert, "Interview with Michelangelo Antonioni."
21. The larger legal issues raised by the action would not be sorted out until 1989 when a separate case, *California v. Freeman*, finally established that paid performance of sex acts in a motion picture (whether real or simulated) is not, at least according to the law in the United States, tantamount to prostitution.
22. Walker, "Michelangelo and the Leviathan," 48.
23. Antonioni as cited by Walker, "Michelangelo and the Leviathan," 48.

24. Charles Champlin, "Movie Review: Plight of U.S. Basis of Plot in 'Zabriskie,'" *Los Angeles Times*, March 18, 1970, F1 and F13.

25. Roger Ebert, "*Zabriskie Point*" (review), *Chicago Sun-Times*, January 1, 1970, www.rogerebert.com/reviews/zabriskie-point-1970.

26. Vincent Canby, "Screen: Antonioni's *Zabriskie Point*," *New York Times*, February 10, 1970, www.nytimes.com/movie/review?res=9E04E2DB1F3FE034BC4852DFB466838B669EDE.

27. I turned fifteen in 1970. It's been a while, but I remember being pissed off, a lot of the time.

28. Sam Tweedle, "Return to *Zabriskie Point*: The Mark Frechette and Daria Halprin Story," *Confessions of a Pop Culture Addict* (blog), http://popcultureaddict.com/movies-2/zabriskiepoint-htm/.

29. Well worth a look is Frechette's appearance with Halprin on *The Dick Cavett Show* in 1970, along with Rex Reed and Mel Brooks. The interview is awkward (to put it mildly), part of a press junket during which Frechette and Halprin continued to play their roles as disaffected, cynical young Americans. See www.youtube.com/watch?v=-jyzFfrtLRk.

30. Ebert, "Interview with Michelangelo Antonioni."

31. David Felton, "The Lyman Family's Holy Siege of America: Inside the Cult Led by Mel Lyman, the East Coast Charles Manson," *Rolling Stone*, December 23, 1971, www.rollingstone.com/culture/features/the-lyman-familys-holy-siege-of-america-19711223.

32. Ebert, "Interview with Michelangelo Antonioni."

33. In the film, Mark steals an airplane. When he tries to return it, he's cornered and then gunned down by the police. Antonioni ends the scene as the police and other onlookers peer into the cockpit at Mark's dead body, which we never see. His death is affirmed not by blood or a corpse or a scene at the hospital. Instead we hear news of his death on Daria's car radio.

3. "Jason's No Businessman . . . I Think He's an Artist"

1. Including *The Graduate* (1968), *Catch-22* (1970), and *What's Up, Doc?* (1972). Henry also turned in some fine performances (e.g., *The Man Who Fell to Earth*). On Henry's early prominence see Marcia Seligson, "Hollywood's Hottest Writer—Buck Henry," *New York Times Magazine*, July 19, 1970.

2. For more on the background, development, and practices of BBS see Mitchell S. Cohen, "7 Intricate Pieces: The Corporate Style of BBS," *Take 1* 3, no. 11 (September 1973); Bo Burlingham, "Politics under the Palms," *Esquire*, February 1977; and Teresa Grimes, "BBS: Auspicious Beginnings, Open Endings," *Movie* 31/21 (Winter 1986); Carmel Dagan, "Steve Blauner, Who Helped Bring 'Easy Rider,' 'Five Easy Pieces' to Screen, Dies at 81," *Variety*, June 17, 2015.

3. Phillip Lopate, "Anticipation of *La Notte*: The 'Heroic' Age of Moviegoing," in Lopate, *Totally, Tenderly, Tragically: Essays and Criticism from a Lifelong Love Affair with the Movies* (New York: Anchor Books, 1998); Monica Raesch, "Let Me Put It This Way: It Works for Me" (interview with Rafelson), *Journal of Film and Video* 65, no. 3 (Fall 2013): 55; Ronald Bergan, "Bert Schneider Obituary," *Guardian*, December 14, 2011.

4. Jeff Corey with Emily Corey, *Improvising Out Loud: My Life Teaching Hollywood How to Act* (Lexington: University Press of Kentucky, 2017); Patrick McGillan, *Jack's Life: A Biography of Jack Nicholson* (New York: Norton, 1994), 23, 90, 93, 179–80; Beverly Walker, "The Bird Is on His Own" (interview with Nicholson), *Film Comment*, May/June 1985, 54, 46; Michael Goodwin, "Camera: Lazlo Kovacs," *Take One* 2, no. 12 (October 1971): 14; Bruce Dern, with Christopher Fryer and Robert Crane, *Things I've Said but Probably Shouldn't Have: An Unrepentant Memoir* (Hoboken, NJ: John Wiley, 2007); Peter Biskind, *Easy Riders, Raging Bulls: How the Sex-Drugs-and-Rock 'n' Roll Generation Saved Hollywood* (New York: Simon & Schuster, 1998), 77 (Jaglom).

5. Tod Lippy, "Writing *Five Easy Pieces*: Interview with Carole Eastman," *Scenario* 1, no. 2 (Spring 1995): 166, 188; Nick Pinkerton, "Bombast: Carole Eastman," *Film Comment*, November 21, 2014; Jay Boyer, *Bob Rafelson: Hollywood Maverick* (New York: Twayne, 1996), 36, 38, 45; Rainer Knepperges and Franz Müller, "The Monologist and the Fighter: An Interview with Bob Rafelson," *Senses of Cinema*, May 2009.

6. John Russell Taylor, "Interview with Bob Rafelson," *Sight and Sound* 45, no. 4 (Autumn 1976): 202, 203; Goodwin, "Camera: Lazlo Kovacs," 16; Boyer, *Bob Rafelson*, 40.

7. Alex Simon, "Karen Black Dances the Missouri Waltz," *Venice*, June 2007.

8. Stephen Farber, "Easy Pieces," *Sight and Sound* 40, no. 3 (Summer 1971): 128–29.

9. Lippy, "Interview with Carole Eastman," 187; Boyer, *Bob Rafelson*, 38; Jackson Browne, "Your Bright Baby Blues," from *The Pretender* (Asylum, 1976).

10. Roger Ebert, "Great Movies: *Five Easy Pieces*," *Chicago Sun-Times*, March 16, 2003.

11. Vincent Canby, "Nicholson's 'Drive, He Said': Movie Marks Actor's Debut as Director," *New York Times*, June 14, 1971; Roger Ebert, *"Drive, He Said," Chicago Sun-Times*, January 1, 1972; Cynthia Grenier, "Reaction to Movie by Nicholson Is Most Violent of Cannes Fete," *New York Times*, May 25, 1971; Dern, *Things I've Said*, 91, 92.

12. Walker, "The Bird Is on His Own," (Nicholson quote). *Drive* has two extended scenes that feature full frontal male nudity, virtually taboo then and for many years after. And its sex scenes, like those in 1971's *Carnal Knowledge* (released the same month as *Drive*), are stripped of typical Hollywood gloss and tend to challenge and confront, rather than titillate. During one ragged episode of intercourse in a cramped car-bound encounter, Olive (Karen Black) exclaims "I'm coming." While American censors were taken aback by male nudity, British censors insisted only on cutting those two words, suggestive of the distinct anxieties of the two cultures.

13. McGillan, *Jack's Life*, 175-76, Jeremy Larner, *Nobody Knows: Reflections on the McCarthy Campaign of 1968* (London: Macmillan, 1970).

14. Jeremy Larner, *Drive, He Said* (New York: Dial, 1964), see for example 18, 105, 110, 139, 161, 170. McGillan, *Jack's Life*, 217-18.

15. Butler also shot *The Rain People* (1969), *Hickey and Boggs* (1972), *The Conversation* (1974), and *Jaws* (1975).

16. Stephen Farber, "The Man Who Brought Us Greetings from the Vietcong," *New York Times*, May 4, 1975.

17. Peter Tonguette, ed., *Peter Bogdanovich Interviews* (Jackson: University Press of Mississippi, 2015), 17, 79.

18. Cecile Starr, "Peter Bogdanovich Remembered and Assessed," *Filmmakers Newsletter* 6, no. 11 (September 1973): 20; Biskind, *Easy Riders, Raging Bulls*, 112.

19. Tonguette, *Peter Bogdanovich Interviews*, 6, 7, 22 (quotes); Cohen, "7 Intricate Pieces," 19.

20. Rachel Abramowitz, *Is That a Gun in Your Pocket? Women's Experience of Power in Hollywood* (New York: Random House, 2000), 25, 27-28, 36; Heather Hendershot, "Losers Take All: On the New American Cinema," *Nation*, May 11, 2011.

21. Tonguette, *Peter Bogdanovich Interviews*, 49 (quote). Bogdanovich wisely avoided the scene in which a group of boys have sex with a cow; he also shows Duane and Sonny only leaving and returning from Mexico, leaving an offensive, cringe-inducing whorehouse scene to the imagination. Several passages in the book elaborate on the miserable home life of Ruth Popper; the film, with more grace and power, intimates this solely through the character of Ruth. And in a terrible dramatic choice, in the novel Sonny and Lois have sex; in the film even the transgressive Lois has the wisdom to recognize the empty foolishness of such a gesture. Larry McMurtry, *The Last Picture Show* (New York: Simon & Schuster, 1966), 102-6 (heifer), 153 (Sam at the reservoir), 167-78 (Mexico), 253 (Sonny and Lois).

22. Hendershot, "Losers Take All"; Ellen Burstyn, *Lessons in Becoming Myself* (New York: Riverhead Books, 2006), 181-83, 187; Tonguette, *Peter Bogdanovich Interviews*, 48, 50.

23. Cinematographer Bruce Surtees had a foot in both camps; with a career that reached back to the days of the studio system, he was nevertheless unfazed by the experimental setups favored by Mike Nichols in *The Graduate* (1968).

24. Jean Douchet, *French New Wave* (New York: Distributed Art, 1999), 93; J. Hoberman, "One Big Real Place: BBS from *Head* to *Hearts*," *Current* (Criterion Collection), November 28, 2010.

25. Paul Zimmerman, *"The Last Picture Show," Newsweek*, October 12, 1971.

26. Peter Tonguette, "Obituary: Bert Schneider," *Sight and Sound* 22, no. 3 (March 2012); Boyer, *Bob Rafelson*, 6, McGillan, *Jack's Life*, 178, 204; Dennis McDougal, *Five Easy Decades: How Jack Nicholson Became the Biggest Movie Star in Modern Times* (Hoboken, NJ: John Wiley & Sons, 2008), 99.

27. J. Hoberman, "One Big Real Place," (nonnarrative); McDougal, *Five Easy Decades*, 124-25.

28. Gunther Stuhlmann, ed., *The Diary of Anaïs Nin*, vol. 7, *1966-1974* (New York: Harcourt Brace Jovanovich, 1980), 233 (quote), 255, 300 (quote), 316, 318.

29. John Russell Taylor, "Interview with Bob Rafelson," *Sight and Sound* 45, no. 4 (Autumn 1976): 203 (quote); Boyer, *Bob Rafelson*, 2, 47, 53.

30. Bryant Simon, *Boardwalk of Dreams: Atlantic City and the Fate of Urban America* (New York: Oxford University Press, 2004); Directors Guild of America, "Conversation with Bob Rafelson and Neil LaBute," November 12, 1998; American Film Institute, *Dialogue on Film* 4, no. 1 (October 1974): 2-4 (interview with Kovács).

31. Burstyn, *Lessons in Becoming Myself*, 231; See also Dern, *Things I've Said*, 121, 123-25.

32. Jay Cocks, *"The King of Marvin Gardens," Time*, October 30, 1972.

33. American Film Institute, *Dialogue on Film* 4, no. 1 (October 1974): 4, 7, 11; "Conversation with Bob Rafelson and Neil LaBute"; Boyer, *Bob Rafelson*, 5, 56–57.

34. David Thomson, *Overexposures: The Crisis in American Filmmaking* (New York: William Morrow, 1981), 234–35, 239.

35. "I knew there would be a realism to the scene if I were chopping off my own long hair that would be difficult to equal." Burstyn, *Lessons in Becoming Myself*, 243.

36. On the *Marvin Gardens* monologues see Boyer, *Bob Rafelson*, 55; McGillan, *Jack's Life*, 232; American Film Institute, *Dialogue on Film* 4, no. 1 (October 1974): 9.

37. Foster Hirsh, well aware he was in the minority, offered a spirited defense of the film: "I loved . . . every stubborn temperamental minute of it," he wrote, in "I Know I Shouldn't Like It, But . . . ," *New York Times*, November 11, 1972. But the official *Times* review ("pretentious . . . empty bombast") was more representative of the general critical response. Roger Greenspun, "The King of Marvin Gardens," *New York Times*, October 13, 1972. Andrew Sarris, "Films in Focus," *Village Voice*, November 9, 1972.

38. Interview with Peter Davis, www.documentaryisneverneutral.com/words/peterdavisham.html; J. Hoberman, "Vietnam, Real and Imagined," *New York Times*, July 6, 2014; Tonguette, "Obituary: Bert Schneider."

39. Begelman was caught in a "bizarre check forging scheme," including one for $10,000 written to the actor Cliff Robertson that proved his undoing. Begelman pleaded no contest to the criminal charges that followed; dismissed from Columbia in 1978, two years later he would be named president of MGM. Robert McG. Thomas Jr., "David Begelman, 73; Headed Columbia Pictures," *New York Times*, August 9, 1995.

40. "Documentary on Vietnam Fails to Open," *New York Times*, December 19, 1974; "'News' Editors Vex Rex," *New York Magazine*, July 1, 1974; Burlingham, "Politics under the Palms," 119, 120, 123.

41. Burlingham, "Politics under the Palms," 124; Bergan, "Bert Schneider Obituary." Text and video links of the acceptance speeches by Schneider and Davis can be accessed at http://aaspeechesdb.oscars.org/link/047-9/.

42. Farber, "Man Who Brought Us Greetings"; Burlingham, "Politics under the Palms," 50, 120; McGillan, *Jack's Life*, 266, 267, 292.

43. Marc Norman, *What Happens Next: A History of American Screenwriting* (New York: Three Rivers, 2007), 390, 398; Tonguette, *Peter Bogdanovich Interviews*, 118, 153.

4. Robert Altman

1. Mikhail Bakhtin, *Problems of Dostoevsky's Poetics*, trans. Caryl Emerson (Minneapolis: University of Minnesota Press, 1984), 202, 160.

2. Gilles Deleuze and Félix Guattari, *Anti-Oedipus: Capitalism and Schizophrenia*, trans. Robert Hurley, Mark Seem, and Helen R. Lane (London: Continuum, 2004), 20. Emphasis in original.

3. Patricia Pisters, "Delirium Cinema or Machines of the Visible?," in *Deleuze and the Schizoanalysis of Cinema*, ed. Ian Buchanan and Patricia MacCormack (London: Continuum, 2008), 112.

4. Max Horkheimer and Theodor Adorno, *Dialectic of Enlightenment*, trans. John Cumming (London: Allen Lane, 1973), 124.

5. Mark Minett, "Sponsoring the Hollywood Renaissance: Reappraising Altman's Industrial Films," in *A Companion to Robert Altman*, ed. Adrian Danks (Malden, MA: Wiley Blackwell, 2015), 36–37, 39–40.

6. David Thompson, ed., *Altman on Altman* (New York: Farrar, Straus and Giroux, 2005), 29.

7. Michael Wilmington, "Robert Altman and *The Long Goodbye*," in *Movie Talk from the Front Lines: Filmmakers Discuss Their Works with the Los Angeles Film Critics Association*, ed. Jerry Roberts and Steven Gaydos (Jefferson, NC: McFarland, 1995), reprinted in David Sterritt, ed., *Robert Altman: Interviews* (Jackson: University Press of Mississippi, 2000), 140.

8. Thompson, *Altman on Altman*, 38.

9. Thompson, 12–13.

10. Jonathan Rosenbaum, "Improvisations and Interactions in Altmanville," in *Essential Cinema: On the Necessity of Film Canons* (Baltimore: Johns Hopkins University Press, 2004), 91.

11. Thompson, *Altman on Altman*, 44.

12. Thompson, 60.

13. Thompson, 61.

14. Gilles Deleuze and Félix Guattari, *A Thousand Plateaus: Capitalism and Schizophrenia*, trans. Brian Massumi (London: Continuum, 2004), 23, 27.

15. Elaine M. Bapis, *Camera and Action: American Film as Agent of Social Change, 1965–1975* (Jefferson, NC: McFarland, 2008), 139.

16. Stephen Teo, "Altman and the Western, or a Hollywood Director's History Lesson of the American West," in Danks, *Companion to Robert Altman*, 263. Emphasis in original.

17. Robert Altman, dir., *3 Women*, audio commentary (2003), DVD, Blu-ray edition by the Criterion Collection, New York, 2004/2011.

18. Bakhtin, *Problems of Dostoevsky's Poetics*, 202, 129–30. Emphasis in original.

19. Virginia Wright Wexman, "*Nashville*: Second City Performance Comes to Hollywood," in Danks, *Companion to Robert Altman*, 378; Alex Lewin, "It Happened in *Nashville*," *Premiere* 13, no. 11 (July 1995): 88–95, 101–2.

20. Robert Self, "Robert Altman," *Senses of Cinema* 34 (February 2005), http://sensesofcinema.com/2005/great-directors/altman/.

21. Christie Milliken, "Movies and the Counterculture," in *American Cinema of the 1960s: Themes and Variations*, ed. Barry Keith Grant (Piscataway, NJ: Rutgers University Press, 2008), 229.

22. Molly Haskell, "*Nashville*: America Singing," *Current*, December 2, 2013, www.criterion.com/current/posts/2978-nashville-america-singing.

23. Self, "Robert Altman."

24. Jennifer Dunning, "The Man Who Painted Robert Altman's *3 Women*," *New York Times*, April 24, 1977, www.nytimes.com/1977/04/24/archives/the-man-who-painted-robert-altmans-3-women.html?_r=0.

25. James C. Edwards, *The Plain Sense of Things: The Fate of Religion in an Age of Normal Nihilism* (University Park: Pennsylvania State University Press, 1997), 190–91.

26. Bakhtin, *Problems of Dostoevsky's Poetics*, 59.

27. Richard Combs and Tom Milne, "Altman Talking," *Sight and Sound* 3 (Summer 1981), reprinted in Sterritt, *Robert Altman: Interviews*, 103.

28. Altman, *3 Women* DVD audio commentary.

29. Robert Kolker, *A Cinema of Loneliness: Penn, Stone, Kubrick, Scorsese, Spielberg, Altman* (New York: Oxford University Press, 2000), 329; Robert T. Self, *Robert Altman's Subliminal Reality* (Minneapolis: University of Minnesota Press, 2002), 276.

30. David Sterritt, "*3 Women*: Dream Project," *Current*, September 14, 2011, www.criterion.com/current/posts/319-3-women-dream-project.

31. Hamish Ford, "On Slippery Ground: Robert Altman, beyond Hollywood or Modernism," *Screening the Past*, August 12, 2015, www.screeningthepast.com/2015/06/on-slippery-ground-robert-altman-beyond-hollywood-or-modernism/.

5. City of Losers, Losing City

1. James Sanders, "Adventure Playground," in *America's Mayor: John V. Lindsay and the Reinvention of New York*, ed. Sam Roberts (New York: Columbia University Press, 2010), 86.

2. Robert Colaciello, "Turn-Offs That Turn On," *Village Voice*, August 19, 1971, 51.

3. Molly Haskell, *From Reverence to Rape: The Treatment of Women in the Movies*, 2nd ed. (Chicago: University of Chicago Press, 1987), 28.

4. Patti Smith's story of her relationship with Robert Mapplethorpe in the city in those same years offers a similar picture. Consider their first apartment together: "We had the entire second floor, with windows facing east and west, but its aggressively seedy condition was out of my range of experience. The walls were smeared with blood and psychotic scribbling, the oven crammed with discarded syringes, and the refrigerator overrun with mold." Patti Smith, *Just Kids* (New York: HarperCollins, 2010), 43.

5. Sherman Square is located at the intersection of Seventieth Street West, Broadway, and Amsterdam Avenue. It was in the 1970s—and is now—little more than a wide concrete traffic median with a few trees and benches.

6. *Serpico* opens with the hero being rushed into a dilapidated New York City hospital that would have seemed completely average to New York viewers at the time. Lindsay ran a 1965 campaign commercial that resonates here; a Bronx truck driver whose grandmother had recently died says, "These are some of the things that I witnessed as I went to the hospital: cockroaches crawl all over the walls. If a person is incapable of feeding themselves, the food is just left there. If a person is dirty in their bed, they just lay there." Cited in Roberts, *America's Mayor*, 31.

7. *All the President's Men* (Alan Pakula, 1976) also fits in this camp.

8. Heather Hendershot, "Strikes, Riots, and Muggers: How Mayor Lindsay Weathered New York City's Image Crisis," Peabody anthology (Athens: University of Georgia Press, forthcoming).

9. *Midnight Cowboy* likewise points to this notion. If this deeply sad film conveys one optimistic idea, it is that even the saddest of losers can connect and take care of each other. Hustler Joe Buck is a miserable failure as a gigolo, but when he offers the dying Rico a mug of soup, heated over Sterno and served in a filthy mug, we know that he is not a miserable failure as a human being.

10. Homer Bigart, "War Foes Here Attacked by Construction Workers," *New York Times*, May 9, 1970.

11. Apparently the scene was improvised, and Pacino had a tough time keeping a straight face. *I Knew It Was You: Rediscovering John Cazale* (Richard Shepard, 2009).

12. Moretti is played by dependable character actor Charles Durning, who also appeared in small roles in a few other New Hollywood films, such as *Sisters* (Brian De Palma, 1972) and *The Sting* (George Roy Hill, 1973). He never achieved leading-man status and ended up working more in TV than in film. Arguably, Durning gave the best, most nuanced performance of his career in *Dog Day*.

13. Lee Wengraf, "A Prison Uprising and Its Brutal Suppression," review of 1993 reissue of *A Time to Die: The Attica Prison Revolt*, by Tom Wicker (1975), *International Socialist Review*, issue 81 (January 2012). On Attica see not only Wicker but also Heather Ann Thompson's Pulitzer Prize–winning *Blood in the Water: The Attica Prison Uprising of 1971 and Its Legacy* (New York: Pantheon, 2016).

14. Carol Wikarska, "Attica," *Women & Film* 2, no. 7: 60–66.

15. Wikarska, 60–66.

16. Wikarska, 60–66.

17. Sanford Schwartz, ed., *The Age of Movies: Selected Writings of Pauline Kael* (New York: Penguin, 2011), 537.

18. Kael specifically declares that Sonny "got into this mess by trying to raise money for Leon . . . to have a sex-change operation, yet the audience doesn't laugh" (Schwartz, *Age of Movies*, 537). I believe that the sex-change operation is supposed to be over the top—the straw that breaks the camel's back where Sonny's responsibilities are concerned—but that the film is not intended to be understood as homophobic.

19. "The Exorcising of Cruising," DVD extra, *Cruising*, dir. William Friedkin, Warner Home Video, 2007.

20. By the time Lumet's *Prince of the City* is released in 1981, just one year after *Cruising*, New York is still dirty and decrepit, but the cops are portrayed as fairly sympathetic; improbably, they don't even use the n-word in private conversations.

21. "Writing a decade later, Charles Morris, a former Lindsay budget aide, concluded: 'City tax spending on higher education was the fastest-growing area in the city budget, jumping from $35 million in 1966 to $200 million in 1973. It was much more than the city could afford.'" Vincent J. Cannato, *The Ungovernable City: John Lindsay and His Struggle to Save New York* (New York: Basic Books, 2001), 458.

22. See Nicholas von Hoffman, *Citizen Cohn* (New York: Doubleday, 1988). Cohn was disbarred, to boot, for patent ethics violations, notwithstanding character witness (and favorite client) Donald Trump coming to his defense. Jonathan Mahler and Matt Flegenheimer, "What Donald Trump Learned from Joseph McCarthy's Right-Hand Man," *New York Times*, June 20, 2016.

7. Cinematic Tone in Polanski's *Chinatown*

1. There are attempts. Many of the indoor scenes are latticed with bars of shadow from blinds; a sepia tone colors some daylight scenes; the last scene set in Chinatown is classic noir. And some of the noir references are both clear and ironic, as if even the fatalism so prominent in noirs is not sufficient to express the degree of impotence of all the characters other than Cross. Jake assumes that Evelyn Mulwray must be the murderess (as if Jake has seen too many noirs) whereas she is, multiply, a victim, guilty of nothing but love for her daughter, raped by her father, and shot dead by the police.

2. Most of the criticism was about the bleak ending, and the sense of hopelessness it left us with. The screenwriter Robert Towne called it "the tunnel at the end of the light." It was not the ending he scripted. Peter Biskind, "The Low Road to Chinatown," *Premiere*, June 1994, 72.

3. Robert Evans, *The Kid Stays in the Picture* (London: Aurum Press, 1994), 257.

4. See the helpful account by Michael Eaton, *Chinatown* (London: BFI, 1997), 32–35.

5. Like many other femme fatales, Evelyn shares the fate of being bound to a man she cannot abide and cannot escape, in this case her father. She shares, that is, the same fate as the femme fatale in *The*

Killers, *The Lady from Shanghai*, *Out of the Past*, *The Big Heat*, *Double Indemnity*, *The Postman Always Rings Twice*, and many others.

6. There are of course several noir heroes who do not fit the type portrayed by Humphrey Bogart, Dick Powell, or, in a near parody of the type, Ralph Meeker's Mike Hammer in *Kiss Me Deadly* (1955). Dana Andrews especially, say in *Laura*, and Robert Mitchum in *Out of the Past* (1947), play against this type. See the discussion of the significance of the difference in my *Fatalism in American Film Noir: Some Cinematic Philosophy* (Charlottesville: University of Virginia Press, 2012).

7. Evelyn, no doubt, because her avowed promiscuity is tied in various ways to the trauma of incest, and Jake because, we sense, the woman he tried to help in Chinatown was so important to him that he isn't "over" it.

8. He is clearly so traumatized by the event, it is likely that he got her killed.

9. This can be a noir theme apart from any Chinatown-like problematic. One of the best examples is Nicholas Ray's *In a Lonely Place*. See my "Passive and Active Skepticism in Nicholas Ray's *In a Lonely Place*, at nonsite.org, http://nonsite.org/issue-5-agency-and-experience.

10. Of course, Chinatown *is* also a police district smack in the middle of LA, also a separate place. But the stake for the characters in so isolating it and mystifying it as another universe is defensive and self-deceived, and it is truly distinct only by being paradigmatic of corruption, especially the corruption of the police, a force actually and famously one of the most corrupt in the country. Perhaps Cross is allegorically indicating something of his understanding of the Chinatown-LA relation when he tells Jake later that if you can't bring the water to LA, bring LA to the water.

11. But he only begins to trust her. When he follows her and discovers Katherine, the daughter/sister, he is back to claiming to know that she is the murderess of her husband.

12. Of course, victims of incest are simply and unqualifiedly victims, no matter how successful the perpetrator is in making them think the two of them were equally responsible. Creating such a feeling of guilt on the part of the victim helps protect the abuser, and adds another level of evil to what is already an unspeakable crime. This issue here is the burden Evelyn *thinks* she bears.

13. T. Adorno, *Minima Moralia: Reflections on a Damaged Life*, trans. E. F. N. Jephcott (London: Verso, 20016), 39. And, *Minima Moralia, Reflexionen aus dem beschädigten Leben* (Frankfurt: Suhrkamp, 1951), 59.

14. "Das Leben lebt nicht," quoting Ferdinand Kürnberger.

15. Far and away the best discussion of the double plot, and the relation of the themes in each, that I have found is Vernon Shetley's "Incest and Capital in *Chinatown*," *MLN* 114 (1999): 1092-1109. Aside from his thoughtful interpretation itself, Shetley provides a concise and illuminating summary of these different approaches.

16. Felicity Barringer, "The Water Fight that Inspired 'Chinatown,'" *New York Times*, April 25, 2012.

17. Shetley, "Incest and Capital," 1094.

18. Quoted in Eaton, *Chinatown*, 64. No textual source is given.

19. Jake may be right, and Cross may be trying to create a diversion, but it is true that Hollis and his wife are clearly trying to hide the girl from Cross, that he is clearly hunting for her aggressively, that that attempt to hide her is ruined by Jake's photograph, and that Huston's line reading suggests a kind of pathos that seems genuine. At any rate, it is another instance where the two plots seem congruent in some way.

20. Shetley, "Incest and Capital," 1098. Cf. "Its [Chinatown's] power arises from the way in which the institution of private property itself, the very foundation of the capitalist economic and social order, becomes identified with the horror of incest" (1100). This seems to me a rare overstatement. Nothing in the film that I can see (nothing in the point of view we are encouraged to adopt) justifies this as a claim about "private property itself," although it is true that one might say that Cross's debased understanding of the entitlement that comes with property is a possible pathological implication of the institution, an implication that becomes hard to resist if great wealth is concentrated in a few hands. Shetley also makes illuminating use of Levi-Strauss on the incest taboo as the basic dividing line between nature and culture, the basic affiliation not based on any biological imperative.

21. Noah Cross can seem to know what is going on in "Chinatown" in all its dimensions, because he makes the rules. But he doesn't seem to understand his own motives, doesn't seem to understand anything about human attachments, and so ends up murdering his old partner, and getting his daughter killed. In general, whatever *can* be made intelligible about Chinatown always comes "too late." We still don't understand what we need to understand when we need to.

22. It is worth noting that, for all of what appear to be Escobar's good intentions, it is still the case that the police in the film end up "doing as little as possible," little that is of any use, at any rate.

23. I do not share what I take to be the "conclusion" the film seems to leave us with. I mean, I think that this *is* its conclusion, but I would prefer to take it as a prophetic warning about the world of late capitalism rather than as some now view climate change: it is real and it is already too late. There is nothing effective left to be done.

8. "I Don't Know What to Do with My Hands"

1. Ben Gazzara, quoted in Tom Charity, *John Cassavetes: Lifeworks* (London: Omnibus, 2001), 147.
2. Al Ruban, quoted in Charity, *John Cassavetes*, 147–48.
3. Ray Carney, in *Cassavetes on Cassavetes*, ed. Ray Carney (London: Faber and Faber, 2001), 384.
4. Gilberto Perez, "Imperfection," *Senses of Cinema*, no. 16 (September 2001), http://sensesofcinema.com/2001/book-reviews/cassavetes_imperfection/.
5. Ivone Margulies, "John Cassavetes: Amateur Director," in *The New American Cinema*, ed. Jon Lewis (Durham, NC: Duke University Press, 1998), 279.
6. John Cassavetes, dir., *The Killing of a Chinese Bookie*, audio recording of an interview with Michel Ciment and Michael Wilson, DVD, Criterion Collection, 2004.
7. See the contributions by Refn, Sayles, Almodóvar, Bogdanovich, and Assayas in Charity, *John Cassavetes*. Scorsese discusses his relationship to Cassavetes in a number of contexts, for example, Martin Scorsese, "Three Portraits in the Form of a Homage: Ida Lupino, John Cassavetes, Glauber Rocha," in *Projections 7: Film-Makers on Film-Making*, ed. John Boorman and Walter Donohue (London: Faber and Faber, 1997), 89–91. In *Cassavetes on Cassavetes*, Carney provides an interesting account of Cassavetes's working relationship with May during the shoot and editing of *Mikey and Nicky*. See Carney, *Cassavetes on Cassavetes*, 350.
8. Apart from the works already cited, I refer to books such as Ray Carney, *American Dreaming: The Films of John Cassavetes and the American Experience* (Berkeley: University of California Press, 1985) and *The Films of John Cassavetes: Pragmatism, Modernism and the Movies* (Cambridge: Cambridge University Press, 1994); Laurence Gavron and Denis Lenoir, *John Cassavetes* (Paris: Rivages, 1986); Thierry Jousse, *John Cassavetes* (Paris: Seuil / Cahiers du Cinéma, 1989); Nicole Brenez, *Shadows* (Paris: Nathan Université, 1995); Vincent Amiel, *Le corps au cinéma: Keaton, Bresson, Cassavetes* (Paris: Presses Universitaires de France, 1998); George Kouvaros, *Where Does It Happen? John Cassavetes and the Cinema at the Breaking Point* (Minneapolis: University of Minnesota Press, 2004); Marshall Fine, *Accidental Genius: How John Cassavetes Invented American Independent Film* (New York: Miramax Books / Hyperion, 2005); Michael Ventura, *Cassavetes Directs: John Cassavetes and the Making of "Love Streams"* (Harpenden, UK: Kamera Books, 2008); Robert Furze, *The Visceral Screen: Between the Cinemas of John Cassavetes and David Cronenberg* (Bristol, UK: Intellect, 2014); Gilles Mouëllic, *"Meurtre d'un bookmaker chinois" de John Cassavetes: Striptease* (Paris: Yellow Now, 2017). This is just a selection. There are many other books, brochures, and special issues of journals where discussions of Cassavetes's work feature prominently.
9. Thomas Elsaesser, "The Pathos of Failure: American Film in the 1970s; Notes on the Unmotivated Hero," in *The Last Great American Picture Show: New Hollywood Cinema in the 1970s*, ed. Thomas Elsaesser, Alexander Horwath, and Noel King (Amsterdam: Amsterdam University Press, 2004), 280. Further page references given in parentheses in text.
10. See Carney, *American Dreaming*, 226; and Richard Combs, review of *The Killing of a Chinese Bookie*, dir. John Cassavetes, *Sight and Sound* 40, no. 1 (Winter 1976–77): 61.
11. Alexandre Astruc, "Fire and Ice," *Cahiers du Cinéma in English* 1 (January 1966): 7.
12. Gilles Deleuze, *Cinema 1: The Movement Image* (Minneapolis: University of Minnesota Press, 1986), 207.
13. François Dagognet, quoted in Leo Charney, "In a Moment: Film and the Philosophy of Modernity," in *Cinema and the Invention of Modern Life*, ed. Leo Carney and Vanessa R. Schwartz (Berkeley: University of California Press, 1995), 290.
14. Nicole Brenez, "Shops of Horror: Notes for a Visual History of the Reification of Emotion in a Capitalist Regime, or (to Put It More Bluntly) 'Fuck the Money,'" *Rouge* 11 (2007), http://rouge.com.au/11/shops_horror.html.
15. Patricia Patterson and Manny Farber, "Kitchen without Kitsch," *Film Comment*, November/December 1977, 47.
16. Patterson and Farber, 47.

17. André S. Labarthe, "A Way of Life: An Interview with John Cassavetes," *Evergreen Review* 64 (March 1969): 47.
18. Yann Lardeau, "Flux d'amour," *Cahiers du Cinéma*, no. 367 (January 1985): 7.
19. Jousse, *John Cassavetes*, 85.
20. Jonathan Rosenbaum, *Essential Cinema: On the Necessity of Film Canons* (Baltimore: Johns Hopkins University Press, 2008), 365. In *A New Leaf* (1971) and *The Heartbreak Kid* (1972) this occurs in the context of two newlyweds. In *Ishtar* (1987) and *Mikey and Nicky* the couple is composed of two heterosexual men.
21. Citing Janet Coleman's history of improvisational theater, *The Compass*, Rosenbaum notes that the origins of *Mikey and Nicky* lie in a play of that name that May was working on in 1954. See www.jonathanrosenbaum.net/2017/04/mikey-and-nicky-liner-notes/. According to Charity, the script for the film had been shown to Falk prior to the production of *Husbands*. See Charity, *John Cassavetes*, 80.
22. Todd Berliner, "Hollywood Movie Dialogue and the 'Real Realism' of John Cassavetes," *Film Quarterly* 52, no. 3 (Spring 1999): 8.
23. Maurice Merleau-Ponty, *Phenomenology of Perception* (London: Routledge, 2002), xviii.

9. The Spirit of '76

1. The most celebrated born-again Christian was Richard Nixon's special counsel and hatchet man Charles Colson, who, sentenced to prison for his part in the Watergate cover-up, underwent a jailhouse conversion and, in 1976, published a best-selling book, *Born Again*, about his experience.
2. *The Last Tycoon* was part of a bicentennial cycle in which Hollywood recalled, sometimes through a glass darkly, its glory days. Others included *The Day of the Locust, Inserts, Hearts of the West,* and *Won Ton Ton: The Dog Who Saved Hollywood* (all 1975) and *Gable and Lombard, Nickelodeon, W. C. Fields and Me*, and *That's Entertainment II* (all 1976). *Film Comment*'s industry columnist Stuart Byron was struck by the magical thinking behind such nostalgia. See Byron, "Second Annual Grosses Gloss," *Film Comment*, March/April 1977, 35. None of these movies, he declared, had been a hit or even made money. "What is this collective madness that has gripped Hollywood's pocketbooks? No trend in Glitter City has ever been more irrational, or financially disastrous." These movies were inept avatars. It would remain for Steven Spielberg, George Lucas, and—of course—Ronald Reagan to successfully recapture classic movie magic.
3. In addition to *Nashville* and *One Flew over the Cuckoo's Nest*, 1975 brought Hal Ashby's *Shampoo*, Ralph Bakshi's scurrilous animation *Coonskin*, John Cassavetes's *A Woman under the Influence*, Walter Hill's *Hard Times*, Sidney Lumet's *Dog Day Afternoon*, John Milius's *The Wind and the Lion*, and Arthur Penn's *Night Moves*—all small, "serious" movies bound neither by genre nor formula that were mostly made from original screenplays.
4. *Taxi Driver* is nakedly opposed even to itself, as well as the culture that produced it. For Travis, all movies are essentially pornographic; had he met his creators, he would, as noted by Marshall Berman in his history of Times Square, surely have considered them purveyors of "scum and filth." It's the slow deliberation with which this lunatic kicks over his TV and terminates his connection to social reality that signals his madness—and the filmmakers'.
5. James Bond was another Secret Agent of History, as were the equally glamorous spies in midsixties movies and TV shows like *The Man from U.N.C.L.E.*
6. Byron, "Second Annual Grosses Gloss," 35.
7. *Taxi Driver* capped the Hollywood new wave launched by *Bonnie and Clyde* in 1967 and, like *Bonnie and Clyde*, projected a violent, sexually frustrated scenario that people—or at least some people—wanted to live.
8. That the presidential candidate Senator Charles Palantine is played by TV commentator Leonard Harris enhances *Taxi Driver*'s media verisimilitude.
9. Indeed, Coppola had actually made an inadvertent contribution to the war, having written the screenplay for the 1970 movie *Patton*—a film portraying the World War II field commander as megalomaniacal war lover and hero that President Nixon screened at least twice, the second time being the night before he invaded Cambodia.
10. The project was produced by Redford. William Goldman, who had written the script for *Butch Cassidy and the Sundance Kid*, and who received considerable help from Woodward, delivered the first draft of his screenplay the very month that Nixon resigned.
11. *The Final Days* was understood as a sort of TV miniseries waiting to happen. In his April 18, 1976, *New York Times* review, Richard Reeves would call *The Final Days* a "high-grade *Backstairs at the*

White House" and a "film of bureaucratic rats on a sinking ship," comparing its style to "the recreated dramatic history being presented these days on television," such as ABC's 1974 docudrama on the Cuban Missile Crisis, *The Missiles of October,* and the more recent NBC telefilm *Truman at Potsdam.* The six-part miniseries *Washington behind Closed Doors* with Jason Robards Jr. as President Richard Monckton was telecast by ABC in September 1977—anticipating an official TV adaptation by twelve years.

12. The saga of this Johnny Reb was based on a novel by another, unrelated Carter, namely Forrest, a self-identified Cherokee storyteller who, it was revealed after the movie's release, was Asa Carter, a white supremacist ideologue, Ku Klux Klan agitator, and onetime speechwriter for Alabama governor and presidential candidate George Wallace. The revelation of Forrest Carter's past caused no stir during the movie's release; the big deal was Eastwood's firing of Philip Kaufman, doubtless chosen to direct on the strength of his 1972 Nixon western *The Great Northfield Minnesota Raid*, and replacing him as director. Eastwood was fined, and the Directors Guild added a new clause to its standard contract designed to preclude any recurrence.

13. Stallone's choice of Philadelphia as a setting was as significant as Scorsese's decision to shoot *Taxi Driver* in New York. Philadelphia (where Stallone had spent a measure of his adolescence) was not only the city that produced America's Declaration of Independence but also a city riven by racial tension and suffering a prolonged economic slump, ruled by the tough-talking ex-cop Frank Rizzo—like Rocky, if not Stallone, a product of Italian American South Philadelphia. Rather than a party, the bicentennial gave the city a rough time. Sanitation workers staged a job action, and the streets were filled with uncollected trash. Rizzo predicted violence and called for fifteen thousand federal troops. He was ignored. In any case, the expected disturbances were mainly orderly rallies and marches held by African American and Native American activists, Puerto Rican nationalists, feminists, gay rights groups, and other leftist organizations. *Rocky* showed Rizzo another way. The morning after his movie's New York premiere, Stallone presented Rizzo with a pair of red boxing gloves (*Philadelphia Bulletin*, December 19, 1976). At one point, Stallone imagined that *Rocky*'s inevitable sequel would end with the lovable pug being elected Philadelphia mayor.

14. See Frank Rich, "'Rocky' Hits a Nerve," *New York Post*, December 4, 1976, 22; Guy Flatley as cited in Stuart Byron, "Rocky and His Friends," *Film Comment*, January/February, 37; Pete Hamill, "Rocky KOs Movie Biz," *Village Voice*, November 8, 1976, 12; Janet Maslin, "Knockout," *Newsweek*, November 29, 1976, 113; Stallone, quoted in Judy Klemesrud, "'Rocky Isn't Based on Me,' Says Stallone, 'But We Both Went the Distance,'" *New York Times*, November 28, 1976, 17; Beth Gillin Pombeiro, "'Rocky' Is a Film for Our Times—with a Real Hero," *Philadelphia Inquirer*, November 21, 1976, 1-H; Vincent Canby, "Cynical Cinema Is Chic," *New York Times*, November 21, 1976, 89; Canby, "'Rocky,' Pure 30's Make-Believe," *New York Times*, November 22, 1976, https://www.nytimes.com/1976/11/22/archives/film-rocky-pure-30s-makebelieve.html; Kathleen Carroll, "'Rocky' Is a Reel Contender," *New York Daily News*, November 22, 1976, http://www.nydailynews.com/entertainment/movies/archives-reel-contender-article-1.2040336; and Pauline Kael, *When the Lights Go Down* (New York: Holt, Rhinehart and Winston, 1980), 213.

15. Stallone was apparently referring to the show *Both Sides Now*, which Sahl cohosted with *Los Angeles Times* reporter George Putnam. Profiled by the *New York Times* (November 28, 1976), Stallone again expressed his admiration for the president-elect: "Carter never gets rattled. Rocky never gets rattled either," adding that "a peanut farmer has just become President of the United States. That's the greatest inspiration story of all time."

16. *Rocky* went wide on December 3, supplanting *Carrie* as the nation's number one film. It held the top spot for only for a week before being replaced by the comedy-thriller *Silver Streak*, but, no less than its protagonist, the movie was resilient. Within a year, domestic grosses were estimated at $100 million.

17. Joe Flaherty, "Calling 'Fix!' on *Rocky*," *Film Comment*, July/August 1982, 60. The redemption of this happy-go-lucky club fighter was far more satisfying for audiences than the revenge of the pampered bourgeois couple (Jane Fonda and George Segal) who, deprived of their class privileges, turn to social banditry in Ted Kotcheff's comic revenge film *Fun with Dick and Jane*, sneak-previewed in New Jersey on September 11 and dumped the following February.

18. Not until 2015, in the last year of Barack Obama's presidency, were *Rocky*'s racial wrongs acknowledged, if not righted, in the reboot *Creed*.

19. John Simon, "Stallone's Ring of Truth," *New York Magazine*, November 29, 1976, 70.

20. Carter's second movie was *One Flew over the Cuckoo's Nest* (January 28); his third was *Network* (February 5), and his fourth was *Rocky* (February 19). He does not appear to have screened either *Taxi Driver* or *Bound for Glory*, at least not in the White House.

21. "Today's cinematic wish fulfillment comes not in an abrupt and gratuitous final moment," Miller writes in an essay linking Hollywood movies to advertising. The "calculated piling up of surplus triumphs" isn't "a quick way to end the film [but] its very purpose." Mark Crispin Miller, *Seeing through Movies* (New York: Pantheon, 1990), 214.

Coda

1. This counterintuitive insight is based on a hunch that so many of the New Hollywood movies revolved around a protagonist freaking out, which gave talented actors like Jack Nicholson and Dustin Hoffman and Robert De Niro and Faye Dunaway and Warren Beatty and Gena Rowlands a chance to chew the scenery. Just to cite one example, *Taxi Driver*, the collaboration of two auteurist minds (Scorsese and Schrader) produced a narrative full of implausibles, which had to be rescued by De Niro's compelling performance. This point was brilliantly made by Molly Haskell, in her appreciation of De Niro:

> The movie that has made him a byword doesn't make much sense even as the study of a psychopath (Arthur Bremer and Jeffrey Dahmer had more consistent MOs and recognizable urges). Why would smirky princess Betsy go out on a date with creepy cabbie Travis in the first place? And why would he take her to a porn film? And then be shocked when she walks out on it and him? And then be shocked when she rejects it and him? Travis is part Paul Schrader ascetic, part Scorsese wise-guy (not to mention the indigestible melding of Ford and Bresson), and totally sexless; the ending is farcical. But despite all this, Travis Bickle lives, and thanks to the untethered nature of De Niro's instinctive performance, breathes, flourishes, threatens, as myth: the savage male underbelly endlessly renewable and terrifying. (Molly Haskell, "A Man Apart," *Film Comment*, May/June 2017, 30)

There were also the new matinee idols like Steve McQueen and Paul Newman and Robert Redford who profited contrastingly by conveying old-fashioned restraint, and who could hold together a mediocre picture simply by underacting and looking cool. Though the New Hollywood is often posited as an auteurist haven, when the dust settled the stars came to hold a lot more power in the studio's decision-making process than directors or cinematographers (Dustin Hoffman being a classic case), and that pattern has held up to the present.

2. Pauline Kael, *For Keeps: 30 Years at the Movies* (New York: Dutton Books, 1994), 141–57, 224–26.

3. Mark Greif, *Against Everything: Essays* (New York: Pantheon Books, 2016), 36.

4. William S. Pechter, *Movies Plus One: Seven Years of Film Reviewing* (New York: Horizon, 1982), 160–68.

5. Stuart Klawans, *Film Follies: The Cinema out of Order* (New York: Cassell, 1999), 160.

6. Peter Biskind, *Easy Riders, Raging Bulls: How the Sex-Drugs-and-Rock 'n' Roll Generation Saved Hollywood* (New York: Touchstone, 1999).

INDEX

Page numbers in *italics* refer to figures.

3 Women (1977), 13, 69, 73, 76, 81–85, *82,* 170
20th Century Women (2016), 34–35

Academy Awards (Oscars), 2–3, 5–6, 9–10, 15, 24, 31, 33, 39, 40, 57, 60, 67, 70, 102, 151, 160, 163, 191n1
Ådalen 31 (1969), 43
Adorno, Theodor, 115, 122–23, 126
African Americans, 9–12, 150, 162–63. *See also* blaxploitation; race and racism
Against Everything (Grief), 169
AIDS epidemic, 99–100
Akerman, Chantal, 28–29, 169, 170
Aldrich, Robert, 5, 116
Ali, Muhammad, 159, 162
Alice Doesn't Live Here Anymore (1974), 9, 18, 20–22, 24–25, 27, 30–33, *32,* 35
Alice's Restaurant (1969), 4, 94
Allen, Dede, 4
Allen, Woody, 7, 24
Allison, Arlene, 137
All the President's Men (1976), 6, 102–3, 106, 108, 113, 156–58, 163
Almodóvar, Pedro, 133
Altman, Robert, 4, 19, 42, 69–85, 133, 140, 146, 150. See also *3 Women* (1977); *MASH* (1970); *McCabe & Mrs. Miller* (1971); *Nashville* (1975)
American dream, 64, 163, 173
American Graffiti (1973), 155, 159
American International Pictures (AIP), 13, 52
American society, 1, 6, 12–16, 18–19, 53, 78, 80, 113–14, 166, 174–75; in 1976, 149–63;

iconography, 110–11; urban conditions, 13–14, 63–64, 86–92, *87, 88,* 151–53, 158–59, 173, 197nn4–6, 198n20, 202n13. *See also* assassinations; conspiracies; corruption; counterculture; gender; paranoia; race and racism; sexuality; Vietnam War; Watergate; youth culture
Anatomy of a Murder (1959), 166, 168
Anderson, Patrick, 154
Angelopoulos, Theo, 169
Angels in America (2003), 99–100
Annie Hall (1977), 7
Anspach, Susan, 33, 55
antiheroes, 34, 76, 87, 96, 127, 149, 151–53
antiwar movement, 91, 167–68, 174
Antonioni, Michelangelo, 4, 15, 36–50, 164. See also *Blow-Up* (1966); *L'avventura* (1961); *Zabriskie Point* (1970)
Apocalypse Now (1979), 5, 6, 155–58, 163, 174, 191–92n12
Apu Trilogy (1955,1956,1959), 164
art films, 15–16, 164, 174. *See also* European art films
Ashby, Hal, 4, 133, 150
assassinations, 14, 18, 53, 78–79, 103–5, 111, 138, 151, 153, 172
Assayas, Olivier, 133
Assis, Machado de, 175
Astruc, Alexandre, 134
Atlantic City, 63–64
Attica (1974), 96
Auberjonois, René, 75

Aubrey, James, 47–48
auteur films, 3–19; contracts, 41–42; psychodramas, 155, 158
Avildsen, John, 15, 91. See also *Rocky* (1976)

Bakhtin, Mikhail, 69, 76, 77, 83
Band Apart (1964), 170
Bapis, Elaine M., 76
Bazin, André, 2, 165
BBS (production company), 13, 51–68
Beatty, Ned, 144
Beatty, Warren, 2, 4, 8, 67, *74*, 75, 103, 106–10, *107*, *111*, 168, 191n1, 203n1
Beauvoir, Simone de, 28
Begelman, David, 196n39
Bening, Annette, 34
Benjamin, Richard, 33
Bennett, Joan, 172
Benton, Robert, 2, 8, 19, 43, 191n1
Bergman, Ingmar, 7, 29, 82, 169, *170*
Berliner, Todd, 147
Bernstein, Carl, 102–3, 106, 113, 150, 156
Bertolucci, Bernardo, 39, 43
Beware of the Holy Whore (1971), 141
Beyond Therapy (1987), 70, 85
Bigger Than Life (1956), 165
Big Heat, The (1953), 115
Big Sleep, The (1946), 112, 114
biker pictures, 52
Bingo Long Traveling All-Stars & Motor Kings, The (1976), 150
Birkin, Jane, 36
Birth of a Nation, The (1915), 162
Biskind, Peter, 174
Bitter Tears of Petra von Kant, The (1972), 29
Black, Karen, 54, 56, *57*, 61, 195n15
Black Caesar (1973), 11
Black Gunn (1972), 10
blacklist, 1, 47, 52, 150
Blakely, Ronee, 79, 172
Blauner, Steve, 13, 51, 52
blaxploitation, 10–12, 89, 151
Blow-Up (1966), 7, 13, 36, 38–41, *41*, 43, 45, 105, 193n12
Bluhdorn, Charles, 3–4
Blume in Love (1973), 33
Bob & Carol & Ted & Alice (1969), 19, 42, 169
Bogart, Humphrey, 168
Bogdanovich, Peter, 19, 42, 43, 58–61, 68, *133*, 167, 195n21
Bogert, William, 95, *95*
Bonnie and Clyde (1967), 1–5, 8, 21, 42, 43, 70, 108, 153, 166, 168, 201n7
Boorman, John, 5, 62
Borzage, Frank, 165
Bottoms, Timothy, 60
Bound for Glory (1976), 150, 163, 202n20
Boyle, Peter, 57, 153

Boys in the Band, The (1970), 8
Brackman, Jacob, 63
Brando, Marlon, 150, 156, 158, 161
Breathless (1960), 170, 193n2(ch.2)
Bremer, Arthur, 153, 203n1
Brenez, Nicole, 139
Brennan, Eileen, 60
Bresson, Robert, 15, 42, 43, 164
Brewster McCloud (1970), 73
Bridges, Jeff, 59
Bring Me the Head of Alfredo Garcia (1974), 100
Brocka, Lino, 169
Broderick, James, 94
Brown, Jerry, 157
Brown, Jim, 5, 10–11
buddy films, 88, 108
Bunny Lake Is Missing (1965), 165
Buñuel, Luis, 15, 43, 134, 164
Burns, Ken, 114
Burstyn, Ellen, 9, 18, 22, 25, 27, 30–32, *32*, 60, *60*, 63, 64
Butch Cassidy and the Sundance Kid (1969), 80, 140
Butler, Bill, 58
Byron, Stuart, 153, 201n2

Caan, James, 159
California Split (1974), 133, 171
California v. Freeman, 193n21
Calley, John, 25, 35, 67
Calvin Company, 71–73, 76
Canby, Vincent, 48, 56, 57, 150, 156, 160–61
Candidate, The (1972), 57
Cannes Film Festival, 39, 43, 52, 56, 67, 70, 157, 193n17
Capra, Frank, 161
Carey, Timothy, 138
Carlin, Lynn, 142
Carlito's Way (1993), 99
Carnal Knowledge (1971), 5, 165, 195n15
Carney, Ray, 132, 134
Carradine, David, 150
Carradine, Keith, 75
Carrey, Jim, 112
Carrie (1976), 84, 202n16
Carrington, Virginia, 130
Carroll, Kathleen, 161
Carstensen, Margit, 29
Carter, Forrest, 202n12
Carter, Jimmy, 6, 15, 34, 154–58, 160–63, 202n15, 202n20
Casablanca (1942), 35, 112
Cassavetes, John, 5, 15, 27, 130–48, *144*. See also *Faces* (1968); *Husbands* (1970); *Killing of a Chinese Bookie, The* (1976); *Love Streams* (1984); *Mikey and Nicky* (1976); *Opening Night* (1978); *Woman under the Influence, A* (1974)
Cassel, Seymour, 142
Catch-22 (1970), 5, 151, 165

INDEX   207

Cazale, John, 93
Celine and Julie Go Boating (1974), 141
censorship, 1, 5, 8, 13, 38–41
Chabrol, Claude, 42, 43
Champlin, Charles, 48
Chaplin, Geraldine, 79, 172
Chianese, Dominic, 98
Chicago Sun-Times, 3, 48
Chinatown, 117–23, 135, 199n10
Chinatown (1974), 4, 5, 14, 67, 115–29, *118, 120, 128,* 198n5, 198nn1–2, 199n11, 199n15, 199nn19–21, 200nn22–23
Chloe in the Afternoon (1972), 169
Christie, Julie, 75, 110
Cimino, Michael, 6, 16, 42, 174
Cinémathèque Française, 2–3. *See also* French New Wave
cinematography, 21, 58, 60–61, 64, 71–72, 74, 109, 166–67
Claire's Knee (1970), 169
Clayburgh, Jill, 25
Cleaver, Kathleen, 43–44, 46
Cleopatra Jones (1973), 11
Close Encounters of the Third Kind (1977), 157
Cocks, Jay, 63
Coffy (1973), 11
Cohen, Larry, 100
Cohn, Roy, 99–100, 198n22
Colson, Charles, 201n1
Columbia Pictures, 51, 52, 58, 66, 67, 196n39
Combs, Richard, 134
Company, The (2003), 75
"Confessions of a Republican," 95, *95*
Conrad, Joseph, 155
conspiracies, 14, 101–13, 153, 167, 173–74. *See also* paranoia
Contempt (1963), 170
Conversation, The (1974), 4, 14, 43, 68, 109, 174
Cooper, Gary, 168
Coppola, Eleanor, 156
Coppola, Francis Ford, 4–6, 13, 41, 54, 68, 165, 201n9. *See also Apocalypse Now* (1979); *Conversation, The* (1974); *Godfather, The* (1972); *Godfather II, The* (1974)
Corey, Jeff, 52
Corman, Roger, 13, 52, 53, 59, 192n16
corruption, 102, 118, 122, 127, 157–58, 167. *See also* police corruption
Cortázar, Julio, 36
Cosby, Bill, 11
Costa-Gavras, 42
Cotton Goes to Harlem (1970), 11
Countdown (1967), 72
counterculture, 13, 36, 38, 43–50, 56–58, 150–51, 154, 156–57. *See also* youth culture
Creed (2015), 202n18
Cronyn, Hume, 103
Crothers, Scatman, 64

Crowther, Bosley, 3
Cruising (1980), 87, 98–99, 198n20
Cukor, George, 165
Cutter's Way (1981), 173

Dagognet, François, 137
Daisy Miller (1974), 68
Darin, Bobby, 52
Davis, Judy, 25
Davis, Ossie, 11
Davis, Peter, 66–67
Day, Doris, 18
Day of the Locust, The (1975), 172
Day of Wrath (1943), 164
Deleuze, Gilles, 69, 75, 136
Deliverance (1972), 5
Demy, Jacques, 54, 59
De Niro, Robert, 30–32, 80, 150–54, *152, 154,* 159, 168, 203n1
De Palma, Brian, 71, 84, 99, 165, 167
Dern, Bruce, 13, 53, 56, 63, *65*
Dern, Laura, 34
Diary of a Country Priest (1951), 164
Diary of a Mad Housewife (1971), 19–20, 25, 28, 29, 33
Didion, Joan, 9, 25, 61, 88
Directors Company, 68
Dirty Dozen, The (1967), 5, 10
documentary approach, 71, 77, 89, 99, 110
Dog Day Afternoon (1975), 4, 14, 171, 198n12
Donny Brasco (1997), 99
Double Indemnity (1944), 115
Dreyer, Carl Theodor, 164, 174
Drive, He Said (1971), 56–58, *57,* 195n15
Dr. Strangelove (1964), 156, 167, 168
Dunaway, Faye, 4, 22, 54, 128, *173,* 174, 191n1, 203n1
Dunne, John Gregory, 88
Dunning, Jennifer, 82
Durning, Charles, 198n12
Duvall, Shelley, 79, 81
Dylan, Bob, 150, 154, 157

Earrings of Madam De, The (1953), 164, 169
Eastman, Carole, 9, 13, 22, 53, 54
Eastwood, Clint, 150, 157–58, 202n12
Easy Rider (1969), 44, 52–54, 56, 61, 70, 140, 167
Ebert, Roger, 3, 45, 48, 49, 55, 56, 191n11
Edgerton, Joel, 27
Elsaesser, Thomas, 133–34, 140–41, 146
Enlightened, 34
European art films, 13, 28–29, 39–43, 51, 134. *See also* French New Wave
Eustache, Jean, 168–69
Evans, Robert, 4, 117, 121
Exorcist, The (1973), 192n13
experimental works, 73, 84, 134, 195n23

Faces (1968), 28, 136, 141–42, 170
Fahrenheit 451 (1966), 2
Falco, Edie, 34
Falk, Peter, 15, 142, 144, 145, 174
Farber, Manny, 140–41, 146
Farber, Stephen, 54
Fassbinder, Rainer Werner, 29, 141, 169
FBI, 44, 46
Fear of Fear (1975), 29
feel-good movies, 6, 58, 163
Fellini, Federico, 37, 39, 193n2(ch.2)
Felton, David, 49
Feminine Mystique, The (Friedan), 28
feminism, 19, 25, 28, 32, 34–35, 160
femme fatales, 115, 119, 198n5
Ferrara, Abel, 100
Film Follies (Klawans), 174
"film generation," 12
film industry, 1–4, 16, 39, 42, 193n6; classical Hollywood, 15, 113, 133–34, 164–65, 201n2; international, 2–3, 7, 15. *See also* European art films; foreign films; New Hollywood (1967–1976)
filmmaking techniques, 134–35, 139, 166–67, 198n1; close-ups, 141–42, 147–48, 166; multilayered dialogue, 72, 77. *See also* cinematography
Final Days, The (Woodward and Bernstein), 156, 201n11
Five Easy Pieces (1970), 13, 22, 51, 53–56, 63, 65, 133, 168
Flaherty, Joe, 162
Flatley, Guy, 160
Fonda, Jane, 9, *23*, 23–24, 27, 102, 202n17
Fonda, Peter, 44, 52, 53, 68
Ford, Gerald, 150, 152, 153, 157, 158, 160
Ford, Hamish, 84
Ford, John, 59, 122, 157, 165, 167, 175
foreign films, 37–41, 61, 164, 169–70. *See also* European art films; French New Wave
Forman, Miloš, 68, 151
Fortier, Robert, 81
Foster, Jodie, 31, 153
Foxy Brown (1974), 11
Frampton, Hollis, 140
Frankenheimer, John, 7, 61, 70
Frechette, Mark, 44, 48–50, 194n29
Free Woman, A (1972), 29
French Connection, The (1971), 4, 99, 151, 192n13
French New Wave, 2–3, 5, 7, 42, 61, 168–69, 174
Freud, Sigmund, 25, 29, 168
Friedan, Betty, 28
Friedkin, William, 4, 8, 68, 87, 98–99, 173, 192n13
Friedland, Alice, 135
Friends of Eddie Coyle, The (1973), 173
From Reverence to Rape (Haskell), 12–13, 20

Front, The (1976), 150
Fun with Dick and Jane (1977), 202n17

gangster films, 130–33, 144
Gardner, Fred, 44
Gazzara, Ben, 130–31, 145
gender, 18–20, 76, 79. *See also* masculinity; women
generational divide, 4–5, 191n11. *See also* youth culture
genres, 112, 116, 192n18; innovation in, 134, 146
Gentleman Tramp, The (1976), 67
German, Alexi, 169
Germany: Year Zero (1948), 89
Getchell, Robert, 30
Getting On, 34
Gibson, Henry, 78, *78*
Gilda (1946), 115
Giler, David, 106
Gilliat, Penelope, 8
Girlfriends (1978), 9
Glenn, Scott, 77
Godard, Jean-Luc, 2, 7, 8, 15, 42, 43, 164, 169–70, 193n2(ch.2)
Godfather, The (1972), 4, 16, 75, 84, 86, 89, 113, 155, 159, 174
Godfather II, The (1974), 5, 89, 93, 98, 113, 167, 174
Goldblum, Jeff, 77
Goldman, William, 201n10
Gone with the Wind (1939), 16, 162
Gordon, Donna Marie, 135
Gould, Elliot, *71*, 168
Graduate, The (1967), 5, 21, 43, 70, 165–66, 169, 174, 195n23
Grant, Cary, 168
Green Berets, The (1968), 157
Grier, Pam, 11
Griffith, D. W., 155
Grosbard, Ulu, 173
Guattari, Félix, 69, 75
Guerra, Tonino, 44
Guess Who's Coming to Dinner (1967), 10
Guffey, Burnett, 191n1
Gun Crazy (1950), 166
Guthrie, Woody, 150

Hackman, Gene, 4, 100, 109, 191n1
Hahn, Kathryn, 34
Halprin, Daria, 44, 48, 49, 194n29
Hamill, Pete, 160
Hammer (1972), 11
happy endings, 20, 25, 97, 158, 163
Harlan County U.S.A. (1976), 9
Harris, Barbara, 79
Harris, Leonard, 80, 201n8
Haskell, Molly, 12–13, 20, 80, 88, 203n1
Hawks, Howard, 59, 72, 112

Hayden, Sterling, 168
Hayward, David, 78
Head (1968), 52
HealtH (1980), 85, 171
Hearst, Patty, 149
Heartbreak Kid, The (1972), 22
Heart of Darkness (Conrad), 155
Hearts and Minds (1974), 66–67
Heaven's Gate (1980), 6, 16, 42, 174
Heidegger, Martin, 83
heist movies, 93–94
Hellman, Monte, 53, 133, 146
Hell's Angels on Wheels (1967), 52–53
Hemmings, David, 36, *41*
Hendershot, Heather, 13–14, 60
Henricksen, Lance, 94–95
Henry, Buck, 5, 51, 68
heroes, 160–62; folk, 150, 154; noir, 199n6. See also antiheroes
Hester Street (1975), 9, 22, 29
Heston, Charlton, 150
Hickey & Boggs (1972), 14
Hill, George Roy, 80, 140
Hired Hand, The (1971), 68
Hirsh, Foster, 196n37
Hitchcock, Alfred, 15, 59, 82, 122, 165
Hoberman, J., 15, 61
Hoffman, Dustin, 5, 87, 100, 150–51, 156, 165–66, 168, 203n1
Hollywood. *See* film industry; New Hollywood (1967–1976)
Hollywood Reporter, 47
homosexuality, 8, 97–99, 198n18
Hope, Bob, 67
Hopper, Dennis, 44, 52, 53, 61, 70, 140, 158
Hou Hsiao-hsien, 169
Hugh, Soto Joe, 138
Humphrey, Hubert, 153
Husbands (1970), 136, 142, 145, 171
Hustler, The (1961), 167
Huston, John, 116, *120*

Ice Station Zebra (1968), 10
I Love Dick, 34
Images (1972), 73, 75, 76, 83
Imamura, Shohei, 169
Imitation of Life (1959), 165
incest, 119, 121–26, 199n7, 199n12, 199n20
insanity, 107–8, 114, 143, 163, 170–71, 201n4
In the Heat of the Night (1967), 10
In the Realm of the Senses (1976), 140–41
inward turn, 54–55
Iosseliani, Otar, 169
Italianamerican, 30
Italian Americans, 30, 159, 162, 202n13. *See also names of individual actors and directors*
I Walk the Line (1970), 61

Jaglom, Henry, 22, 56, 59, 61, 62, 67
Jarmusch, Jim, 133
Jaws (1975), 6, 151
Jeanne Dielman, 23, quai de Commerce, 1080 Bruxelles (1975), 28–29, 170
Joe (1970), 91, 96, 159
Johari, Azizi, 130
Johnson, Ben, 60
Johnson, Laura, 143
Johnson, Lyndon B., 156
Josephson, Erland, 29, *170*
Jousse, Thierry, 143
Joyce, Adrien (pseudonym for Carole Eastman), 53
Just Tell Me What You Want (1980), 171

Kael, Pauline, 3, 16–17, 37, 42, 97, 161, 163, 165, 166, 192n21, 193n15, 198n18
Kane, Carol, 22, 29
Kanfer, Stefan, 42
Katzelmacher (1969), 141
Kaufman, Philip, 165
Kaufmann, Stanley, 12, 37
Kazan, Elia, 111, 150, 161
Keaton, Diane, 169
Keitel, Harvey, 30, 31, 153, 156, 157
Kennedy, John F., 14, 103–5, 153
Kennedy, Robert, 53
Kennedy, Ted, 153
Kerkorian, Kirk, 47–48
Kershner, Irvin, 19, 24, 25
Kesey, Ken, 151
Kiarostami, Abbas, 169
Killing of a Chinese Bookie, The (1976), 15, 130–40, *131, 137, 139,* 144–48, 171
King, Martin Luther, Jr., 53
King of Marvin Gardens, The (1972), 13, 51, 63–66, *65,* 196n37
Kirshner, Jonathan, 13
Kissinger, Henry, 156
Kiss Me Deadly (1955), 116
Klawans, Stuart, 174
Klute (1971), 14, 20, *23,* 23–25, 27, 33, 101–2, 108, 169
Knapp Commission, 90
Knight, Shirley, 22
Knute Rockne All American (1940), 158
Kolker, Robert, 84
Kopple, Barbara, 9
Kouvaros, George, 15
Kovács, László, 13, 53, 54, 63, 64
Kristofferson, Kris, 25, 30–33
Kubrick, Stanley, 167

Ladd, Diane, 31, 34
La dolce vita (1961), 37, 193n2(ch.2)
Lady from Shanghai, The (1947), 115

La femme infidel (1969), 42
Laing, R. D., 28
Lane, Mark, 105
Lang, Fritz, 59, 166
Lange, Jessica, 34
Langella, Frank, 33
Langlois, Henri, 2
Larner, Jeremy, 57, 58
Last Detail, The (1973), 67, 133
Last Hard Men, The (1976), 150
Last Picture Show, The (1971), 13, 51, 58–61, 60, 167
Last Tycoon, The (1976), 150, 201n2
Late Spring (1949), 164
Laura (1944), 165
L'avventura (1961), 37–38, 44–45, 193n2 (ch.2)
Leachman, Cloris, 60
Leadbelly, 150
Lear, Norman, 150
Lebrun, Françoise, 169
Le cercle rouge (1970), 93
Le doulos (1963), 168
leftist/communist politics, 1, 46, 168
Le gai savoir (1969), 42
Legend of Nigger Charlie, The (1972), 11
Leone, Sergio, 169
Le samouraï (1967), 168
Lewis, Jerry, 112, 165
Lewis, Jon, 13
life: art and, 49; as false, 122–23, 127–29
lighting, 20, 30, 71, 76, 134–35, 139, 166–67, 198n1
Lindsay, John, 14, 86, 87, 89–92, 99–100, 197n6, 198n21
Lion's Love (1969), 43
Little Big Man (1970), 4, 167
Loden, Barbara, 8–9, 26–27, 173. See also *Wanda* (1970)
Long Day's Journey Into Night (1962), 171
Long Goodbye, The (1973), 14, 140, 171
Lopate, Phillip, 12, 15
Lords of Flatbush, The (1974), 159
Los Angeles Times, 48
Lost Honor of Katharina Blum, The (1975), 29
Love Streams (1984), 142
Loving (1970), 24
Loving (2016), 27
Lubitsch, Ernst, 164, 175
Lucas, George, 6, 13, 71, 155, 157
Lumet, Sidney, 4, 70, 97–98, 136, 171. See also *Dog Day Afternoon* (1975); *Network* (1976); *Prince of the City* (1981); *Serpico* (1973)
Lupino, Ida, 8, 30, 173
Lusty Men, The (1952), 165
Lutter, Alfred, 31
Lyman, Mel, 49–50
Lynch, David, 84, 122

Maas, Peter, 89
Mack, The (1973), 11
Mad Housewife genre, 19–20. See also insanity
Malick, Terrence, 84
Maltese Falcon, The (1941), 115–16
Man Called Horse, A (1970), 150
Manchurian Candidate, The (1962), 153
Man Escaped, A (1956), 114
Mann, Anthony, 15, 165
Mann, Michael, 173
Marcuse, Herbert, 28
Marey, Étienne-Jules, 137
Margotta, Michael, 56
Margulies, Ivone, 132
Marley, John, 141
marriage and family, 18–35, 169–70, 173, 175
Marrying Kind, The (1952), 165
Martha (1974), 29
Marvin, Lee, 5
Mary Hartman, Mary Hartman (television show), 150
masculinity, 160, 168
MASH (1970), 4, 11, 43, 69, 70, 71, 75
Mason, James, 172
May, Elaine, 5, 8–9, 15, 22, 133, 146. See also *Mikey and Nicky* (1976)
Mazursky, Paul, 7, 19, 21, 24, 33, 42
McCabe & Mrs. Miller (1971), 4, 13, 69, 73–77, 74, 108, 110, 141
McCarthy, Eugene, 57
McMurtry, Larry, 59
McQueen, Steve, 203n1
Mean Streets (1973), 30, 31, 141, 168
Meet Me in St. Louis (1944), 164
Melville, Jean-Pierre, 168, 173
Merleau-Ponty, Maurice, 148
Metcalf, Laurie, 34
MGM, 36, 38, 41–43, 45, 47–48, 196n39
Mickey One (1965), 7, 167
Midnight Cowboy (1969), 8, 70, 86, 87, 90, 96, 100, 198n9
Mikey and Nicky (1976), 15, *144*, 144–45, 173–74, 201nn20–21
Milius, John, 155
Miller, Mark Crispin, 163, 203n21
Mills, Mike, 34–35
Mineo, Sal, 59
Minett, Mark, 71
Minnelli, Liza, 32, 101
Minnelli, Vincente, 164, 165
Mirren, Helen, 34
misogyny, 151, 169
Missouri Breaks, The (1976), 4, 5, 150
Mitchum, Robert, 168
Mizoguchi, Kenji, 15, 164, 175
Model Shop (1969), 54
Monkees, The (television show), 52
Moretti, Nanni, 169

Morgenstern, Joseph, 3
Morris, Charles, 198n21
Mother and the Whore, The (1973), 168–69
Motion Picture Association of America (MPAA), 7, 36, 38–42
"movie brats," 13, 40, 71
M rating (for "Mature Audiences"), 7, 40
Mulligan, Robert, 101
Murnau, F. W., 134
music, 1, 77, 80–81, 109, 118
My Brilliant Career (1979), 25
My Lai Massacre, 53
My Night at Maud's (1969), 42, 169

narrative, 18, 21, 45, 69; classical, 133–34; de-dramatizing of, 140–42; new possibilities of, 80, 81, 84, 138, 171; nonnarrative films, 36, 61. *See also* plot
Nashville (1975), 13, 22, 69, 75, 77–81, *78*, 83, 151, 156, 171–72
Nashville, A Wedding (1978), 70
National Catholic Office of Motion Pictures (NCOMP), 40
National Society of Film Critics Awards, 42
neo-noir, 14, 115
neo-woman's film, 18–35
Network (1976), 4, 6, 95, 96, 149, 160, 163
Newell, Mike, 99
New Hollywood (1967–1976): beginning and end of, 1–7; critique of, 164–75; definition of, 4; marginalized voices in, 7–12; period genres, 192n18; retrospective view of, 16–17; social and political context (*see* American society); timelines, *88*, 177–88. *See also* film industry
New Leaf, A (1971), 22
Newman, David, 2, 8, 191n1
Newman, Paul, 150, 151, 161, 203n1
New Republic, 3, 37
Newsweek, 3, 61, 157, 161
Newton, Huey, 67
New York, New York (1977), 174
New York City, 13–14, 86–100, *87*, *88*, 151–53, 197nn4–6, 198n20, 198n21
New York Daily News, 67, 152
New Yorker, 3, 8, 42
New Yorker Theater, 59
New York Film Critics Circle, 54
New York Film Festival, 42, 55
New York Magazine, 160, 163
New York Post, 160, 161
New York Times, 3, 48, 90, 96, 150, 154–55, 160, 196n37, 201n11
Nichols, Jeff, 27
Nichols, Mike, 5, 7, 70, 99–100, 191n11. *See also Graduate, The* (1967)
Nicholson, Jack, 13, 51–58, 61–68, *65*, *120*, 150, 203n1
Night Moves (1975), 4, 14, 100

Nin, Anaïs, 62
Nixon, Richard, 14, 46, 53, 80, 91, 105, 156, 201nn9–10
noir, 14, 20, 109, 111–12, 115–17, 119, 123, 134, 172, 198n1, 198n5, 199n6
nostalgia, 7, 16, 149, 201n2
Nostalgia (1969), 140
Notorious (1946), 165
nouvelle vague, 151, 168
Novick, Lynn, 114
Nurse Jackie, 34

Oates, Warren, 100, 134
Obsession, 167
O.C. and Stiggs (1985), 70
O'Connell, Jack, 48
Omen, The (1976), 150
On Dangerous Ground (1951), 173
O'Neal, Ryan, 159
One Flew over the Cuckoo's Nest (1975), 151
One from the Heart (1981), 174
On the Town (1949), 86
On the Waterfront (1954), 161
Opening Night (1978), 136, 142–43
Ophüls, Max, 164, 172, 175
Oscars. *See* Academy Awards
Oshima, Nagisa, 140
Oswald, Lee Harvey, 104, 153
Outlaw Josey Wales, The (1976), 157–58
Out of the Past (1947), 115
Ozu, Yasujirō, 164, 174

Pacino, Al, 87–100, 113, 159, 168, 171, 198n11
Paint Your Wagon (1969), 193n15
Pakula, Alan, 4, 101–14. See also *All the President's Men* (1976); *Klute* (1971); *Parallax View, The* (1974)
Panic in Needle Park, The (1971), 14, 87–89
Paper Moon (1973), 59, 68
Parallax View, The (1974), 4, 5, 14, 101–14, *104*, *107*, *111*, 153, 161, 167
Paramount case, 1
Paramount Pictures, 3–4, 68
paranoia, 101–10, 116–17, 127–29, 167. *See also* conspiracies
Parker, Alan, 169
Parks, Gordon, 11, 150
Parks, Gordon, Jr., 11, 89
Parsons, Estelle, 191n1
Pasolini, Pier Paolo, 43
Passenger, The (1975), 68, 193n12
Passer, Ivan, 173
Patterson, Patricia, 140–41, 146
Patton (1970), 201n9
Pechter, William S., 172
Peck, Gregory, 61, 168
Peckinpah, Sam, 42, 70, 100, 165
Pelican Brief, The (1993), 105

Penn, Arthur, 1-4, 7, 8, 19, 70, 100, 150. See also *Bonnie and Clyde* (1967)
Penn, Sean, 133
Peploe, Clare, 44
Perez, Gilberto, 132
Perkins, Anthony, 62
Perry, Frank, 62
Persona (1966), 7, 82
Philadelphia, 63, 158, 202n13
Phillips, Julia, 9, 152, 153
Phillips, Thomas Hal, 78
Pialat, Maurice, 169
Pigpen (1969), 43
Pippin, Robert, 14
Pisters, Patricia, 70
Platt, Polly, 9, 59
Player, The (1992), 70, 73, 77, 83
Play It as It Lays (1972), 9, 20, 22, 25, 26, 61-62
plot, 49; double, in *Chinatown*, 123-27, 199n15. *See also* narrative
Point Blank (1967), 5, 62
Poitier, Sidney, 10
Polanski, Roman, 4, 42, 115-29. See also *Chinatown* (1974)
police corruption, 89-91, 98-99, 125, 129
politics: 1976 presidential campaign, 153-58. *See also* American society; assassinations; Watergate
Pollack, Sydney, 173
Pollard, Michael J., 191n1
Pombeiro, Beth Gillin, 160
Ponti, Carlo, 36
pornography, 45-46, 151-52, 201n4, 203n1
Postman Always Rings Twice, The (1946), 115
Postman Always Rings Twice, The (1981), 67
Potter, Dennis, 116
Premier Films, 38
Preminger, Otto, 15, 165
Prentiss, Paula, 103
Pretty Poison (1968), 62
Prince of the City (1981), 7, 171, 198n20
Proctor, Phil, 62
Producers, The (1967), 86
Production Code Administration (PCA), 8, 18, 36, 38, 40
prostitution, 23, 28, 76, 110, 151-53, 193n21
Psycho (1960), 153
Psych-Out (1968), 53
Puzzle of a Downfall Child (1970), 20, 22, 54, 170

Quintet (1979), 70, 73, 81, 85

race and racism, 10, 117-20, 151, 162-63, 168, 198n20, 202n13, 202n18. *See also* African Americans
Rafelson, Bob, 13, 43, 51, 53, 54, 61, 63, 68, 133
Rafelson, Toby Carr, 9, 64
Raging Bull (1980), 7

Rainbow Pictures, 67
Rain Man (1988), 165
Rain People, The (1969), 20, 22, 29-30
Rameau's Nephew (1974), 141
Rampling, Charlotte, 34
rape, 33, 57, 122
ratings system, 4, 7, 39-40, 46
Rauschenberg, Robert, 1, 3
Ray, Nicholas, 15, 165, 173
Ray, Satyajit, 16, 164
Raybert Productions, 52
Ready to Wear (1994), 70, 75, 79
Reagan, Ronald, 6, 15, 99, 152, 153, 156-58
realism, 21, 76, 89, 102, 113-14, 142-48, 171
Reckless Moment, The (1949), 172
Redford, Robert, 57, 150, 156, 159, 161, 163, 173, 174, 201n10, 203n1
Redgrave, Vanessa, 36, *41*
Reed, Rex, 67
Reeves, Richard, 201n11
Refn, Nicolas Winding, 133
Regarding Henry (1991), 165
Remick, Lee, 167
Renoir, Jean, 174
Republic Studios, 72
Resnais, Alain, 5, 62
Resnick, Patricia, 81
Revolution (1968), 48
Reynolds, Burt, 159
Rich, Frank, 161
Ride in the Whirlwind (1966), 53
Rivette, Jacques, 73, 134, 141
Robards, Jason, Jr., 102
Roberts, Meade, 130
Robertson, Cliff, 196n39
Robinson, Julia Anne, 64
Rocky (1976), 6, 15, 158-63, *159*, 202n13, 202nn15-18
Rocky Horror Picture Show, The (1975), 151
Rocky II (1979), 163
Rocky III (1982), 162
Rohmer, Éric, 42, 169
Roiphe, Anne, 25
Rolling Stone, 49
Ronstadt, Linda, 157
Roots (miniseries), 150, 162
Rosemary's Baby (1968), 42
Rosenbaum, Jonathan, 73, 144, 201n21
Rossellini, Roberto, 169
Rossen, Robert, 167
Rowlands, David, 145
Rowlands, Gena, 22, 27, 28, 141-43, 203n1
Ruban, Al, 132, 147
Ruby, Jack, 104
Rudolph, Alan, 72
Rule, Janice, 81
Rush to Judgment (Lane), 105
Ryan, Robert, 173

Safe Place, A (1971), 22, 61–62, *62*
Safire, William, 155
Sarris, Andrew, 37, 66, 165
Saturday Night Live (television show), 150, 158
Sayles, John, 133
Scarecrow (1973), 4, 43, 89
Scarlet Street (1945), 115
Scenes from a Marriage (1973/1974), 29, 169, *170*
Schatzberg, Jerry, 4, 19, 43, 54, 87, 170
Schier, Ernest, 161
Schlesinger, John, 8, 70. See also *Midnight Cowboy* (1969)
Schlöndorff, Volkor, 29
Schneider, Bert, 13, 51, 52, 58, 59, 61, 66–68
Schrader, Paul, 15, 151, 153, 203n1
Scoppa, Peter R., 144
Scorsese, Martin, 7, 13, 15, 30–32, 42, 71, 84, 133, 146, 159, 165, 174. See also *Alice Doesn't Live Here Anymore* (1974); *Mean Streets* (1973); *Taxi Driver* (1976)
Screen Gems, 52
Seale, Bobby, 53
Searchers, The (1956), 165
Seconds (1966), 7
Second Sex, The (Beauvoir), 28
Secret Honor (1984), 80
Segal, George, 33, 202n17
Self, Robert T., 79, 80, 84
Semple, Lorenzo, Jr., 106, 174
Serpico (1973), 4, 14, 89–91, 99, 136, 171, 197n6
sex scenes, 38, 45–47, 56, 193n21, 195n15, 195n21
sexuality, 8, 38, 59, 97–99, 169, 198n18; women and, 19, 26, 32–33
Seyrig, Delphine, 28
Shaft (1971), 11
Shampoo (1975), 4, 5, 108
Sharp, Alan, 68
Shawn, Wallace, 3
Sheen, Martin, 156, 157
Shepard, Sam, 43–44
Shepherd, Cybill, 59, 60, *60*, 153
Shepitko, Larisa, 169
Shetley, Vernon, 199n15, 199n20
She Wore a Yellow Ribbon (1949), 165
Shooting, The (1966), 53
Shootist, The (1976), 150
Shoot the Moon (1982), 169
Shop around the Corner, The (1940), 114, 164
Short Cuts (1993), 70
Sight and Sound, 38
Silver, Joan Micklin, 9, 22
Simon, John, 163
Sinatra, Frank, 67
Singer, Loren, 106
Sirk, Douglas, 15, 122, 165
Slaughter (1972), 10
Small, Michael, 109

Smith, Patti, 197n4
Snodgress, Carrie, 19–20, 28, *33*
Snow, Michael, 141
Sopranos, The (television show), 98
Sorcerer (1977), 173
Sorvino, Paul, 98
Spacek, Sissy, 81, *82*
Spielberg, Steven, 6, 71, 157
Stallone, Sylvester, 15, 158–63, *159*, 202n13, 202n15
Star is Born, A (1954), 165
Star Wars (1977), 6, 155, 157, 163
Stay Hungry (1976), 67
Stendhal, 175
Sterile Cuckoo, The (1969), 101
Sterritt, David, 13
Stewart, James, 156, 167–68
Stockwell, Dean, 53
Stolen Kisses (1969), 42
Straight Time (1978), 173
Strangers When We Meet (1960), 167
Straub, Jean-Marie, 134
Streamers (1983), 70
Streep, Meryl, 34, 100
Streisand, Barbra, 25
Sturges, Preston, 111
Sunday Bloody Sunday (1971), 8
Super Fly (1972), 11, 89
Surtees, Bruce, 195n23
Sutherland, Donald, *71*, 102
Svevo, Italo, 175
Sweet Sweetback's Baadasssss Song (1971), 11–12

Taking Off (1971), 68
Tannen, Ned, 68
Tanner '88 (1988), 80
Targets (1968), 59
Tarkovsky, Andrei, 169
Tati, Jacques, 73
Tavoularis, Dean, 4
Taxi Driver (1976), 6, 15, 31, 43, 79–80, 136, 149, 151–54, *152, 154,* 157, 163, 168, 170, 201n4, 201nn7–8, 203n1
television, 72, 95–96, 150
Teo, Stephen, 76
Tepper, William, 56, 58
Tewkesbury, Joan, 9, 22, 79
They Live by Night (1948), 166
Thief (1981), 173
Thieves Like Us (1974), 140
Thomas, B. J., 80
Thomson, David, 12, 14, 64
Three Days of the Condor (1975), 14, 67, 150, 160–61, 173, *173*
Three the Hard Way (1974), 11
thrillers, 38, 102, 150, 156
Time magazine, 1, 3–4, 42, 63, 157, 160
To Live and Die in L.A. (1985), 173

Tomlin, Lily, 79
Touch of Evil (1958), 115–16
Towne, Robert, 5, 53, 56, 106, 117, 121, 124
Tracks, 61
Trip, The (1967), 53
Trotta, Margarethe von, 29
Trouble in Paradise (1932), 164
Truffaut, François, 2, 8, 42, 43
Trump, Donald, 111, 113, 198n22
Twentieth Century Fox, 81
Two-Lane Blacktop (1971), 29, 68, 133–34, 140

Udall, Morris, 154, 156, 157
Ugetsu (1953), 164
Ullmann, Liv, 29, *170*
Uncommon Denominator, The (1963), 61
underdog films, 162–63
Une femme douce (1969), 42
United Artists (UA), 6, 191n12
Universal, 68
Unmarried Woman, An (1978), 7, 25
Up the Sandbox (1972), 20, 25

Valenti, Jack, 7, 38–40, 42
van Peebles, Melvin, 11–12
Van Runkle, Theadora, 191n1
Varda, Agnès, 43
Variety, 38, 40
Vertigo (1958), 165, 167
Veruschka, 36
Vietnam War, 53, 105, 151, 160; films on, 66–67, 114, 155–57. *See also* antiwar movement
Vietnam War, The (2017), 114
Village Voice, 15, 37, 87, 160
Vincent & Theo (1990), 77
violence, 79–80, 129, 143, 151, *154*, 168, 201n7. *See also* assassinations
Voluntary Movie Rating System, 4, 39–40, 46

Wakeford, Kent L., 30
Walker, Beverly, 46
Wallace, George, 153, 156, 202n12
Wall Street Journal, 152
Walsh, M. Emmet, 144
Walsh, Raoul, 165
Wanda (1970), 9, 20, 23, 24, *26*, 26–27, 29–30, 33, 173
Warner, Jack, 2–3
Warner Bros., 67, 72
Warren Commission, 14, 104
Washington Post, 102, 113
Watergate, 90, 102, 105, 149–50, 153–54, 156, 161, 201n1

Watermelon Man, The (1970), 11–12
Wayne, John, 150, 168
Wedding, A (1978), 70, 80, 81, 171
Weill, Claudia, 9
Weld, Tuesday, 22, 61, 62, *62*
Welles, Gwen, 61, 79, 171
Welles, Orson, 58, 59, 61, 62, *62*, 72, 115, 116
Wepner, Chuck, 159
West, Nathaniel, 172
westerns, 74–75, 112, 122, 150, 157–58; anti-westerns, 74, 80
Westmorland, William, 66
Wexman, Virginia Wright, 79
What's Up, Doc? (1972), 59
"white events," 136
Who's Afraid of Virginia Woolf (1966), 7, 40
Wicker, Tom, 96
Widerberg, Bo, 43
Wikarska, Carol, 96
Wild Angels, The (1966), 52, 59
Wild Bunch, The (1969), 42
Williamson, Fred, 10–11
Willis, Gordon, 109
Wind, Bodhi, 82
Winkler, Henry, 160
Winning Team, The (1952), 158
Woman under the Influence, A (1974), 20, 22, 27, 28, 142–43, 170
women, 18–35; as actresses, 12–13, 22, 33–34; as directors, 8–9; as femme fatales, 115, 119, 198n5; misogyny and, 151, 169; representations of, 12–13, 60, 72, 76, 79, 88, 116; studio system and, 12–13, 20–21
women's movement. *See* feminism
Woodward, Bob, 102–3, 106, 113, 150, 156, 201n10
world creation, 132–33
Written on the Wind (1956), 165
Wyler, William, 165

Yang, Edward, 169
Yardbirds, 36
Yates, Peter, 173
Young Turks, 19, 30, 175
You're a Big Boy Now (1966), 54
youth culture, 4–5, 52, 54, 167–69, 194n29. *See also* counterculture; generational divide

Z (1969), 42
Zabriskie Point (1970), 4, 13, 41–50, *44*, *46*, *48*, 167, 193n12
Zoetrope studio, 155
Zsigmond, Vilmos, 68, 74